# Problems in Middle and High School Teaching

# Problems in Middle and High School Teaching

## A Handbook for Student Teachers and Beginning Teachers

**Adam M. Drayer**
King's College
Wilkes-Barre, Pennsylvania

**Allyn and Bacon, Inc.**
Boston · London · Sydney

Portions of this book first appeared in *Problems and Methods in High School Teaching*, by Adam M. Drayer, copyright © 1963 by Allyn and Bacon, Inc.

**Library of Congress Cataloging in Publication Data**

Drayer, Adam M
  Problems in middle and high school teaching.

  Includes bibliographies and index.
  1. High school teaching.  2. Student teaching.
3. First year teachers.  I. Title.
LB1777.D72     373.1'1'02     78-19029
ISBN 0-205-06146-X
ISBN 0-205-06131-1 pbk.

**To My Students**

# Contents

| | | |
|---|---|---|
| | List of Problems | ix |
| | Preface | xv |
| Chapter 1 | **Common Mistakes of Beginning Teachers** | 1 |
| | The Teacher's Qualities | 2 |
| | The Classroom Environment | 8 |
| | Discipline | 9 |
| | Classroom Procedures | 11 |
| | Evaluation | 19 |
| | Handling Problems | 21 |
| | Attitude Toward Theory Courses | 23 |
| | Maintaining Proper Morale | 24 |
| Chapter 2 | **Problems of Discipline** | 27 |
| | Suggestions for Maintaining Discipline | 29 |
| | Handling Disorderly Pupils | 32 |
| | Twenty Problems of Discipline | 37 |
| | Selected Readings | 66 |
| Chapter 3 | **Problems of Motivation** | 67 |
| | Suggestions for Motivating Pupils | 68 |
| | Other Sources of Motivation | 72 |
| | Twenty Problems of Motivation | 75 |
| | Selected Readings | 102 |

Chapter 4    **Problems of Emotional Adjustment**    **103**

Symptoms of Emotional Problems    105

Suggestions for Handling
Emotional Problems    109

Twenty Problems of Emotional
Adjustment    112

Selected Readings    137

Chapter 5    **Problems Related to Individual Differences**    **139**

Some Common Physical Defects    139

Suggestions for Dealing with
Physical Defects    143

Differences in Mental Ability    144

Suggestions for Dealing with Mentally
Superior Students    147

Suggestions for Dealing with Mentally
Slow Students    149

Learning Disabilities    150

Twenty Problems of
Individual Differences    151

Selected Readings    177

Chapter 6    **Problems of Evaluation**    **179**

Evaluating by Tests    180

General Suggestions on Evaluation
and Testing    182

Twenty Problems of Evaluation    187

Selected Readings    209

Chapter 7    **Problems of Adjustment to School Personnel**    **211**

Suggestions for Developing
Good Relationships    212

Twenty Problems of Developing
Good Relationships    217

Conclusion    241

Selected Readings    242

Index    243

# List of Problems

**Problems of Discipline**

1. Class discussions bring an unruly class to order.   **37**
2. A student teacher's sense of humor solves a disciplinary problem.   **39**
3. A ringleader is won over by a private talk.   **41**
4. Corporal punishment is used to quiet a boy.   **42**
5. Special problems in the biology laboratory.   **43**
6. The student teacher uses questionable disciplinary procedures.   **45**
7. Classroom fisticuffs.   **46**
8. A girl fears her teachers.   **47**
9. A student with ability is hampered by being in a problem group.   **49**
10. A student teacher changes from meanness to firmness.   **51**
11. Cheating on a test.   **53**
12. A student is pre-judged by teachers.   **54**
13. A belligerent boy is overprotected by his mother.   **55**
14. A ninth grade student dislikes student teachers.   **57**
15. A teacher realizes his mistake.   **58**
16. An unruly boy refuses to be helped.   **59**
17. A delinquent girl breaks down.   **61**
18. A language laboratory creates special problems for the teacher.   **62**
19. A senior causes trouble in a sophomore class.   **63**
20. The student teacher is unsuccessful with a disruptive pupil.   **64**

## Problems of Motivation

21. Vocational students dislike English grammar.   **75**
22. A potential drop-out is saved.   **77**
23. A sense of pride is restored to an economically deprived student.   **79**
24. Student participation in experiments arouses a previously uninterested student.   **81**
25. Encouragement and outside interests help motivate an unruly boy.   **82**
26. A private talk stimulates a girl to do better work.   **83**
27. An entire class is motivated to work.   **84**
28. An English teacher capitalizes on a troublesome student's art ability.   **85**
29. A bowl contest generates interest in English grammar.   **87**
30. A class clown turns into a source of motivation.   **89**
31. The student teacher's persistence finally motivates a boy.   **90**
32. Making use of televisio   programs watched by pupils.   **92**
33. A disinterested student is shown the value of education.   **93**
34. A history class makes use of relatives' war experiences.   **95**
35. The student teacher's personal interest motivates a boy.   **95**
36. Consideration helps to motivate an unruly pupil.   **97**
37. A slow student feels cheated on a test.   **99**
38. Special projects and a pupil-conducted class add interest.   **99**
    A superior student with failing grades needs motivation.   **100**
40. Use of improper sources of motivation causes trouble.   **101**

## Problems of Emotional Adjustment

41. A girl tries to escape from poor home conditions.   **112**
42. A stutterer is helped to relax.   **113**
43. A boy's desire for attention is channeled in the proper direction.   **115**
44. A bright student worries about his parents.   **117**
45. Unexplained illnesses are developed by a student.   **118**
46. An only child creates disturbances.   **120**
47. Unfavorable home conditions affect a boy's work.   **121**
48. A withdrawn boy comes out of his shell.   **122**
49. A shy girl is helped to recite.   **124**
50. A boy is helped to overcome his stuttering.   **124**
51. A change of home environment helps a girl.   **126**

52. A girl has no friends.    **127**
53. An unresolved personality problem.    **128**
54. A pupil changes from an introvert to an extrovert.    **130**
55. A student teacher is exposed to a serious case of emotional maladjustment.    **131**
56. A girl seems to feign illnesses.    **132**
57. An eighth-grade boy feels lost after his mother dies.    **134**
58. A broken home leaves a girl without supervision of her home study.    **134**
59. Little progress is made with a juvenile delinquent.    **135**
60. Worry causes a boy's work to suffer.    **136**

## Problems of Individual Differences

61. A bright girl is not challenged sufficiently.    **151**
62. A slow student is given some pride.    **152**
63. Eyeglasses make a difference.    **154**
64. The student teacher enjoys a well-rounded superior student.    **155**
65. Superior students stump the student teacher.    **156**
66. A slow group "makes good" by putting on a play.    **158**
67. A girl lacks control of her voice.    **159**
68. A pupil's special ability in art is used to advantage.    **161**
69. Very little success is experienced in handling a slow student.    **162**
70. A boy is self-conscious about an eye defect.    **164**
71. A superior seventh-grade student needs an enriched course.    **165**
72. A pupil with several physical handicaps makes a good adjustment.    **166**
73. A student teacher sees advantages in homogeneous grouping of superior students.    **168**
74. A possible undetected brain injury changes a pupil's life.    **169**
75. The teacher tries to evaluate individually prescribed instruction.    **171**
76. A class of mentally slow pupils presents problems.    **173**
77. A superior student is disliked by his peers.    **174**
78. A student teacher finds it difficult to adapt his methods to a heterogeneous group.    **175**
79. A student teacher dislikes homogeneous grouping of dull students.    **176**
80. A mentally slow class lacks knowledge of simple facts.    **176**

**Problems of Evaluation**

81. A student takes advantage of a "no failures" policy.   **187**
82. Pupils accuse a student teacher of prejudice in grading.   **189**
83. A student thinks her grade on a test is too low.   **190**
84. A student claims he is checking his answers, not cheating.   **191**
85. Daily quizzes are found to improve work.   **192**
86. The student teacher evolves a grading system.   **194**
87. A student is resentful because his grade was lowered.   **195**
88. A bright pupil teaches the student teacher to be careful in making up test items.   **196**
89. The student teacher bets a failing pupil that he can pass.   **197**
90. A student thinks his teachers are unfair in grading him.   **199**
91. The student teacher gives help to a pupil during a test.   **200**
92. The student teacher prefers essay questions.   **201**
93. A pupil graded low in effort refuses to do any work.   **202**
94. A pupil tries to take advantage of a policy of automatic promotion.   **203**
95. The student teacher decides that spelling and grammar should not enter into a pupil's mark.   **204**
96. Textbook questions confuse a slow pupil.   **205**
97. Grading is based on a pupil's I.Q. rather than on achievement.   **206**
98. The student teacher experiments with tests and grading.   **207**
99. A student is caught cheating on a test.   **208**
100. The cooperating teacher insists on a lower grade for a below average pupil.   **208**

**Problems of Developing Good Relationships**

101. A young student develops a "crush" on the student teacher.   **217**
102. A student teacher receives threatening telephone calls.   **218**
103. Pupils appreciate being treated as young adults.   **220**
104. The student teacher is self-conscious in the presence of the cooperating teacher.   **221**
105. A sarcastic comment arouses the wrath of a parent.   **223**
106. A girl resents a teacher's joke.   **224**
107. Teachers do not relate to a "wise guy."   **225**

108.  Two cooperating teachers are contrasted by the student teacher.   **227**
109.  The student teacher thoughtlessly criticizes another teacher.   **228**
110.  A student teacher seeks preferential treatment.   **229**
111.  The student teacher unwittingly dates a student.   **231**
112.  The question of how long a cooperating teacher should observe the student behavior.   **232**
113.  The student teacher tries to mend broken fences.   **233**
114.  A teacher dislikes team teaching.   **234**
115.  The son of a school board member assumes he does not have to work.   **236**
116.  The student teacher becomes unnerved by the continual interruptions of the cooperating teacher.   **237**
117.  A pupil threatens to hit the student teacher with a chair.   **238**
118.  The cooperating teacher's son becomes a problem.   **238**
119.  The cooperating teacher gives the student teacher no authority in grading pupils.   **239**
120.  The student teacher is enchanted by a student.   **240**

# Preface

*Problems in Middle and High School Teaching* describes 120 problems experienced by student teachers in grades 6 through 12. Ninety of the problems show how each teacher attempted to solve the problem, whereas the other 30 are presented as unsolved, open-ended problems which permit the reader to offer possible solutions.

The material in this book is directly applicable in both student teaching seminars and in-service training seminars dealing with problems in middle and high school teaching. The issues presented supply an abundance of material for discussion, and expose the beginning teacher to enough different problems to anticipate almost any type of situation. Although these problems were experienced by student teachers, they are typical of those that are experienced by any beginning teacher, and even by some experienced teachers.

The problems should also prove highly useful in methods courses, for they illustrate the application of principles in actual classroom situations. The theories taught become real, and more meaningful, when students see them applied in situations which they themselves will very likely meet. Instructors of other professional education courses, especially educational psychology and tests and measurements, will find this book a useful supplementary source. The cases described provide many illustrations of the problems and principles discussed in those courses.

Although nothing can adequately replace actual classroom experience to bring about full realization of the many problems involved in teaching, much can be learned through vicarious experience. It is through such experience that this text seeks, in a modest way, to ease the sometimes rough transition from theory to practice in teaching. The beginning teacher will be able to project himself into problem situations and decide how he would have handled them if they had been his own. Moreover, he will have the opportunity to see how other beginning teachers worked out solutions which are not necessarily the *only* way to approach or solve these problems. Consequently, the cases presented readily lend themselves to a discussion of other measures that might be taken. Except for the open-ended problems, each problem is followed by lead-off questions which provide a starting point for discussion.

Most of the problems encountered by new teachers may be grouped into problems of discipline, motivation, emotional adjustment, individual differences, evaluation of progress, and relationships with school personnel. The illustrative cases are therefore grouped into those categories, with twenty problems in each group. As a further aid to the beginning teacher, the first chapter is devoted to a discussion of mistakes most commonly made by beginners, and suggestions for dealing with them. Each of the last six chapters includes suggestions for dealing with the specific type of problem being discussed.

The emphasis in this book is on the problem approach. Through it, prospective teachers are encouraged to apply principles of education which they are learning, or have learned, in their theory courses. On the other hand, discussion of the problems should lead to the development of other principles and ideas. It is therefore a deductive-inductive process. Such an approach has the obvious merit of compelling education students or beginning teachers to think through and evaluate their solutions.

In the problems described, it will be noted that in many instances the student teachers consulted the personal records of pupils in order to obtain information that might help to understand and solve the pupils' problems. Student teachers are cautioned that the Buckley Amendment, which has been federal law since November, 1974, requires the permission of the parents, or the student if he or she is over the age of eighteen, to consult those records.

With no intention of slighting the female sex, the grammatical rule of using the masculine pronoun when it applies to both sexes has been observed in this book. The use of the masculine alone eliminates the many cumbersome references that would have to be made to "he/she" or "him/her."

The author is indebted to former students for the experiences described herein. Although they suffered varying degrees of anxiety in trying to solve their problems, they have the satisfaction of knowing that their experiences may relieve the growing pains of those who follow them.

# 1

# Common Mistakes of Beginning Teachers

"To err is human . . ." All beginning teachers make errors, some more frequently than others, some more seriously than others. They should not be overly concerned at the prospect of making mistakes, because even experienced teachers sometimes fall into error. The beginning teacher, lacking the experience and perhaps the maturity of judgment of older teachers, will make mistakes more often, and will make them in areas which are no longer a problem to most experienced teachers. When the student teacher first takes charge of a classroom, there are so many things for him to think about simultaneously in a new environment that he may become confused. He is like an inexperienced automobile driver wending his way through heavy traffic for the first time, somewhat bewildered by the rush of movement in all directions. He experiences tension and apprehension, trying to attend to all the little details of his performance, while at the same time striving to remain aware of the activities of others about him. He will make an occasional mistake, but as he gains experience, many actions will become habitual. He will make fewer errors in performance and judgment, he will become more relaxed, and he will be able to consciously focus more fully on the main tasks of maintaining smooth operation and achieving maximum performance. Thus, the possibility of error should be accepted by the student teacher, even though he may minimize it by careful advance preparation.

There are perhaps a thousand and one mistakes possible in teaching, because it is possible to err, at one time or another, in every aspect of classroom activity and in every phase of human relationships. In this chapter, only some of the more common errors made by student teachers are discussed. They are categorized into errors centering around the teacher's qualities, classroom environment, discipline,

1

classroom procedures, evaluation, handling of problem cases, and attitude toward theory courses. Not all the mistakes described are made by all student teachers, nor even necessarily by the majority of them, but the errors have occurred frequently enough to deserve special mention. Interspersed with the discussion of errors are practical suggestions for avoiding them, or overcoming them. Thus, the prospective teacher may at the same time be both forewarned and forearmed.

## THE TEACHER'S QUALITIES

A considerable number of shortcomings emanate from the personal equipment of the teacher. These can be overcome with a moderate amount of effort on the part of the student teacher.

*Poor Voice.*   Many student teachers have difficulty in judging the volume of their voices. The more common error is to speak too softly, resulting in students straining to hear what is being said, or not hearing at all. In many classrooms where the students are unable to hear, they will begin glancing at each other questioningly, and shifting about restlessly. When this situation is later brought to the attention of the student teachers, they always say that they are not aware of it. They should have been aware of it, and might have checked on it by simply asking the pupils in the rear whether they could hear clearly. The student teacher should not wait for a pupil to ask him to speak louder, as sometimes happens. In some rare cases, this error is fostered by a cooperating teacher who believes if the pupils are straining to hear, they will give more attention to what is being said. The device is undesirable, however, because too much of the pupil's attention is diverted to the teacher's voice, whereas full attention should be given to the lesson.

In some cases, the student teacher speaks so loudly that his voice booms and reverberates around the room. Although the pupils have no difficulty in hearing, such a manner of speaking can be as distracting as speaking too softly. Usually the student teacher is able to modulate his voice as soon as his attention has been called to it. If he is unable to do so, he may seek help from the speech department at his college.

*Elevated Vocabulary.*   Fairly often, student teachers make the mistake of talking over the heads of their students. This is largely a problem of the student teacher using terms which are familiar to him, but strange to middle and high school pupils. Unless he is introducing new terms appropriate to the subject, the student teacher should replace polysyllabic words with more simple terminology. This does not mean that he should go to the other extreme of talking down to his students. A little experience and careful observation will enable him to strike the happy medium. Whenever the student teacher uses a word which he thinks might be unfamiliar to the pupils, he should write it on the chalkboard, explain it, or call on a pupil for its meaning.

*Errors of Expression.*   In communicating with their students, prospective teachers often lose their effectiveness by speaking too rapidly or too slowly. In the one case, pupils are unable to keep up with the teacher; in the other case, the pupils are impatiently waiting for the teacher to move along. In either situation, instruction becomes ineffective. The cooperating teacher will usually help the student teacher to acquire a pace which is consistent with the understanding of the class. The more common error of the two is for the student teacher to give his pupils "too much, too fast."

The prospective teacher should try not to sound as if he were giving a speech when he is explaining material to his students. He should talk *to* them, not *at* them. This may be accomplished by using a conversational tone and manner, and by looking directly at the pupils instead of at the chalkboard, the floor, or the ceiling. Some student teachers find it distracting to look pupils in the eye. They can obtain the same effect by looking between pupils; the class then has the feeling that the teacher is maintaining contact with them as his eyes move around the room. As the teacher gains confidence, he can start to make direct visual contact with individual pupils.

Because the beginning teacher has not acquired facility of expression, there are pauses and gaps in his speech. He may have a tendency to fill in those gaps with "Uh ... Uh ..." Other student teachers acquire pet words or phrases which they repeat with disturbing regularity. One student began almost every other sentence with "Now, we see that ..." or ended with "See?" Another student made inordinate use of "All right ..." in going from step to step in the lesson. Most student teachers are unaware of these peculiarities of expression until they are brought to their attention. After being made conscious of it, they usually are able to eliminate or minimize the use of these pet phrases or words.

As one would hope, most student teachers use correct grammar. Occasionally, however, a student teacher lapses into a grammatical error, recognizes the error as soon as he has spoken, but fails to correct himself. It is a mistake not to rectify the error, because there are certain to be pupils in the class who will notice the incorrect expression and conclude that he is ignorant of the proper form.

Similarly, the student teacher should be positive of the spelling of words that he writes on the chalkboard. There is no excuse for not looking up unfamiliar words in advance, but occasionally the teacher will make a purely mechanical error in writing on the board. For that reason, after he has written on the board, he should stand back to read what he has written.

*Distracting Mannerisms.* Many teachers unconsciously develop distracting or annoying little mannerisms or actions. There is the nervous pacer, who walks back and forth as if on sentry duty, with leather heels beating a tattoo on the floor. The chalk tosser may keep shaking chalk in his cupped hand, or may actually send it aloft for short distances. Occasionally, too, we find the coin jingler, who continuously toys with coins in his pocket. The gesturer is distracting because he continuously saws the air with an emphatic motion. There are also other actions involving fumbling with eyeglasses, a lock of hair, buttons, belts, and so on, which draw attention to themselves and weaken the attention pupils give to the lesson. These should be eliminated as soon as they are called to the notice of the student teacher.

*Neglect of Personal Hygiene.* Although most student teachers report for duty with a bright, scrubbed look, occasionally there is one who, although tastefully and neatly dressed, has a problem with body or mouth odors. The body chemistry of some individuals may be such as to require more frequent cleansing of the skin; or it may be that the individual has simply been negligent in airing or cleaning his clothes. Offensive mouth odors may be the result of mouth or stomach disorders, over-indulgence in smoking, or too heavy an onion garnish on food. Whatever the cause, the prospective teacher should work diligently to remove it. Otherwise, he will find his students becoming more distant, both figuratively and literally.

*Lack of Discretion.* Student teachers have occasionally been guilty of indiscreet remarks in and outside of their classrooms. An indiscreet remark ultimately receives a wide audience. It affects not only the student teacher, but also the pupils, the personnel of the cooperating school, college personnel, and even sometimes members of the community. One student teacher in a mining community, in discussing a piece of controversial mining legislation, expressed an opinion unfavorable to the miners. His students apparently carried home what he had said, because the telephone lines began to hum. The parents called the cooperating school; the cooperating school called the college; the student teacher had the matter brought to his attention by everyone. Since it was a controversial issue, he should not have committed himself to the class. The issue could have been handled by pointing out advantages and disadvantages for both sides, and then permitting the students to draw their own conclusions. Such a procedure should be followed on all controversial issues.

It is quite likely that a student teacher may occasionally observe an act or a procedure in the school that could be legitimately criticized. Although criticism may be justified, it should never be given by the student teacher. He should not make negative comments about the school, the supervisors, or the teachers to anyone, with the possible exception of his college supervisor, who can advise the student concerning his difficulties and who will maintain a discreet silence about what he has been told. If the student teacher criticizes one teacher in the presence of another, or if he makes negative comments about the administration, he will arouse antagonisms which will shatter the cooperative relationship which has existed between the student teacher and the personnel of the cooperating school. The student teacher will find himself facing an attitude of hostility, manifested by comments such as, "That young upstart! Who does he think he is, criticizing us?" I recall one student teacher who failed to heed this admonition. After he had been student teaching for several weeks, he criticized one of the regular teachers whom he had been permitted to observe, by saying that he could do a better job than the teacher in question. His comment spread throughout the staff. Thereafter, his stay at the cooperating school taught him a lesson in humility, because the teachers involved in his training program bared to him his every weakness in no uncertain terms.

The future teacher must bear in mind that there is no such thing as a perfect school, administration, teacher, or person. If one searches for weaknesses, he will find them. The student teacher can be sure that teachers and administrators are aware of their shortcomings, and are continuously trying to overcome them. To be criticized by a neophyte can have no other effect than to arouse resentment. If the student teacher wishes to be critical, he would do well to turn his eyes inward, examining himself to discover his own shortcomings. He will find so many things within himself that need improvement, that he will have no time to criticize others. (See problem 109.)

*Lack of Knowledge of Pupils.* A teacher cannot hope to be successful without knowing his pupils as individuals. Although a great deal of his preparation and instruction is directed toward the group, he should at the same time cultivate a knowledge of individual students and their problems. Some student teachers do not give evidence of this aware-ness to the degree that they should; they think of their pupils as a class, rather than as individuals making up a class. This outlook is erroneous, for the student teacher should try to help each pupil develop whatever potentialities he has as a unique person.

It is unbelievable, but true, that an occasional student teacher knows so little about his pupils that he is unable to identify them by name, even though he has been instructing them for several weeks. This is inexcusable negligence. Most student teachers learn the names of their pupils before they finish their period of observation, and are able to address pupils by name as soon as they begin to teach. During their pre-teaching period, too, they have acquired a great deal of infor-mation about the pupils from records, teachers, and their own observa-tion. The student teacher who, during his second or third week of teaching, is still calling on pupils by using terms such as "the second pupil in the third row" has been very remiss in becoming acquainted with his pupils. One must consider, too, how much better a pupil feels and responds when identified by name.

*Disproportionate Individual Help.* Even though most student teachers do a creditable job of identifying and resolving individual problems ex-perienced by their pupils, they occasionally become so engrossed with the problems of one individual that they neglect the others. A case in point is the student teacher who spent all his study periods and most of his free time outside of class helping one pupil. This was unfair to the other pupils who, although their problems were less spectacular, nevertheless also needed help. The student teacher should budget his time so that he can give at least some help to all who need it.

*Unprofessional Manner.* In their desire to be accepted and well liked, a considerable number of student teachers err in the direction of being too friendly with their pupils. In some cases of this type, student teachers need not be surprised to hear themselves addressed by their first name outside of class. Although pupils do not usually address teachers by their first name, this type of behavior is encouraged by the student teacher's familiarity. It should be emphasized once again that, although the student teacher should be friendly, he should maintain enough dignity and formality to discourage students from taking liber-ties in their relationship with him. Once the student teacher has over-stepped the bounds of propriety in this matter, it is very difficult for him to retrace his steps. It is better to err by being too formal at first than being too familiar. Students will welcome the change from exces-sive formality to warm friendliness, whereas a change in the other direction, from familiarity to at least a temporary unbending formality, will produce strained relationships. The student teacher therefore should avoid fraternizing with his pupils. (See problem 120.)

Sitting on the desk, with legs dangling, is likewise unprofessional. Other undesirable posturings include resting a foot on a chair or an open lower drawer of the desk, or partially sitting on a pupil's desk. Besides being undignified behavior, these actions hardly encourage proper respect for property among the pupils, who might imitate this type of action in the school, home, and society.

*Negative Approach.*   Some student teachers concentrate on "don't" rather than "do." They focus their attention on the mistakes of pupils, but seldom commend them on their good efforts or performances. This approach may betoken the hypercritical, nagging, complaining type of teacher who expects little, and gets less from his pupils. As he prepares to teach, the student teacher should regard education as a growth, not a withering process. He must nurture, not destroy, the pupil's confidence and motivation in developing his powers. He should be sure to praise a good answer or piece of work. Even if a pupil's answer is not wholly correct, the teacher can try to lead the pupil to the desired response, thus helping him to success. Indeed, even if the pupil's answer is incorrect, and the teacher is unable to help him to a correct answer, his approach can still be positive by using comments such as "Not quite," or "Can someone add to that answer?" This device leaves the pupil feeling that he may have contributed something to the recitation. Most pupils seek approval and commendation. If they never receive it, if they hear only negative comments, they themselves will develop a negative attitude toward the teacher, expressed by comments such as, "Why should I work? You can't satisfy him no matter what you do."

*Lack of Emotional Control.*   Since he is human, the student teacher will at times find strong emotions welling up within him, but he should guard against permitting his emotions to rule his actions. Since his pupils are also human, mischievous, and sometimes downright perverse, they will at times tax the teacher's patience to the limit. The student teacher must learn to control his anger, and deal with the pupil on a rational, rather than on an emotional, basis. Most of us remember teachers in high school who threw chalk or erasers at pupils, who slammed books on the desk, who lifted pupils bodily out of their seats, or who cuffed pupils over the head or ears. These, of course, are extremes of behavior manifested by teachers who had little emotional control. They might have resulted in physical injury to the pupils, but, beyond that, they produced a classroom atmosphere which was not conducive to learning.

The student teacher must also guard against allowing his actions to be influenced by his affection for certain pupils. Some pupils are more naturally likable than others, and there will be an occasional pupil who attempts to influence the teacher's judgment by "polishing the apple." Some student teachers have "pets" or "old reliables" on whom they depend excessively for correct responses, or for the performance of errands and chores. Since the other pupils are quick to notice and resent such preferential treatment, it should be scrupulously avoided.

Emotional control is a matter of self-control, achieved through practice. When the student teacher feels anger surging up within him, he can control it by shifting his attention and thoughts to something else. For example, if he feels that he is about to lose his temper with a pupil, he should terminate the incident by telling the pupil to report to him after class, and then proceed with the lesson. Or if he does not wish to do this, he should wait a few moments before addressing the pupil in question. Just a few seconds are enough for the student teacher to gather himself together sufficiently to deal with a pupil on a rational, rather than on an emotional, level. In doing so, he not only deals with the situation more effectively, but also provides a good example to his pupils. A teacher cannot expect self-control from his pupils unless he himself practices it.

**THE CLASSROOM ENVIRONMENT**

The environment in which pupils learn should be aesthetically and physically comfortable, and should contain the essential tools of learning. Although the student teacher cannot remedy basic defects in the classroom, such as walls that need painting, he should at least make the most effective use of what is available.

*Untidiness.* The classroom should always be kept neat. Books, periodicals, desks, and chairs should be kept in orderly array. A student teacher who has books and papers strewn all over his desk, or who has flung his hat and coat atop a cabinet, is hardly a good example to his students. A half-erased chalkboard can make an otherwise neat room appear sloppy. These are things that can be easily avoided. He can also take positive measures to eliminate signs of disorder for which he was not responsible.

*Poor Lighting.* Not all student teachers are as sensitive to proper lighting conditions as they should be. There are those prospective teachers who fail to turn on the classroom lights on dreary days; the students seated near the windows may have sufficient light, but the pupils on the other side of the room could be in deep shadows. Besides interfering with vision, poor lighting may be reflected in the attitude of the pupils; a dark room is not conducive to bright spirits. Sunny days may also present problems. Unless the shades are properly drawn, some students may be sitting in direct sunlight, while others are subject to the discomfort of glare of reflected light.

*Improper Temperature and Ventilation.* In one classroom a pupil raised his hand to ask if he could open a window. In another room, a strong breeze through an open window was causing papers to flutter. There is no reason why a student teacher should wait for complaints from his students before adjusting the temperature or ventilation in the classroom. He should automatically check the temperature when he enters the room, and immediately make appropriate adjustments. If changes in temperature occur during the period, he should be sensitive enough to notice and take action.

*Inadequate Supplies.* Quite frequently, student teachers have to pass out supplies, though these needs should have been met before the recitation began. Confusion is further compounded if the student teacher has no definite system for the distribution of supplies. In one class, the student teacher was interrupted by a pupil who requested additional paper. When the student teacher asked if others needed paper and the majority had raised their hands, he gave a ream of paper to the first pupil in the first row, telling him to help himself and then pass it along. After the lesson had continued for a few minutes, another hand shot up, the pupil saying that more paper was needed. Two rows of students had consumed a ream of paper! The student teacher had to stop the lesson again, gather in the surplus paper, and distribute it equitably throughout the class. When he had finished, he still had half of the original ream left. Thus, lack of system produced not only waste of valuable class time, but also needless waste of material.

## DISCIPLINE

Generally speaking, student teachers do not make any serious errors in handling discipline. This is probably because disciplinary problems are the ones most feared; acceptable principles for dealing with this type of problem consequently receive considerable attention and careful practice from student teachers. Among the errors they do make, three occur with greater frequency than others.

*Lack of Regulations.* It is a great mistake for a student teacher to take over a class without telling its members what is expected of them. Lack of regulations breeds disorder. The pupils, knowing neither what to expect nor what is expected, may experiment to find out what is required—a process which causes needless disorder in the class. At the outset, the student teacher should outline to the class a set of reasonable regulations and standards under which they will operate, explaining that these are necessary for order and for effective learning. He should also inform the class that he will have to take action against anyone who acts in such a way as to jeopardize the welfare of others. Many student teachers who fail to state their regulations at the start, have to pause after a week or two of teaching to do so. In the meantime, there has been much misunderstanding and inefficiency which could have been avoided.

*Imprudent Leniency.* One of the more common errors made by student teachers is to assume that if they are lenient, they will be well-liked, and that if they are well-liked, better learning will result. The latter conclusion is generally true, but the first one rests on false premises. Strange as it may seem to the new teacher, pupils like moderate strictness better than leniency. As a matter of fact, they lose respect for a teacher who is lenient, regarding it as a sign of weakness. Student teachers discover this sooner or later, sometimes so late that they never regain a desirable type of control over the class. Being lenient is unfair to the pupils because it does not foster self-control, and because it produces undesirable learning conditions which deprive them of the training they should be receiving. The student teacher, therefore, should begin by being strict, but should temper strictness with justice and charity.

*Belligerent Attitude.* Although it is well to be strict with new groups, the teacher should guard against tyranny. It sometimes happens that a student teacher is so fearful of not being able to control his class that he overdoes strictness. He takes over the class with an "I'll show you who is boss" manner, not permitting the rustle of a paper, and treating the shuffle of a foot as if it were a thunderclap. This type of student teacher has no difficulty maintaining discipline unless he meets a student who is as belligerent as he. However, the apprehension, tension, and resentment that build up within the students frustrate the main purpose of the classroom meetings. The pupils cannot or will not learn as well as they should because of these emotions. Thus, the student teacher maintains order, but interferes with the learning process.

An excessively belligerent attitude is sometimes a manifestation of a student teacher's lack of confidence in himself. He holds an excessively tight rein because he fears that if he relaxes his hold, the class will run away from him. He should realize that he will lose control only if he goes to the other extreme of holding a fairly loose rein. Quite often an overly strict student teacher mellows to the proper degree after he sees that he has little to fear from the class. (See problem 8.)

Another type of student teacher sometimes found is the half-hearted belligerent. He is the one who uses threats to quell disorder, but does not have the heart to follow through with his promises of punishment. Since the pupils learn that he does not mean what he says, his threats become meaningless and fail to act as a deterrent to disorder. Such student teachers finally reach a point where they must take action that should have been taken a long time before. A student teacher should never issue a threat unless he intends to act upon it. If he does act promptly, pupils will not misbehave because they will know that punishment will be swift and certain.

## CLASSROOM PROCEDURES

The ideal classroom is one in which the pupils and teacher are cooperatively and interestedly engaged in learning activities that lead to desirable and accepted goals. Many things contribute to the attainment of this ideal, such as the teacher's competence, the classroom environment, and the nature of the pupils. Also contributing greatly toward a desirable learning situation are the methods and procedures used by the teacher. Although prospective student teachers have studied these, and may have had some previous experience in their use, they often fail to use, or they misuse, these effective instruments of learning. Because methods and procedures are so numerous, more errors are made in this area than in any other. Again, the discussion is confined to those errors most commonly made by student teachers.

*Insufficient Material.* Beginning teachers have difficulty in judging the amount of material they will need for discussion during a class period, or they do not pace themselves properly with an adequate amount of material. As a rule, they go over a lesson much faster than they thought they would, with the result that they are left with time on their hands toward the end of the class period. The obvious remedy is to prepare more than they think they will use—a good rule of thumb for the beginner. Later, as the student teacher becomes adept at raising questions and leading discussions, he will find himself covering less, but uncovering more of the material.

Should the student teacher find that he has run out of material before the end of the period, he may profitably spend the remainder of the time with a review of the work of the period, or he may call on pupils to answer questions based on the day's work. If he is unprepared to do this, he may make the next day's assignment and permit the students to spend the rest of the period working on it.

*Improper Lesson Planning.*   No student teacher should walk into a classroom without a written lesson plan. The written plan provides him with a guide for the day's work, as well as making provision for aims, review, content, procedure, and an assignment for the next day. In thinking through and writing up lesson plans, student teachers make several common errors.

1.   The aims are not properly stated. The aim of a lesson should be stated concisely, and should relate only to that particular lesson. Most student teachers state their aims in such broad terms that it is difficult to relate them specifically to what is being learned or taught. Even though a teacher has general aims for a unit or a course, he must achieve those aims step by step through daily work. It is obviously advantageous to him and his pupils if he has thought through these steps well enough to be able to express them. Moreover, in the statement of aims, student teachers make the mistake of stating what they hope to accomplish with the material rather than what they expect to do with the students. In education we hope to bring about desirable changes in pupils; subject matter is but one instrument in this process. Consequently, the aim should state what the student teacher is trying to do for and with his pupils.

Recently, in the statement of aims, emphasis has been placed on stating what a pupil will be *able to do* after completing an instructional activity. Aims or objectives expressed in this way have been termed as behavioral or performance-based objectives. These objectives are expressed in concrete terms to show specific learning tasks the pupil is expected to be able to perform. They may also state the level of proficiency expected of the student, as well as the conditions under which it will be done. Following are examples of behavioral objectives:

- Given a written composition, the student shall be able to identify errors in spelling and punctuation with at least 90 percent accuracy.

- Given a column of ten three-digit numbers, the student shall be able to add them with 100 percent accuracy.
- After having read Shakespeare's *Hamlet*, the student shall be able to summarize its plot in writing.
- After having studied the elements of a good short story, the student shall be able to evaluate Poe's *The Pit and the Pendulum*.
- The student shall be able to describe how animals adapt to their environment.
- The student shall be able to research a topic in the library, and present his findings orally to a class of peers.
- The student shall be able to dissect a frog, and identify its organs.

It will be noted that the first two objectives listed not only state what the student shall be able to do, but they also specify the conditions under which it is to be done and the level of proficiency expected. The conditions and level of proficiency may not be necessary in the statement of some objectives. Thus, the third and fourth objectives state the conditions and the activity, but do not specify the level of proficiency expected. The last three objectives simply specify the activities.

The student teacher will need to think through and state carefully on his lesson plan the objectives for a particular lesson. In all cases, the objectives must state specifically what the pupil is expected to be able to do after he has completed the lesson.

2. Procedures are not specific enough. Most student teachers make an adequate outline of the material to be taught, but they do not state clearly how it is to be taught. For example, in outlining procedures and methods, student teachers use phrases such as "Explanation," "Chalkboard will be used," "Passage will be read," and so on. Such descriptions of procedure are too vague. Better statements would be "Explanation by the teacher, with examples," "Students will work these exercises on the chalkboard," and "Passage will be read by the teacher; then he will question pupils on it." The procedure should show what activities will be performed and by whom. Some student teachers outline their own activities very well, but fail to state what the pupils will be required to do during the class period. An outline of both is necessary. The lesson plan should therefore show not only what is to be taught, but also how it will be taught. In describing the how, the activities of both the teacher and the pupils should be shown.

3. Assignments are not detailed enough. Very frequently, the only notation found on the assignment section of the lesson plan is a brief, "Read pages 276–284," or "Read Chapter VI." Certainly, the teacher's intention is not to require mere reading of a certain number of pages, but rather to have pupils read them meaningfully and critically. To help or stimulate the pupils to do so, the teacher should give them a general preview of the material, point out things to look for, and indicate how the new assignment relates to what has been studied. As a study aid, the teacher may ask the students to prepare answers to questions on the material. Or he may wish to test their understanding by giving an oral or written quiz at the beginning of the next period. Whatever he intends to do with and about the assignment should be set down in written form on the lesson plan. He should be sure to leave enough time at the end of the period, or at some time during the period, to be able to explain the assignment adequately and to answer any questions the pupils may have on it.

The lesson plan is an important part of a student teacher's work. If he makes it out properly, it is evidence that he has devoted sufficient attention to all phases of the work of the day. It enables the cooperating teacher, or any other observer, to see in a moment what the student teacher hopes to accomplish on that day, and how he expects to go about it. It also serves as a guide to the student teacher as he progresses with the day's work. (See figure 1.1.)

The lesson plan is a general outline. As such, it cannot possibly include all the details of content and procedure. The beginning teacher, therefore, will find it helpful to keep a set of notes to which he can keep referring if necessary. In these notes he can include important details on content obtained from supplementary sources. He may wish to include actual examples and illustrations that clarify and explain the material, or jot down a reminder to refer to a particular source. Details of procedure may be added in his notes. At a certain point he may wish to remind himself: "Throw this open to discussion," or "Get pupil reaction to this," or "Have pupils put this in their notebooks." Notes of this type assure the teacher that he will not forget important items of content and procedure. Such thorough preparation will also add to his confidence. In the beginning, of course, the student teacher will find himself including much more in these notes than he will after he has acquired experience.

*Overuse of the Lecture Method.* After they overcome their initial timidity about talking before a group, some student teachers never stop talking. Whether they are bewitched with the sound of their voices, or

**Figure 1.1  Sample Lesson Plan**

Teacher _____ Date _____ Subject _____

*Title of this lesson:*  The Life of Abraham Lincoln

*Objectives:*  1) The student shall be able to describe the main events of Lincoln's life;
2) The student shall be able to give examples of Lincoln's honesty, integrity, and industry;
3) The student shall evaluate Lincoln as a person and as a president.

*Points to be reviewed:*  None. This is a special lesson for Lincoln's birthday. (An assignment was made a week ago for students to write a 500-word composition on Lincoln's life.)

| Content | Procedures |
|---|---|
| 1. Lincoln's life<br> a. Ancestry<br> b. Boyhood<br>  1) Log cabin<br>  2) Schooling<br> c. Early years of manhood<br>  1) His first look at slavery<br>  2) His dry-goods and grocery store<br>  3) His study of law<br>  4) His marriage to Mary Todd<br> d. Rise on politics<br>  1) Election to state legislature<br>  2) Election to presidency<br> e. Lincoln as president<br>  1) The Civil War<br> f. His death | 1. The teacher will briefly relate the general facts of Lincoln's life, describing instances of his honesty, integrity, and industry. Pupils will take notes on Lincoln's life.<br><br>The teacher will pause occasionally to ask questions, or to respond to questions raised by pupils. |
| 2. Evaluation of Lincoln's life | 2. The teacher will lead a class discussion, calling on students to evaluate Lincoln as a man and as a president. In supporting their opinions, the students will make use of the material they researched for their compositions.<br><br>3. The teacher will collect the compositions written by students. |

*Assignment:*  The students will read pages 167–173 in the textbook, and write out answers to questions 1, 5, 6, at the end of the chapter. (The teacher will give a preview of the assignment.)

At the beginning of the next period, the students will be questioned orally on the assigned reading.

whether they are over-zealous in imparting knowledge, the practice is undesirable. Rare is the teacher who is able to sustain attention through the exclusive use of the lecture method. If it is necessary for the student teacher to lecture (as it often is), he should periodically interrupt with other activities such as questions, discussions, or summaries. The student teacher should always keep in mind that the *pupil* must be kept busy with a variety of activities if his interest is to be maintained, and if effective learning is to take place.

*Improper Questioning Technique.* In spite of the fact that student teachers know they should not take their pupils' understanding for granted, they are often careless in the matter. After explaining material, it is common to hear a student teacher ask, "Are there any questions?" and, if there are none, to move on with the lesson. The fact that no one volunteered a question does not necessarily imply that the material was understood, because many pupils hesitate to ask questions, especially of a new teacher. Instead of addressing such a broad question to the entire class, the student teacher should spot-check the pupils' understanding by addressing questions to individual pupils. If it appears that they understand the material, the teacher may safely move on to new grounds, but, if the questions show that they do not understand, further explanation is in order.

It is sometimes apparent that pupils are repeating verbatim what they have read, or what the teacher has said. Some student teachers are satisfied with this type of answer, while others more properly ask the pupils for a further interpretation of what they have said. Ability to repeat words does not necessarily imply understanding. Unless the purpose of the question is to drill the pupils, the student teacher should keep probing for meanings. This he can do by asking questions that call for evaluation, analysis, comparison, contrast, generalization, or criticism. Too often student teachers are satisfied if their pupils accumulate facts. Although facts are important, they are but a foundation for the higher intellectual processes—namely, the ability to form concepts and make valid judgments and conclusions. The effective use of the questioning technique is one of the best means to attain that goal.

Other frequent errors in the use of the question are to designate the respondent before asking the question, or to allow insufficient time for the formulation of an answer. When the student teacher begins a question with "Jimmie, explain what is meant by . . . ," only Jimmie is really challenged to think. If, instead, the teacher addresses his question as follows, "Explain what is meant by . . . ," and then pauses before calling on Jimmie, all the pupils are thinking of an answer during the pause. Sometimes, too, the student teacher errs in not allowing enough time during the pause for the pupil to frame a suitable answer. Thought questions require the pupil to gather and organize ideas, a process which is not instantaneous. Often a pupil will respond, "I don't know," simply because he was not given sufficient time to think through an answer.

*Neglect of Drill.*    Occasionally a student teacher will state with some degree of satisfaction, "My class is doing very well. We are one chapter ahead of schedule." A serious question could be raised as to whether the class is really doing well. To be sure, it has covered material extensively, but has there been as intensive study as there should have been, and has there been a proper degree of mastery of material? In every course, there are important facts, ideas, habits, or skills, which should be made a certain possession of the student. One of the ways to assure mastery is through drill, by repetition and practice. This takes time. Consequently, if a student teacher is running well ahead of the schedule of experienced teachers, it can safely be assumed that he has neglected something. Either he has not probed deeply enough into the material, thus exposing his students to superficial learning, or he has not dwelled long enough on the mastery of important elements of the course.

*Improper Review.*    Drill concerns itself with initial learning, whereas review is a view backward over material already learned. Although there is an element of drill in review, the function of review goes beyond repetition of previously learned material. Review, if properly conducted, integrates and correlates material, thus adding new meanings and broader understanding. The threads of each individual lesson are woven together into a fabric wherein a pattern emerges. It is this pattern which is neglected by some student teachers, perhaps because they have not yet achieved skill in the weaving process, or because they have made no attempt to do so. The student teacher should ask himself: "How do these things fit together? What is the total picture?" When he has answered these questions for himself, he will be able to lead his students also to the answers.

*Insufficient Illustration.*    One of the most powerful allies a teacher has is illustration. Even a rough diagram drawn on the chalkboard can often make things clearer to the pupils than a carefully detailed verbal description. Though there is an abundance of concrete materials that can be obtained within the school and from outside sources, one occasionally finds a student teacher who will discuss geographical locations without referring to a map, who will describe the strategy of a battle without outlining on the board the positions of the belligerents, who will discuss Shakespeare without a picture or a model of an Elizabethan theatre, who wi¨ discuss plant life without bringing in specimens, and so on. Every teacher, and especially a beginning teacher, needs all the aids he can muster in the learning process. Wise use of illustration makes learning easier, more vivid, and more interesting. No student teacher should neglect its use.

*Failure to Help Pupils with Note-taking.*   One of the best aids to study is a good set of notes. Proper note-taking has several advantages. It gives the pupil practice in organizing material into main ideas and their subdivisions. In doing this, the pupil must look at material for its meaningful elements, and thus exercise logical thinking in placing ideas in their proper perspective. Moreover, a concise set of notes saves the student considerable time whenever it is necessary for him to review the material. Also, in studying and reviewing the material, the pupil is able to see, almost at a glance, the main ideas and their relationship to one another. The material thus outlined may be from the textbook, from supplementary material introduced by the teacher, or from research work assigned to the pupils.

The mistakes made by student teachers in this area consist largely of acts of omission. In the first place, some student teachers assume that pupils are accustomed to taking notes and will do so without being reminded of it. Secondly, they mistakenly assume that their pupils know how to take notes. Finally, student teachers assume that their pupils can take notes faster than they are really capable of doing. One has but to observe a few high school classes to know that all of these assumptions are unfounded. There are always pupils who are doodling instead of taking notes on the teacher's explanations. Some are taking down the trivial and omitting the important, while still others may be trying to take down everything the teacher says. At times, too, one notices that the pupils are unable to keep up with the teacher because he is proceeding too rapidly.

Student teachers can do a great deal to help their pupils to take notes correctly and efficiently by observing the following practices:

1.   Announce that note-taking will be required, that notebooks will be checked periodically, and that their quality will be an element in grading.

2.   Show the pupils how to make a topical outline if they do not already know how to do so.

3.   As a guide to the students, place an outline of the day's material on the chalkboard.

4.  Inform the pupils that they should not try to take down everything that is said in class. For a while, actually tell them what should be placed in their notebooks.
5.  Require them to outline each chapter in the textbook.
6.  Proceed deliberately enough to allow time for note-taking.
7.  Be sure to check notebooks at regular intervals.

These procedures will require extra effort on the part of the student teacher and his pupils, but the benefits derived make it worthwhile. The training received by the pupils will have the immediate value of facilitating learning, but in addition, it will help build habits of systematic thinking of benefit to them throughout life.

## EVALUATION

In spite of the fact that student teachers are usually very careful and conscientious about testing and grading their students, there are several mistakes made with disturbing regularity. These are made during the first weeks of teaching, and are gradually overcome through experience and through advice.

*Dictation of Test Questions.* The disadvantage of dictating test questions is obvious: it is not only time-consuming, but also lends itself to misinterpretation. In addition, it deprives the student of time to ponder over the answers he finds difficult. In spite of all this, there are some student teachers who use this procedure of administering tests. In such a classroom, the students' train of thought is continually interrupted by the dictation of the next question. Some students are finished with a question, others are not. Some students have heard and understood the question, while others ask to have it repeated, or look quizzically at their neighbors.

It is a rare school today that does not have duplicating machines for the use of teachers. All the problems and disadvantages mentioned are eliminated if the test is duplicated and a copy distributed to each student. If the cooperating school does not have the necessary equipment, the student teacher can usually make arrangements with his college to have his tests reproduced.

*Unreasonable Tests.* In the beginning, student teachers are prone to give their pupils tests that are either too long or too difficult, or both. This is a discouraging experience for both the pupils and the student teacher, because the grades on such tests are low. The student teacher can avoid such an outcome if, before giving a test, he asks the cooperating teacher for samples of tests previously given so that he can form a judgment on the length and difficulty of the test he should give. Also, after drafting his proposed test, the student teacher should show it to the cooperating teacher, who will judge its suitability. Finally, he should take the test himself. If he finishes it in about one-half the time he allocated for the test, it is probably of reasonable length.

*Subjective Grading.*   Sometimes student teachers allow their grading of certain students to be influenced by personal feelings. "He is a nice boy, and he tried very hard, so I gave him a passing grade." Such a comment is typical in these cases. Whether or not the pupil is a nice boy should have no effect on his grade. As for "trying very hard," how can one possibly evaluate a pupil's degree of effort in relation to his ability and achievement? The student teacher should base his grade on the pupil's achievement. In grading, he cannot concern himself with what could be or might have been; he must deal with what *is*.

*Changing a Grade.*   Assuming that a student teacher has arrived at a grade in a conscientious and careful manner, he should not permit himself to be influenced by students to change it. The student teacher will be confronted with this problem after every test which he returns to the pupils. One or more pupils usually ask for additional credit on answers marked wrong, or partially wrong. A pupil will inform the student teacher, "This is what I meant by my answer," and will proceed to give his answer a twist or a boost which would make it acceptable. I have heard some student teachers concede: "All right, I'll give you the benefit of the doubt." The student teachers raised the grade, and the students gleefully walked away. Other student teachers handled the situation more properly by informing the students: "I cannot grade you on what you *meant* to say. Your answer, as it stands, is incorrect." In these cases, the student teachers did not change the grade. The pupils usually accept this stand. They are hoping, rather than expecting, to get additional credit. After being refused, it is not uncommon to hear pupils say: "Well, it was worth a try, anyway." Student teachers who take a firm stand on the matter of grading discourage further such attempts on the part of the pupils. On the other hand, the student teacher who permits himself to be swayed will find an ever-increasing number of pupils requesting grade changes. (See problem 83.)

*Grade Changes by Cooperating Teachers.*   Sometimes student teachers forget that the grades they submit for students are *recommended* grades, and that the cooperating teacher has the responsibility for ultimate approval of the final grades. Occasionally, but not very often, the cooperating teacher changes a grade recommended by the student teacher. I recall one student teacher who became so resentful of such a change that he came out with remarks in class which made the cooperating teacher appear to be an ogre walking with an axe, chopping down grades. There is no justification for this type of reaction. Student teachers must always keep in mind that, although they are delegated a considerable amount of responsibility, the ultimate responsibility for the welfare of the students rests with the cooperating teacher. Even though the student teacher may not like having a recommended grade changed, he should have enough professional spirit and ethics to accept it graciously. (See problem 100.)

## HANDLING PROBLEMS

There are very few problems that student teachers do not eventually solve. When errors are committed in handling problems, they are usually errors of omission. No matter what the problem, it is safe to say that the student teachers could have saved themselves many heartaches by taking a few positive steps which would have led to an earlier solution of their difficulties.

*Delay in Taking Action.* The most common error made in handling problems is to delay facing them. The problem cases cited in this book are full of incidents about student teachers who did not take action soon enough. It is as if they threw up a mental smoke screen between themselves and the problem, hoping that when the smoke lifted, the problem would no longer be there. Instead, the problem persists. The delaying tactics, in fact, have given it time to grow to more serious proportions. The student teacher, therefore, once having identified a problem, should take appropriate action immediately. When he does, he will experience relief from the anxiety that usually accompanies procrastination in such matters. He will be properly discharging one of his duties as a teacher in helping a pupil with his problems, and, depending on the nature of the problem, he may prevent it from spreading to other pupils. Generally speaking, the student teacher who tries to avoid problems through delay finds, instead, that his problems increase both in number and in magnitude. (See problem 40.)

*Failure to Have a Private Talk with the Student.* Some student teachers fail to make adequate progress in the solution of a problem because they lack information, or because they do not understand the individual well enough. One of the best sources of information is the pupil himself, yet some student teachers try to solve problems on an impersonal basis in public view of the class. Though it is true that many minor problems can be solved in this way, by a word of encouragement or by a reprimand in class, any deep-seated problem of motivation, maladjustment, discipline, or personal relationships must be handled, in part, on an individual basis through a private talk with the pupil involved. It is only through such interviews that the student teacher can learn enough about the pupil to be able to help him with his problems. Since such conferences are conducted on a personal basis, and since it is evident to the pupil that the student teacher is genuinely interested in helping him, they produce a type of information and a degree of rapport which cannot be obtained in any other way. In discussing their unsolved problems with student teachers, I always ask if they had had a private talk with pupils involved. Time after time, the answers have been negative. "I thought I would wait a while," or "I was going to try that next" were typical responses. They should not have waited so long before utilizing this most effective technique of handling problems. No one can help a pupil effectively without first being able to define the problem and without understanding the nature of the individual.

*Failure to Seek Help When Needed.* It sometimes happens that a student teacher has taken all the appropriate measures, including private talks, but has been unable to solve a pupil's problem. For such a failure he is not to be condemned, because not all problems can be readily solved. He is to be criticized, however, if he shelves the problem when he is not able to solve it. Many student teachers fail to seek help with perplexing problems because, they say, "I felt it would be a sign of weakness if I were not able to solve my own problems." Actually, it would be a sign of weakness only if the student teacher kept running to someone for help with every little problem that came up. To seek help with a serious problem after one has exhausted his own resources is, rather, a sign of strength of character. It is not easy to admit one's limitations, but it is a sign of wisdom to do so. After all, even the most experienced teachers consult with their colleagues. Consequently, the student teacher should not hesitate to confer with his cooperating teacher or his supervisors after he has tried to solve a problem and failed. To do otherwise is a disservice to his pupils and to himself. (See problem 65.)

*Neglecting Responsibility.* The prospective teacher should guard against listening to inner or outer voices which urge him: "Forget about her—she doesn't want to be helped," or "Don't bother with him—he isn't worth being helped." In conscience, the student teacher must *try* to help every pupil who has been placed under his care. The girl who does not want to helped probably needs more help than the others, and it might be that the student teacher will strike just the right chord with her. As for the boy who "isn't worth being helped," the student teacher should not try to sit in judgment on the worth of an individual. In his eyes, all pupils should be regarded as equal but unique, each with different problems, and each entitled to the opportunity of being helped. Perhaps the boy who "isn't worth being helped," was too long deprived of this opportunity.

Similarly, the student teacher should not lapse into a frame of mind, sometimes induced by lack of time, which prompts the attitude: "I am going to be with these pupils only a few months. How could I possible help a pupil with a serious problem in that short period of time?" The answer is: "You can help him a *great deal.*" I am continually amazed with the results achieved by student teachers who really *want* to help their pupils and take the time to do so. Even though there are many cases that student teachers are not able to conclude successfully because of lack of time, they walk away from the scene with a feeling of satisfaction, knowing that there are others to continue the help where they left off.

## ATTITUDE TOWARD THEORY COURSES

It is quite probable that the greatest and most common mistake made by future teachers occurs even before they begin student teaching. Unfortunately, students are somehow possessed of the notion that a dichotomy exists between theory and practice. Consequently, in taking their theory courses in professional education, they do not give sufficient attention to the practical application of the principles and theories they learn, even though their instructors attempt to help them do so. They do not ask themselves: "How will I apply this in the classroom? How will this help me in teaching?" Instead, they neatly compartmentalize the information as theory, recall it on their college tests, and then forget to apply it when they enter the classroom as teachers. The truth of this has been demonstrated on countless occasions when student teachers have approached me with problems. Most of these problems were solved by asking these students questions such as the following: "Do you remember what we said in Educational Psychology about causes of emotional maladjustment, and the basic steps to take in dealing with them?" "In the course in Tests and Measurements that you took, do you remember discussing the essentials of a good test?" And so on. In each case the student teacher usually responded with a grin, reached into the compartments of his mind, and pulled out the information necessary to apply to the particular problem.

In their theory courses, then, they have listened but have not heard, and have looked but have not seen. Had they heard and seen, they unquestionably would have avoided many of the errors that were described in this volume.

## MAINTAINING PROPER MORALE

The student teacher should not become discouraged if he makes mistakes now and then, or if his class does not run as smoothly as he would like. If he is a conscientious teacher, he will never be fully satisfied with his efforts. He will always be able to look back at his day's work, analyze it, and mentally note that "I should have spent more time on this," or "It would have been better to do it this way than that." At the same time, he usually will also be able to say, "The pupils were certainly interested in that discussion," or "That explanation went over well." If he is honest with himself, he will always find bad points as well as good in his teaching. It is important for his morale and for his efficiency that the satisfaction received from the good always outweigh the discouragement over the bad. The student teacher need not worry about the direction in which the scale will tip if he always does the best he can, but he should be sure to strive to *do* the best he can. No one can ask for more, and he cannot afford to give less.

•   •   •

The description of student-teacher problems in the following chapters shows that some student teachers handled their problems admirably, while others fell into one or more of the aforementioned common errors. As the reader studies these problems, he should project himself into the student teacher's situation, trying to decide how he would have handled the problems if they were his own.

The 120 problems described in the following chapters were experienced by student teachers who were teaching in grades 6 through 12. Although each problem occurs within the context of a particular academic subject, most of the problems could have occurred in *any* classroom, regardless of the subject being taught.

Each of the following chapters begins with a discussion of theory appropriate to the type of problem under consideration, and is followed by practical suggestions for dealing with such problems. In order to facilitate the correlation of textual material with the problems, reference is made throughout the textual material to specific problems which illustrate the particular points being discussed.

As a starting point for the discussion of the problems, the first fifteen in each chapter are followed by discussion questions. Some of these questions call for general exposition of theory, but most of them are directed toward the specific problem under consideration. Should the instructor wish to emphasize certain points of theory, he can bring these out by adding questions of his own. No discussion questions were provided for the five open-ended problems in each chapter, because such questions would provide direction in the solutions of the problems, thus limiting open-ended responses from the reader.

Reaction to the problems may be either written or oral. Should the instructor wish a written evaluation from his students, two sample worksheets are provided on the pages which follow. The first of these is designed for use with the first fifteen problems in each chapter, and the second for use with the five open-ended problems in each chapter.


Name _____     Problem Number _____

Course_____     Date_____

Section _____



*Evaluation of the student teacher's thoughts and procedures:*




*Additional measures that might have been taken in this case:*

Name _____   Problem Number_____

Course_____   Date_____

Section _____

*Describe alternative courses of action that might be taken in this case. Select the one you would use, and give reasons for your selection.*

# 2

# Problems of Discipline

Nothing causes more anxiety among prospective teachers than wondering if they have the ability to maintain order in the classroom. "Will I be able to keep them interested?" "How strict shall I be?" "Will there be any troublemakers?" "How shall I handle them, if there are any?" These are questions which keep recurring among students who are about to begin student teaching.

Many students become fretful, and in a few instances, their anxiety borders on panic as the first day of teaching approaches. It is not a rare occurrence for a student to ask that he be dropped from the student teaching program, even before it has begun. Usually he is persuaded to try it, and almost always he is happy that he did.

Except for a few extreme cases, students who show signs of anxiety as the day approaches are behaving normally. It is as natural for a student teacher to be under tension while he awaits his first meeting with a class as it is for a speaker to be keyed up before making a speech. It is also a natural process for most of this anxiety and tension to dissipate after the first few days of teaching.

Although there will be problems arising for every student teacher, in most cases they will not be as serious as anticipated if handled properly from the outset. Small problems can become big ones if they are not dealt with immediately, or if they are not managed in accordance with recognized principles. Besides these minor problems which exist in every classroom, a teacher will usually find one or two individuals in each class who require special attention. Inasmuch as these special problems will call forth all the teacher's knowledge of growing children, and all his ingenuity if he is to resolve them adequately, such problems should be regarded as a challenge rather than a source of anxiety.

The prospective teacher's ability to cope with disciplinary problems means a great deal to him in terms of personal happiness and instructional efficiency. The teacher who has tried, but failed, to maintain order in the classroom walks about with the feeling of failure instead of the experience of happiness and satisfaction that can come from teaching. Without an orderly classroom he is assured of failure, because effective instruction cannot take place amid disorder. Moreover, unless he has control of the class, he will lose the respect of his pupils, which in turn will create further problems for him. Under such conditions, many beginning teachers are lost to the profession, either because they have left voluntarily, or because their contracts were not renewed. Thus, in teaching, the ability to maintain discipline is the keystone of success, happiness, and even survival.

What is discipline? There are shades of interpretation of the term, but it is usually associated with helping the student acquire self-control, and with the measures that are taken to bring this about. Hence, discipline may be defined as training in self-control, and the means adopted to foster self-control and orderly conduct. Such a concept implies that the school and the teacher have developed systematic means to help the pupil direct his thoughts, actions, and emotions toward proper goals. It also implies acceptance and active cooperation on the part of the pupil—an acceptance and cooperation which require self-control to do not only what is immediately interesting, but also what at times may be distasteful.

The most desirable and beneficial type of self-controlled activity is that which arises from the pupil's understanding and acceptance of proper values. He actively participates in a lesson because it is interesting, or because he realizes the value of the subject being studied. He abides by rules or procedures because he recognizes that they contribute to his welfare.

Unfortunately, because of their essential immaturity, pupils do not always recognize what is good for them. It is then that external influences are brought to bear on them, to stimulate them to self-control which will help them guide their activities toward conformity with school regulations. Sanctions are imposed upon them for not doing their homework, for disrupting the class, and so forth. In order to avoid these penalties, most pupils work and conform even though they do not have the best type of motivation to do so. It is one of the teacher's never-ending tasks to try to generate the type of motivation which drives the pupil from within.

In spite of the fact that means are taken to train pupils in self-control, an occasional rebellious head will crop up, or there will be an occasional lag in the learning process. It is well to remember that there is always a *reason* for such lapses. Sometimes, the teacher is at fault; at other times, the pupil is at fault. Sometimes neither is to blame, for the cause may be found in the pupil's environment, or in the state of his health. Whatever the cause, if it is uncovered, remedial action will usually return the learning situation to normal.

It would not be possible to list all the causes which might contribute to disciplinary problems. The teacher may err through insufficient preparation, or because he does not understand the characteristics of children at various stages of development. The pupil may be at fault in his desire to be "one of the gang," or, on the other hand, in his desire to achieve recognition by being unpleasantly different. Still other causes of misbehavior may be rooted in physical defects, or in a frustration of basic needs in the home.

The explanation of any particular problem case is complicated by the fact that no two pupils are alike. Consequently, in trying to explain the conduct of a particular pupil, he must be considered as an individual. General knowledge of the characteristics of growing adolescents is useful, general principles of handling them may be applied, but there are also unique factors which are indispensable in understanding and solving the problems of some students.

The following discussion of ways of maintaining an orderly classroom, and some of the ways to deal with problems that do arise, should prove to be a helpful guide in evaluating and discussing the problems which appear in the last part of this chapter.


## SUGGESTIONS FOR MAINTAINING DISCIPLINE

*Set and Maintain Standards.*   A good beginning is extremely important for success in teaching. When meeting a class for the first time, the teacher should explain his procedures, standards, and regulations, and the *reasons for them.* Pupils want to know how the class will be conducted, and what will be expected of them.

Once the teacher has made these matters known to his students, he should insist that they be observed. To make an exception is to invite other exceptions. To accept an untidy paper is to encourage more papers of this type. To assign homework and not collect it is an invitation to the pupils to take the chance that it will not be collected again. To overlook conversation between two pupils is to court further distractions of this type.

*Prepare Thoroughly for Each Class.*   Thorough preparation assures the teacher of knowing, during every minute of the class period, exactly what he will do, and how he will do it. This adds to the teacher's self-confidence, and enables him to unfold the day's activities with assurance. Pupils are less likely to probe for weaknesses in the teacher's armor if he appears to be a competent individual.

*Make Sure Pupils are Attentive Before Beginning a Class.* Unless orderly conditions are present, effective learning cannot take place. No teacher should begin to conduct a class in which any form of disorder is exhibited. The teacher must have the pupils' undivided attention. Whispering, note-passing, giggling, shuffling of feet, pencil sharpening, and other distractions must cease when the teacher is ready to begin a lesson. If the student teacher deals with these problems at the outset, he will have set the tone for his class. He will find that pupils readily recognize and respect a teacher's ability to control his class.

*Make Provisions for Pupil Activity.* Busy pupils have no time for mischief. The teacher's lesson plan should include ways of keeping all pupils active at all times, through oral work, written work, chalkboard work, or through special projects or research work.

Special problems present themselves in a traditional classroom during board work and during recitations. How can the attention of the class be maintained while the few are working at the chalkboard, or while a single pupil is reciting? The problem of board work is solved readily by providing activity for the pupils remaining in their seats. The seated pupils may be required to write exercises similar to those being written on the board, or groups of pupils (a row, or a half-row for each student at the board) may be asked to watch closely to determine the accuracy of the work being done at the board. In this way, all the pupils are actively engaged in the lesson.

An effective way to keep pupils active during a recitation is to tell them at the outset that they will be held accountable for everything that is discussed in class. If the pupils know that they may be checked *at any time* on class material, they will generally give attention to classroom activities. These checks by the teacher may take the form of oral questioning, spot-check test questions, or asking pupils to summarize at any time during a class period.

*Use a Variety of Procedures.* Variety adds spice to teaching, whereas the same routine day after day is flavorless. It is difficult to hold the attention of pupils for long periods of time with an inflexible method of teaching.

Although there is a limit to the number of methods and techniques that can be used effectively in teaching a subject, the teacher should alternate the procedures that are appropriate to him and his course. In addition to lecturing, the teacher may intersperse activities involving chalkboard work, demonstrations, drills, reviews, oral reports by students, class discussions, panel discussions, dramatization, individual and group projects, and appropriate use of audio-visual aids. (These are discussed in more detail in the chapter on motivation.)

A common mistake made by beginning middle and high school teachers is to overuse the lecture method. They explain, describe, or narrate to the students, while their pupils occupy themselves by taking notes. This procedure, if continued without interruption, is deadly to interest and attention, because middle and high school students, still in the process of acquiring self-control, cannot maintain voluntary attention for long periods of time. Consequently, if it is necessary to lecture, the middle and high school teacher should do so only for short periods of time, and then pause to ask questions, or to have pupils summarize, or to start a discussion, or to answer pupils' questions. After interspersing activities of this type, the teacher may again lecture for a short time.

*Know and Treat Your Pupils as Individuals.*  As soon as possible after beginning to teach, the teacher should be able to identify each pupil by name. No student likes to be regarded as a number or a name on a seating chart. If the beginning teacher is able to call each pupil by name, the pupil feels that he is known as an individual, thereby improving the teacher-student relationship.

In addition, the teacher should try to learn something of each pupil's background and interests. This not only gives the teacher a better understanding of the pupil's progress, or lack of it, but also helps the pupil realize that the teacher has a personal interest in him. To be able to ask one pupil, "How is practice for the play coming along?" or to tell another, "That was a pretty flashy set of wheels I saw you driving!" or to ask about the health of the member of the family who is ill, will cause a spark in a student's eyes that can be kindled in no other way. A teacher who does this sincerely seldom has disciplinary problems. (See problem 25.)

*Be Just in Dealing with Pupils.*  A teacher who does not treat his students fairly and objectively is certain to have trouble with them. Although he is sure to like some of his students better than others, he should never allow this feeling to enter into the evaluation of their progress. If he does, the rest of the pupils will readily become aware of the fact that he has "pets" or "pet peeves," and they will become resentful, sometimes to the point of failing to cooperate in classroom activities. It is sometimes necessary for the teacher to consider extenuating circumstances, or to sprinkle justice with charity, but this acceptable practice is altogether different from allowing feelings to influence judgment.

*Have a Sense of Humor.*   There are occasions in the classroom when a pupil may say or do something that is truly humorous, resulting in an uproar of laughter among the pupils. Instead of regarding this as a breach of order, as some teachers do, the teacher should allow a few moments for this type of catharsis to spend itself. In fact, if the situation is appropriate, the teacher may have a good laugh *with* the students. There are times, too, when the teacher may make a humorous blunder, but the pupils hesitate to laugh at the teacher. If he can humorously chide himself for his lapse, the pupils will generally respond with a good-natured laugh—laughing *with* the teacher rather than inwardly laughing *at* him. In such cases, the pupils respect the teacher for admitting his error, and for being able to laugh at himself. This type of attitude on the part of the teacher goes a long way toward establishing good relationships and maintaining discipline. (See problem 2.)

## HANDLING DISORDERLY PUPILS

There are many ways of dealing with disorder in the classroom. Some are more effective than others, but even the more effective means are not equally effective with all pupils. The student teacher, therefore, should try to deal with a problem in a way he thinks appropriate. If this does not solve the problem, he should try another, and another, until he reaches an effective solution in a particular case. The student teacher should recognize, however, that sometimes, no matter how hard he tries, he may fail to solve a particular problem.

The following ways of dealing with disorderly pupils are ones that have been used frequently by teachers. Although there are differences of opinion as to their value, an attempt will be made to evaluate them on the basis of their effectiveness in the experience of a large number of student teachers.

*Private Talk.*   Having a private talk with the individual is by far the most effective way of dealing with disciplinary and other types of problems. A sincere, frank talk with the student has the effect of showing him that the teacher is interested in him as a person, and that, to-gether, they can attempt to solve the problem. In a private talk, the pupil is more likely to cooperate, there being no need for him to resort to face-saving or attention-getting devices, as there would be in the presence of his classmates. (See problem 26.)

*Reproof.*    One of the most frequently used means of restoring order in the classroom with cases of minor disturbance, such as whispering, talking, or lack of attention on the part of the pupil, is reproof. A re-buke from the teacher is usually sufficient, except in the case of the chronic offender, with whom other means would then have to be employed. The effectiveness of a reprimand varies with the individual. Some pupils will do anything to avoid being reprimanded; others merely shrug their shoulders and continue with actions that invite other measures to be taken.

*Sarcasm.*    Whereas reproof is an acceptable way to restore order, sarcasm is not. Reproof is a just rebuke directed at the act of the pupil, but sarcasm is a cutting, caustic remark that belittles the student as a person. Although sarcasm may quiet a disorderly student, it causes resentment within him. If the teacher continues to be sarcastic, the pupil and his classmates may lose respect for the teacher. Also, there is the danger that resentment may build up to the point of exploding into more serious problems. Since nothing positive is accomplished by sarcasm, it should be avoided.

*Frequent Questioning.*    A measure that sometimes produces quick re-sults with a pupil who is talkative or inattentive is to direct questions to him more frequently than to other students. It takes the pupil only a short time to recognize that he is questioned more frequently when he is disorderly than when he is not. Usually, he will then begin to give more attention than he did previously.

*Change from Recitation to a Test.*    Should a considerable portion of the class be involved in disorder, it may be quelled immediately by calling a halt to the recitation and giving a short test on the material being discussed. This is a procedure which immediately both quiets the class and acts as a deterrent to future disorder. The test grades on such an unannounced test will usually be poorer than on a regularly announced test; thus, after correcting the tests, the teacher may point out that little progress is made unless there is order in the classroom. The teacher, however, should give little weight to these tests in making up a student's grade, because the undesirable circumstance under which they were given does not reflect a pupil's true ability.

*Consulting with Parents.* Very often the teacher can receive help with a serious or a chronic problem by conferring with the parents. Frequently, parents do not realize that their children are misbehaving in school, particularly when they make no effort to meet with the teacher or to attend parents' nights. A conference with the parents might be profitable for all parties concerned. The parents become enlightened on the conduct of the student, and the teacher receives information which gives him further insight into the child's problem. After exchanging information, there may be mutual agreement on a plan of action involving the cooperation of the parents. Moreover, the student, knowing that the parents and teacher are working together, will very likely be more cooperative than he was in the past.

In dealing with parents, the teacher must exhibit tact. He should not place the blame on the parents, and should not in any way imply that they are not doing their duty. His approach should be: Here is a mutual problem—what can we do about it together? Tact is especially necessary in the case of parents who think their children "can do no wrong." Unless approached properly, some such parents become highly indignant and refuse to cooperate, even though the child's welfare in involved.

Sometimes, a problem can be solved merely by telling the pupil that, unless he behaves, the parents will be called in. This device is effective to the degree that the student respects the authority of his parents. An interesting variation of this technique was reported by a student teacher who was having difficulty with a student. One day in class, while the pupil was not giving attention to the lesson, he asked the student for his home address, and then continued the recitation. After class, the pupil asked why he wanted his address. When told by the teacher that his parents would be interested in learning about his conduct in class, the student begged that his parents not be informed, and promised to behave. The student teacher agreed, and he had a model pupil thereafter.

*Gaining the Cooperation of the Group Leader.* All groups have recognized leaders. This is particularly true of adolescents, who sometimes blindly look up to their heroes, and as blindly follow their lead. If the teacher can win over the leader of a particular group in class, he should have little difficulty with the others. This might be done by enlisting the aid of the leader with some routine procedure in class. If he cooperates in one thing, he may cooperate in other activities.

Needless to say, it is not always easy to win over the group leader. The basic step would be to have a private talk with him, during which the teacher may take the approach that he has noticed leadership qualities in the student, and that these qualities could be put to good use in helping individuals not as gifted as he. Some form of appeal to his ego, in addition to recognition of his qualities for leadership, may win him over. (See problem 3.)

*Isolation.*   Adolescents wish to be identified with and accepted by a group. Consequently, isolation from the group is effective with individuals who have a strong desire to work with the group. This isolation may be either physical or psychological.

Physical isolation takes the form of placing the individual in a seat which separates him from the rest of the group. It is usually better to place him in the rear of the room, because he is less able to attract the attention of others from that point. It is well also to explain to the student that he has been isolated because he is impeding the progress of the group, and that as soon as he has demonstrated his willingness to cooperate, he will be permitted to rejoin the group.

In cases where it is evident that two or more pupils sitting next to each other are part of a clique, breaking up the group through changes of seats will usually quell disorder or incipient disorder. This change may be made openly, or it may be done unobtrusively by including other students in the seat changes.

In employing psychological isolation, the pupil is permitted to remain in his regular seat, but the teacher does not include him in classroom activities. He is not asked questions, nor is he recognized when he wishes to ask a question or to contribute to a discussion. This is effective to the degree that the student seeks teacher approval.

*Detention.*   Keeping the pupil after school has been a common form of punishment. It is effective when the pupil has other things he wishes to do, or has to do, after school. If a pupil misses a club meeting, or football practice, or if he is late for a part-time job, he will strive to avoid activities that might place him on detention. If, however, he has little else to do after school, the punishment loses its effectiveness.

Detention has several disadvantages which should be noted. First, it may create hardships for students who are dependent on school buses for transportation. Second, the pupil may be deprived of participating in an extracurricular activity which is of more benefit to him than the detention. Third, the detention may jeopardize a pupil's part-time employment, or may interfere with after-school chores which have been assigned to him. Finally, the teacher is also a victim of the punishment in that he must remain after hours.

*Assigning Extra Work.*  It is generally agreed that extra work should not be assigned as punishment for disorderly conduct, although there are teachers who have found it effective and strongly defend its use. The danger cited is that a pupil may begin to associate school work with punishment, which in turn may lead him to dislike all school work. It is possible that this might happen, although the proponents of this form of punishment say that it is unlikely because pupils dislike extra work so much that they will behave in order to avoid it. While this may be true, it is hardly a desirable way to motivate pupils to work, and the student teacher would be wise not to assign extra work as punishment for disorderly conduct.

*Deducting Academic Credit.*  The grade a student receives should be based on his achievement, not on his deportment. Although the threat to "deduct five points from your grade" may sometimes quiet a rebellious student, this practice distorts the picture of the pupil's ability to achieve. Actually, if a teacher *does* deduct the credit, his problems may begin to multiply. The students become resentful, and the teacher may be asked by supervisors and parents to justify his position. He would find it difficult to do so.

*Dismissal from Class.*  Dismissal from class is a serious affair. It is akin to suspension from school, except that the suspension is confined to one class. During his absence from class, the pupil is, of course, missing important instructional activities that are going on during that time. The student teacher should resort to dismissal from class only after he has exhausted his own resources in handling the problem. If he does resort to this measure, it implies that he was *not* able to cope with the situation.

Under no circumstances should the teacher dismiss the pupil without directing him what to do. If the teacher merely tells the pupil to leave the room, the pupil may enjoyably spend the free period he has been given. Instead, the student teacher should tell the student to report to the cooperating teacher or the principal; and the student teacher, as soon as he is free to do so, should check to make sure that the pupil reported as directed. It would be well to tell the pupil at the time he is dismissed from class that he will not be readmitted until he has a slip from the proper authority permitting him to do so. (See problem 9.)

*Public Apology.*  For a pupil to stand before his classmates and publicly apologize to them for a misdeed is a humiliating experience. Usually it accomplishes nothing constructive from the viewpoint of teacher-pupil relationships, and the smouldering resentment the student carries with him certainly is not conducive to willing work on his part. The only circumstance under which a public apology might be justified at all would be in a situation in which the student has affronted the entire class. (See problem 7.)

*Corporal Punishment.* There has been considerable controversy on the use of "physical persuasion" in the classroom. Generally speaking, it should not be used because problems can usually be solved through less drastic measures. It is conceivable, however, that there are occasions when it is necessary for a teacher to use force, for example, to eject a pupil who is causing physical harm to another pupil, or to quiet a pupil who has become excessively abusive. Also, the teacher should have the right to defend himself against a threatening pupil. Such cases are rare, and they are seldom experienced by a good teacher.

Even though the United States Supreme Court ruled that corporal punishment may be used in the schools if the punishment is "reasonable," there are local policies regarding its use. The student teacher should immediately inquire of his supervisors what these policies are. In any event, the student teacher should avoid its use, for pupils and parents generally resent such action. There is the additional danger of physical injury to the pupil, which might expose the teacher to a lawsuit. If a student teacher thinks that a problem can be solved only through the use of corporal punishment (which is unlikely), his most prudent course would be to refer the matter to the cooperating teacher or to the principal. (See problem 4.)

• • •

The examples of disciplinary problems which follow are types frequently experienced by beginning teachers. As the problems are read and discussed, it will become evident that some of them were handled quite well by the student teacher. In other cases, however, it will be equally evident that the student teacher contributed to his problem through improper measures, or by not acting soon enough.

## PROBLEM 1: CLASS DISCUSSIONS BRING AN UNRULY CLASS TO ORDER

Before I had a chance to meet Class 7-3 I heard many things about its members, and what I heard was mostly bad. Several sources described 7-3 to me as a "bunch of marble-heads," "potential dropouts," "future voc-tech punks," "creeps," and other labels I would rather not mention. So, psychologically I tried to prepare myself to meet the "monsters."

My first experience with them is one I will never forget. John insisted on talking all the time. Greg wouldn't sit near Louise because she was a "creepy slob," Joe walked around whenever the spirit moved him, and Ann was more interested in combing her hair and putting on make-up than she was in anything else.

I tried every method I knew to try to bring them to order, and get them interested, but nothing seemed to work. It took me about two weeks before I recognized that my methods were no different than those of other teachers who taught this group. I realized if I were to get anywhere with this class, I would have to think of a different approach.

I gave the matter serious thought for a few days, trying to project myself into the shoes of a twelve-year-old. I decided one of the things I would like most would be to have someone hear my problems and complaints. My next problem was to try to incorporate myself as a "listening post" into my teaching techniques.

My solution to the problem was to accelerate our English lesson each day so as to allow time for discussion at the end of each period. I explained this to 7-3, telling them we would discuss *any* *topic* they wanted during the discussion period. They whooped and hollered their approval.

From that point on, they talked and I listened during the discussion period. I listened and listened, and listened some more. Before long, 7-3 came into my class and behaved—well, almost anyway. We hurried our lessons, and then talked. I found myself learning from them. They talked about pollution, drugs, events in history, boys and girls, and just plain everyday problems. I don't really know how much they learned from the book, but I know they learned something about living. I do know they gave more attention to their English lessons, because they looked forward to continuing the practice of having discussions.

I had my doubts as to whether or not I had done the right thing, but my doubts vanished when I received a letter in the mail from one of those "bad kids":

Dear_____:

Your class is fun to be in. It is the first time I really liked English. And I am getting better grades in English. We can do more in your class than any other. I like the way we have discussions. And I hope you have a long and happy teaching career. It is really a pleasure to be in your class. I would like to be in your class all the time.

Your English student (signed)

I know I haven't performed any miracle, but this letter made me believe that I had reached at least one student, and all the frustrating and exhausting days were well worth it. I'll miss 7-3 very much.

## Points for Discussion

- *What would educators think of allowing discussion of any topic in class?*

- *This student teacher accelerated the English lessons. What disadvantages are there to doing this?*

## PROBLEM 2: A STUDENT TEACHER'S SENSE OF HUMOR SOLVES A DISCIPLINARY PROBLEM

During my first week of teaching eighth grade English, Jerry sat in the rear of my classroom making a nuisance of himself. Even before I had started to teach, other teachers informed me what I could expect of him. He was completely indifferent to schoolwork, teachers, and school itself.

On several occasions, his parents had been summoned to the school to discuss Jerry's poor attitude toward school. However, his parents thought he was a paragon of virtue, and rather than cooperate with the school, they accused the school of mistreating and "picking on" him. With no help forthcoming from the parents, the school tried, but failed, to stimulate him toward desirable goals.

Even though Jerry's reputation had preceded him, I had resolved that the opinions of other teachers would not influence me in my relationships with students. I did not want any student to feel that he had been labeled good or bad, as is so often the case. Consequently, in my classroom procedure, I gave each student the chance to prove himself by calling on each to participate, ignoring none.

By the end of my first week of teaching, each student, except Jerry, knew what was expected of him, and cooperated in all classroom assignments. I received homework, classroom participation, and good behavior from all but Jerry. When I called for homework, he did not have it with him, or admitted not having done it. When I called on him in class, I would have to tell him what page we were on, what sentence we were analyzing, and even how to begin it. It did not take me long to discover that he knew how to do it, but simply would not cooperate in the procedure. I decided that if he wished to be treated like a first grader, being questioned on each step before replying, I would continue the process, hoping it would embarrass him. It didn't. After repeating this procedure several times I gave it up because it was wasting too much class time.

I considered one or two other ways of awakening Jerry. The school where I taught had instituted a demerit system for students who did not do their work or who misbehaved. The number of demerits was shown on report cards, so that parents could be informed of their children's behavior. With Jerry, however, collecting demerits became a hobby; he already had garnered 155. Feeling that an additional five demerits would only add to his proud "collection," I decided against using demerits. The other type of punishment I considered was detention. However, I discovered that Jerry was completely booked with detention for several weeks to come.

Toward the end of my second week of teaching an event took place which completely altered my relationship with Jerry. I had the students making introductory speeches in preparation for writing paragraphs. While one of the students was giving his speech, I stood in the back of the room. Standing there, I saw Jerry put a cough drop box into his mouth. He blew into the box, producing a screeching sound.

When the student finished his speech, I stood there watching Jerry. He slipped the box into his desk. Suddenly, the whole thing struck me as funny. Instead of reprimanding him, I stood there laughing, remembering that I, too, had done the same thing only a few years before. Laughing, I asked him to show the class how he had produced the screeching noise. He did. The class laughed, he laughed, I laughed. Within a short time the laughing subsided, and the class was ready to continue with the speeches.

From that time, Jerry became one of the class. Homework was handed in, and classroom recitation and behavior improved. The answers were not always right, but the attitude was.

### Points for Discussion

- *What means would you take to try to convince Jerry's parents that he was not a "paragon of virtue"?*

- *Discuss the use of demerits and detention as forms of punishment.*

- *How would you have reacted to Jerry's screeching noise?*

## PROBLEM 3: A RINGLEADER IS WON OVER BY A PRIVATE TALK

Every time I entered the classroom after the bell had rung, it took me from five to seven minutes to quell the noise. I had to resort to shouting before order was restored.

Then, after I began the class, the sound of whispering would fill the room, but I was unable to trace it to its source. I knew it was started by one or two students, from whom it would mushroom in all directions. I changed the seats of some of the students, but it still didn't stop entirely.

After a few days, I finally singled out the ringleader. He was a tall boy who looked older than he was. He had been held back in school one year, and the others in the class looked up to him as a "hero." I found out from my supervising teacher that this boy did not like school, and he caused trouble in other classrooms. One teacher in the the school told me the only thing he would understand was corporal punishment, but I did not want to resort to that. I had some vague hope of being able to help him reform.

The next time he caused trouble, I called out his name sharply and reprimanded him in front of the class. Though this device quieted him for a while, he then refused to answer questions during recitations. A few days later he started to get loud again. I changed his seat, but he kept it up. I was at my wit's end when I decided, as a last resort, to have a personal talk with him. My comments were somewhat as follows.

"Look, my friend, I don't know what your trouble is, and I don't know why you take the attitude you do, but I want you to know that I have a job to do here and I intend to do it in spite of you. If you don't like school, I can't help it, but you are going to have to stay here until you are of age to leave, so you might as well be nice instead of nasty. If you don't want to work in class, that is all right with me, but don't disturb the others by talking. I'm not going to tell you again. I expect you to keep absolutely quiet in class from now on. I have asked you like a man to stop, and I expect you to act like a man and obey."

He answered, "All right; I'll keep quiet but I won't do any work, because no matter if I work or not, I'll get the same grade."

I promised him that if he worked for me, he would get exactly what he earned.

At the very next class meeting he behaved perfectly, but he would not answer a question. I continued to call on him everyday. Finally, he began to answer, but he seemed very shy—I think it was because he was giving up his old role, and didn't want the rest of the class to think that he was becoming "soft." Gradually, however, he began participating daily, and even raised his hand to answer every time I asked a question. Though I continued to be firm with him, I made it a point to praise his work whenever the opportunity presented itself. This praise, I think, encouraged him to the point where he now works fairly well for me. Of all the experiences I had in student teaching, this boy's improvement has given me the most personal satisfaction.

### Points for Discussion

- *Do you think a ringleader loses "face" when he decides to stop making trouble? Why?*

- *What probably prompted this pupil to say that he would get the same grade whether he worked or not?*

- *What are the experimental findings on reproof as a means of maintaining discipline?*

### PROBLEM 4: CORPORAL PUNISHMENT IS USED TO QUIET A BOY

My supervising teacher warned me about Donald, a habitually wayward and mischievous boy of fourteen, who was completely indifferent to teachers and studies. He had no interest in anything, including sports. Recreation periods were taken up with fights and quarrels with other children. In the classroom he would sprawl in his seat and yawn intermittently.

After my first week of student teaching, Donald began to disturb me and his classmates by making caustic remarks about them whenever they would answer a question. I reprimanded him and threatened him, but he persisted in his ways. To gain added attention, Donald would start humming, or drumming his pencil on his desk.

I talked with other teachers who had Donald in class. They told me they could not do a thing with him. I then talked to the school psychologist, who told me that mental and personality tests showed Donald to be normal in all respects. However, the psychologist thought that environmental factors in the home were conducive to making Donald a poor student, and at times, an emotionally disturbed student. Donald's mother was a widow who held two jobs to support the children. Nevertheless, the psychologist felt Donald would eventually outgrow his need for attention.

I was left without a definite solution to the problem. After thinking it over, I felt that a lack of firm male guidance may have caused the problem. Force is a last resort, but in this case it seemed advisable.

When Donald persisted in his sarcasm and noise-making, I took the bull by the horns. During the course of a recitation by a student, Donald kept interjecting sarcastic remarks. Very nonchalantly I walked up the row in which he was sitting, and gave him a re-sounding slap which sent his hair flying in all directions. He was frightened and stunned, not uttering a word. I kept right on questioning the other students. There wasn't a sound from Donald for the rest of the period.

From that day on, Donald was a reformed pupil. He took an active part in class work, and even volunteered to decorate the classroom for Christmas.

### Points for Discussion

- *What do educators recommend on the question of corporal punishment?*

- *In this case, was it necessary or not to use corporal punishment? Why?*

- *When should the student teacher have taken action in this case? Why?*

### PROBLEM 5: SPECIAL PROBLEMS IN THE BIOLOGY LABORATORY

Discipline in laboratory work is extremely important. Taking proper precautions and safety measures can be a matter of survival for the students and/or the teacher. Yet, I found that regardless of the detailed instructions I gave, some of the students in my biology labs did not take my instructions seriously.

One of the most dangerous procedures is sterilizing agar in the autoclave. We did not have an automatic autoclave, so it was risky business trying to maintain 21–22 pounds of pressure when this particular autoclave was set to blow at 23 pounds of pressure. When the gauge reached 22 pounds we had to remove the autoclave from the hot plates, let the pressure go down to 20 pounds, and then put it back on the hot plates. This process, lasting thirty minutes, was a potentially disastrous one, especially if the safety devices failed. My college-bound biology students were very cautious about the procedure, but I had to watch the vocational students like a hawk, because the latter acted as if they would have taken delight in seeing the lab blow up.

Blood typing interested the students. Here again, however, problems can arise, because some students are squeamish about pricking their finger with the blood typing lance. One fourteen-year-old boy was so frightened that he flatly refused to do it, and he literally turned white while watching the others. At the other extreme was the boy who wanted to show the others that he was a "he-man." He was not satisfied to prick his finger; instead, he lanced his skin for about 2½ inches, just above the wrist. It was not a serious cut, but since he was bleeding steadily, I sent him to the school nurse to be bandaged. In the meantime, some of the other students panicked when they saw the boy bleeding, so that ended blood typing for the period.

One of the biggest problems in laboratory work is that some pupils will not believe what they are told. They want to experience things for themselves, even though they have been warned of danger. For example, when distilling the water for dissolving agar, wet paper towels must be wrapped around the flask so as not to burn the hands when touching it. However, *in every class I taught* there were unbelievers, or those who wanted to test their threshhold of pain. As soon as I turned by back to them, they reached for the hot flask with their bare hands. Consequently, the lab was periodically disturbed with a yelp or howl of pain.

Small but aggravating things sometimes interfere with experiments. In an experiment on trying to determine family pedigree, I distributed PTC taster strips to the students. They were to take these home to test the members of their family for positive and negative reactions. The main problem here was that some of the students "misplaced" them. They came in with excuses: "It was in my pants pocket, and my mother washed the pants"; "It was in my notebook, and must have fallen out on the way home"; or, "My family would not do the test—they objected to putting anything in their mouths." Since we had a limited amount of taster strips, these students could not perform the experiments.

There are many other problems a student teacher has to cope with in laboratory work. Following are a few of them:

1. Students work in pairs on the experiments. This created two problems: (a) the students socialized, became noisy, and had to be quieted regularly; and (b) in many cases, one of the pair did all of the work while the other did nothing.

2. Some students are allergic to formaldehyde and/or embalming fluid. Even a slight allergy to some of these substances may result in redness, swelling, and tearing of the eyes.

3. Working with specimens is repugnant to some students. A familiar complaint by students in the biology lab is, "Ugh! I'm not going to touch *that*! It's all slimy! And does it smell!"

4. All of my labs were taught on one day. I had very little time between classes to make sure the lab was cleaned up and all materials were ready for the next group.

5. Students would often complain that the scalpel was not sharp enough, or the scissors would not cut, or the forceps were missing. Although I check all of my equipment after lab, it seems that other teachers did not.

There were some lighter moments in the lab, if you can call them that. One day a boy asked me if I would like to see what was in his gym bag. I replied, "Sure." He reached into his bag, pulled out a 1½-foot snake, and waved it in my face. The girls in the lab became hysterical, and I, not too calmly, dispatched him to the principal's office to get rid of the snake.

## Points for Discussion

- *What safety precautions will you take in the lab sections of the science you are going to teach?*

- *Since students often work cooperatively in lab sections, what measures can be taken to minimize noise, roaming about, and other distractions?*

## PROBLEM 6: THE STUDENT TEACHER USES QUESTIONABLE DISCIPLINARY PROCEDURES

A student teacher is confronted with many interesting individuals, some more fascinating than others. One that interested me a great deal was a freshman who was in one of my classes.

From the first day I taught, I noticed Mike tended to isolate himself from the rest of the class. He came in alone, left alone, and made no attempt to mingle with his classmates. Naturally, I wondered why he was a loner.

Within the next few days, I found that he cried readily. He cried in my class, in the hallway, and in the yard. The students, of course, knew that he was a crier, so they teased him about being a "cry baby." This, in turn produced more crying spells.

I felt a private talk with Mike was in order, so I called him aside after class. I told him his classmates looked down on him because of his crying. I pointed out to him that one could expect frequent crying from a baby, but that he was in high school and should have outgrown that type of reaction. I asked him how many of his classmates cried at the slightest provocation, and he replied, "None." He said he would try to stop.

All went well for a few weeks, until I saw him cheating on a test. This naturally called for a strong reprimand by me, and public derision in the presence of the class. He broke down and cried. Again I told him that he must learn to control his emotions.

A short time later, while I was conducting a discussion of *Julius Caesar*, I noticed Mike was reading a magazine instead of paying attention. When I asked him why, he said that he had finished reading the play ahead of time. I asked him if he understood it. He replied proudly that he had. I then proceeded to ask him several questions, showing him how little he knew about the play. I thoroughly embarrassed him in front of his classmates. Again the tears came.

I had another talk with Mike after class. I asked him if he thought he was right in reading a magazine during class. Guiltily he admitted he was wrong. As for his crying, I told him he would have to learn to accept criticism from others without breaking up emotionally, because it was part of living. In essence, I told him to "grow up." I feel I have helped him.

## Points for Discussion

- *Although very little background is given in this case, how would you have handled Mike?*

- *Do you agree or disagree with the student teacher's conclusion that he helped Mike? Why?*

- *What is the attitude of educators toward criticizing pupils in the presence of classmates?*

### PROBLEM 7: CLASSROOM FISTICUFFS

Ronald and Thomas were members of my sophomore English Grammar class, with all the natural exuberance of normal, healthy, sixteen-year-old boys. It was with difficulty that they behaved themselves in class, and I was often forced to reprimand them during my first month of student teaching.

One day, a number of the boys were at the blackboard writing some sentences, while I was working with the rest of the class at their seats. Suddenly a loud commotion began. Tom and Ronnie were fighting! They had had a disagreement over a piece of chalk, and their short tempers had caused them to lose control of themselves.

Almost unconsciously I rushed into the fray. Violently, I grabbed the shoulder of each and separated them. Since I had formulated no plan of action for such a situation, all I could do was to hold them apart while their ruffled feelings were calming down.

I told the boys to resume their seats. Next, I wondered what I should do with them. The obvious remedy was to march them to the principal's office, but I was mindful of the admonition to use such a measure only as a last resort. I asked them, therefore, to act like men, to shake hands with each other, and then apologize not only to me but also to the other members of the class.

By this time the boys were more embarrassed than angry, and I could see that they dreaded the ignominy of an oral apology. To help them out, I made a few remarks on bravery, ending with the question: "Is a person braver if he loses his self-control and begins to fight, or if he makes a public apology for disrupting the class?" Heartened by this, the pair came to the front of the room and shame-facedly shook hands, then apologized to me and to their classmates.

Since that time both boys have been well-behaved in class. Perhaps in this case "the cure was worse than the disease," and may have acted as a deterrent to further outbursts on their part or on the part of the other members of the class.

### Points for Discussion

- *What may have been responsible for the fact that the boys were able to reach the point of fighting?*

- *What are the advantages and disadvantages of a public apology?*

### PROBLEM 8: A GIRL FEARS HER TEACHERS

Shortly after I began my observation period as a student teacher, I noticed that Susan was very much afraid of my cooperating teacher. In fact, Susan went to the guidance counselor about it. Very wisely, the counselor felt that it would be helpful for herself and Susan to meet with the cooperating teacher. The purpose of this meeting, according to the counselor, was to help Susan see this teacher as a person, as well as a teacher, and to show her that the teacher was interested in her and wanted to help her. From what I learned from both my cooperating teacher and the guidance counselor, the meeting was highly successful. Susan began to accept her teacher both as a person and a teacher. The thought then struck me that, although Susan had finally accepted her teacher, she would soon be facing what she would consider another crisis—me!

When I took over the class, Susan's behavior toward me was polite, almost to the point of being obsequious. Within a week, however, I saw that she had become as frightened of me as she had been of my cooperating teacher. Apparently there was something about me or my manner that brought on her fear. True, I was a tall, husky fellow with a booming voice and an authoritative manner, but I had thought this would produce respect, not fear.

During my second week of teaching, my college supervisor came to observe me. One of the things he mentioned after observing the class was that my manner was such that "You even frighten me!" Almost simultaneously, it seems, Susan approached me after class and told me she was afraid of me, and that my teaching method reminded her of the Gestapo. I told her I was sorry if I frightened her, and that this certainly was not my intent. She seemed to take my word for this.

However, another crisis arose when I gave my first test. She had done more worrying than studying for it, and unfortunately scored only 25 percent. Needless to say, she was very upset about it. After class, I talked to Susan, explaining that this was only one test out of many, and that her failure on one did not mean that she would fail the rest. I told her that since we are all human, we all make mistakes and that we cannot expect perfection. That is why, I explained, they put erasers on pencils. She seemed touched by my humor and understanding, and was able to walk away with a genuine smile on her face.

After the next test, Susan really had something to smile about! Her score was 85, and her face expressed pure delight. After class, I casually asked her if she was still "scared stiff" of me, and she laughingly replied "No." Needless to say this was encouraging to me. It proved the validity of the statement that high marks tend to make a student better. "Nothing succeeds like success."

Susan had other problems besides fearing teachers and tests. One of them arose when she crashed into a bus while taking a driving lesson in the school's driver-training car. She took quite a bit of teasing from the other students about that, and was crushed by the experience. I asked the students how they would feel if it had happened to them, and they got the point.

On another occasion, we were discussing the role of religion in American History. Susan boldly proclaimed that she was a disciple of Transcendental Meditation, and that all the religion she had been taught was "sheer bunk." The class pounced on her like a robin on a worm. Several students ridiculed her to the point of tears. I succeeded in calming them by telling them that one of the most beautiful fruits of liberty in this country is that we enjoy freedom to worship as we please.

Toward the end of my student teaching, things were brighter for Susan. The class actually accepted her as a normal peer, and she was doing very well in her school work, ending up with a B in my course. It was extremely gratifying when she approached me just before I finished student teaching to remark that she thought I was a "great teacher," and that she had really learned a lot from me. I thanked her, but quickly explained that the praise was due her since she had overcome many obstacles and had made great progress.

I guess the greatest lesson I learned was that teachers can be the source of the students' problems, as I was in the beginning. I think I changed from a tyrant into an understanding teacher—at least I hope I did.

### Points for Discussion

- *The counselor wanted Susan to see the cooperating teacher as a "person." Considering teachers in general, do you think there is much difference in personality between the "teacher" and the "person"?*

- *Agree or disagree with the statement that "Nothing succeeds like success." Substantiate your position with the findings of educational research.*

- *The other students did not fear the cooperating teacher and the student teacher. What, then, might have been Susan's basic problem?*

### PROBLEM 9: A STUDENT WITH ABILITY IS HAMPERED BY BEING IN A PROBLEM GROUP

Before I met my World History class, I was warned that this group was composed of most of the trouble-makers of the tenth grade. The principal explained to me that these pupils had been segregated as an experiment. In previous years, they were scattered throughout the classes, and had been a source of trouble to teachers and students wherever they were located. The principal indicated that if these students were grouped together, it would be easier to deal with them and they would not be distracting other students. There were twenty-nine boys and five girls in the class.

I found there were a variety of reasons to account for their poor work. In general, they lacked interest in school work, or were unable to do it. One of the most prevalent problems was their inability to read. I found there were cases of stuttering, and in two cases, the students had hearing problems. Because of their unwillingness or inability to do the work, they very often amused themselves with distracting practices such as cat calls, moaning, giggling, hee-haws, loud whispering, and the like.

John, a member of this class, came to my attention because he was one of the best readers in the class. Yet, when called upon to answer a question, he could not, or as I found out later, would not answer. At first I thought that he was shy, but I soon discounted this because of his actions. During the class, he was often talking to those around him, completely oblivious to what we were discussing in class. He seemed to be trying to gain the approval of a certain clique in the room, a group which formed the core of the troublemakers. This began to worry me.

I talked to my cooperating teacher about John, and was informed that he was very capable but that he needed urging in the right direction. I then asked John to see me during activity period. We had a good talk. I asked him if he was having any particular difficulty in the history course and he answered no. I then told him he was on the verge of failing this marking period if he continued his antics. He said he didn't mean any harm—that he was just having a good time. At the end of our meeting, John said he would try a little harder to do better work in my class.

The next day I could see that he had paid only lip service. He continued his disorderly conduct, and received barely a passing grade for the marking period. This seemed to stimulate him to do better work, but only for a few days.

I asked my cooperating teacher to speak to John. It had no effect on his conduct. I gave him repeated warnings, and even changed his seat. I realized then I would have to take drastic action. Finally, his conduct became so bad that I asked him to leave the room and report to the office. The principal gave him a two-day suspension.

The next day, I received a telephone call from John's father who asked what the trouble was. I explained the situation to him. He thanked me for the information, and promised to do what he could to remedy the problem.

After John returned to class he behaved like a different boy. Instead of trying to impress the clique, he teamed up with another boy who is a good student. Sometimes, these two got into heated class discussions about the topics we were covering. It was strange and gratifying to see a boy change from one who refused to answer in class into one who plied me with questions and showed remarkable interest in his work.

I realize the two-day suspension was harsh medicine for John, but it certainly was the proper prescription in his case. He even acted as a sparkplug to a few others in the class who had formerly shown no interest in their work.

### Points for Discussion

- *Discuss the advantages and disadvantages of segregating "trouble-makers" into one class.*

- *What do you think of suspension as a disciplinary measure?*

- *Discuss the role of parents in dealing with their children's misconduct in school.*

### PROBLEM 10: A STUDENT TEACHER CHANGES FROM MEANNESS TO FIRMNESS

My cooperating teacher assigned me to a problem class because she felt that it would be good experience for me. I took over the class, and immediately found out that I was not prepared to take what they were ready to hand out. The class was not violent, but it was filled with constant talkers who made no bones about talking when I was. In fact, it got to the point that I was shouting to get their attention.

What was I to do? I tried standing quietly in front of the class as a way of getting attention, but that did not work. I tried verbal reprimands, but that was equally unsuccessful. Then I took the problem to my cooperating teacher, hoping that she might have a suggestion for me. She did not. However, she offered to stay in the classroom with me, if I thought that would be a help. This I refused, because to do so would be to admit defeat.

One day in desperation, I assigned work to be done in class which was to be turned in at the end of the period. They still continued to talk. Infuriated, I told them that they could expect a test the next day.

Later that afternoon, I had the opportunity to talk to one of the students from the class. He had asked for help with his term paper. After we finished with that, we began talking about the class as a discipline problem. When I expressed my concern, he very politely set me straight. He said what it amounted to was that I was trying to act mean, but it was not my nature to be that way, and the class knew it. So, why didn't I stop acting that way? He suggested that rather than scold and assign extra work, which the class resented, I should simply tell the class that if the noise did not stop I would ask my cooperating teacher to take over. I decided that he might have a point there. Besides, what could I lose at this stage of the game?

The following day, I had a straight talk with the class. Sensing my sincerity and urgency, they listened. No one spoke a word. You could have heard a pin drop in that room. Throughout the episode, I stayed at my desk, and spoke softly. I could feel them straining to hear what I was saying. I explained to them that things could not continue the way they had. I told them I did not want little robots sitting neatly in rows, but neither would I continue to compete with them. I offered them several choices. The first choice was that every time they got out of line, there would be a test and mounds of homework; I explained I would not like this any more than they would, since it meant that I would be stuck with a lot of "busy work." The second choice was that I ask my cooperating teacher to take over the class; this, I said would be admitting defeat as well as failure as a teacher, but I assured them that, if I must, I would do so. The last choice was that we forget the whole thing and start over again. I then told them to choose a leader, think over what I had said, and report their decision to me through their spokesperson.

They chose their leader quietly and efficiently. They spoke among themselves in subdued tones for a short time, after which they gave me their decision. They unanimously chose the third option.

I can honestly say I have not had a problem with them since then. They have become a model group for me.

## Points for Discussion

- *What type of relationship do educators think should exist between a teacher and his pupils?*

- *Do you think it was advisable for the student teacher to threaten to turn over the class to the cooperating teacher? Why? What does this imply about the cooperating teacher?*

- *What do you think of the student teacher's comment to the class that she would be stuck with a lot of "busy work" if she assigned "mounds" of homework?*

## PROBLEM 11: CHEATING ON A TEST

Julie appeared to be a typical girl. She got along well with everyone, and was accepted by "the crowd." However, I found Julie to be quite changeable, almost on a day-to-day basis. One day she might be pleasant, industrious, cooperative, and able to do her work well. The next day she would become disrespectful, lazy, boisterous, and uncooperative. She had the capabilities of a better-than-average student, but she did not always use them.

One day while I was giving a short written test, I noticed Julie staring intently at her cupped hand. I walked to her seat quietly, and found she had notes written on a piece of paper small enough to fit into her hand. She was unaware that I noticed it and that I knew she was cheating, because for the moment I said nothing.

Keeping in mind that she was an above-average student, and that she was in the midst of her best friends, I called her aside privately after class to speak to her. I asked her if the material was too difficult for her to study, and I received the expected "No" for an answer. I then asked if she thought it might be better to spend time studying than to devote time to writing out the material in order to cheat. She agreed that it would be. She could have mastered the material in the time it took her to write it out.

From that moment on, she was consistently an ideal student. Since this was so, I drew several conclusions.

In the first place, it pays to take a conservative approach to a problem. It is much safer to discuss the problem with the student than to employ some drastic action. For example, if I had made a spectacle of Julie in front of her friends, the whole case might have taken a negative turn. Instead of improving her, it might have soured her. In the beginning, I thought her excellent cooperation and effort might have been due to the fact that she considered this incident as a threat which I held over her. I ruled out this possibility because two months have passed and the incident is forgotten.

In the second place, I feel Julie's improvement was due to the fact that she now realized I had an interest in helping her, and that I had treated her perhaps better than she deserved to be treated. She now has renewed faith and confidence in her teachers.

It was truly a reward to see this renewed enthusiasm in Julie, and it made me proud to think I played some part in bringing about the change.

## Points for Discussion

- *What are some of the other ways of handling cheating?*

- *What would you have done if Julie had cheated again instead of improving as she did?*

### PROBLEM 12:  A STUDENT IS PRE-JUDGED BY TEACHERS

Ann is a student in my sophomore College Prep English course. I noticed her on my first day of observation, because she was separated from the rest of the class. When I asked my cooperating teacher why Ann was isolated, I was told that Ann had come into the class with the idea that she was going to "run the class."

During the next few days of observation, I made it a point to pay particular attention to Ann. I noticed she never volunteered to answer a question. However, when she was called on to answer a question, she always gave an intelligent answer.

I looked into Ann's grades, and was surprised to find she was not passing any of her courses. Her marks in conduct were also low. It seemed strange to me that she should be giving such intelligent answers in class, but that her grades were so low. When I asked some of the other teachers about Ann they supported my cooperating teacher's remarks concerning her poor attitude and lack of work.

Checking into Ann's cumulative record, I found she had an I.Q. of 125. Her grades had been high until this year. She was listed as emotionally stable, physically fit, and without any family problems.

Since Ann impressed me as being mature for her age, I decided to have a frank talk with her. During my period of observation I had opened a communications link with Ann, a link which seemed to be lacking with other teachers. I asked her to see me after class. During our talk, we both laid our cards on the table. I told her I knew she could be a better student than she was showing herself to be. I asked her what her problem was, and she openly told me that all of the teachers had pre-judged her because of "grapevine" information they had received about her behavior in the class of one particular teacher. She said she saw no point in working because all of the teachers regarded her as "just a smart aleck." I neither agreed nor disagreed with her, but I told Ann that she and I were on fresh ground. I told her that the reason I was talking to her was that I had not pre-judged her, and that as far as I was concerned it was entirely up to her to succeed or to fail in my class. I also talked to her about having pride in one's achievements. In this way, I hoped to show her that satisfaction in one's work does not come from teachers' marks but rather from the pride of personal achievement.

Ann responded to the talk very well. I tried to involve her in class activities, and whenever she deserved it I praised her for her effort. Her marks improved from a 60 average before our talk to an 82 average after the talk. Her greatest improvement came in interest and participation. She became the class leader in literature discussions. She shows the ability not only to understand and intelligently question the technical aspect of literature but also to understand, discuss, and intelligently question the "living values" of English.

Possibly the greatest lesson I learned from this experience with Ann is not to judge a pupil on the basis of "grapevine" evidence. I know the greatest pleasure I derived from student teaching was to see Ann move from a dormant pupil to an active student in most of her classes.

### Points for Discussion

- *Can you offer any reason why all of Ann's teachers regarded her as a "smart aleck"?*

- *Offer suggestions as to how Ann herself could have improved relationships with her teachers.*

- *What can teachers do to avoid a "halo effect" in their attitude toward pupils?*

### PROBLEM 13: A BELLIGERENT BOY
### IS OVERPROTECTED BY HIS MOTHER

Frank had been disrupting my class continually. He had been talking, shuffling his feet, dropping his books, passing notes, and distracting the other students. I tried reprimands, private talks, detention, and several other things without success. As a last resort I sent him to the principal's office.

Looking into his records, I found that he was rated by his teachers as below average in several personal traits, that he had a D average for the year, and that he had repeated grades seven and eight. The records further revealed he had been dismissed from class ten times during the year. On each occasion, his mother returned to the school with Frank, apologizing for him, and promising that it would not happen again. Also, his mother was in the habit of writing excuses for him, explaining why he had not completed his homework. On one occasion, his mother accused the faculty of being prejudiced against Frank because of his religion.

There were other disappointing incidents. He had had fights with two different boys. Each time it was broken up by members of the faculty, and each time the faculty members reported that Frank threatened to kill the other boy while unleashing a stream of vile language. Also, it was learned that he smoked pot.

Fortunately for me, Frank did not return to my class because the principal convinced the parents that the boy should be sent to a Child Service Center, where he was given psychological tests, and where he began to work with a therapist.

The Child Service Center sent reports of progress back to the school. The results of interviews at the Center showed that Frank was completely dependent on his mother. Each night she would take him to his bedroom and stay with him until he fell asleep. Then, during the night, she got up to take him to the bathroom. This was the extreme of the many ways in which he was dependent on her. The upshot of the situation was that Frank did little for himself, and he had little concept or appreciation of what he might be able to do in the absence of his mother.

As a result, Frank had difficulty in knowing how to deal with his peers. His classmates teased him for not taking part in anything they did. To make matters worse, his parents discouraged him from becoming involved with the other children.

After six psychiatric sessions at the Center, the mother terminated the interviews. She falsely stated that the appointments would not be kept because of her job and the father's illness. The high school principal tried in vain to have the interviews continued.

During the interviews at the Center, it became obvious to the therapist that Frank was highly interested in vocational training, particularly cooking. The principal persuaded the parents to allow Frank to go into vocational training, spending half a day in vocational school and the other half at the high school.

This was the plan being followed when I finished student teaching. At the time I left, Frank's belligerent attitude toward teachers had decreased, but there was little improvement in his relationship with his classmates.

I had no part in Frank's rehabilitation, but I keep wondering how he will fare in school and life. To me it seems a shame that he was not given help earlier in his schooling. It seems to me, too, that his mother should have received psychiatric help early in her life.

## Points for Discussion

- *What do you think Frank could have done about his relation-ship with his mother?*

- *If vocational training had not been available, what could have been done for Frank?*

- *Discuss the findings of psychologists on the effects possessive parents have on their children.*

## PROBLEM 14: A NINTH GRADE STUDENT DISLIKES STUDENT TEACHERS

I had not been teaching long when I noticed a boy in the fourth row, third seat, continuously smirking and acting as if I did not know what I was doing, as if he was the "know-it-all" and I the "know-nothing."

One day I told him to remain after class. When I asked him what was wrong, he replied: "Nothing, nothing at all." I asked him if he enjoyed our ninth grade Civics class, to which he responded, "Yes." I knew he wasn't telling the truth. I told him I didn't want any more of his rudeness in class, and dismissed him.

Although he made no more comments in class, his expression still showed that he resented being taught by me. I called on him frequently, but he never gave the right answer and was acquiring a number of failures in my record book, a circumstance which made no impression on him.

One day, needing some paper, I sent him for it. He went willingly, and returned promptly. I asked him to pass out paper, which he did efficiently. I later put him in charge of the cancer drive which was going on at that time. He handled the assignment as if it were nothing at all, bringing us over our quota.

He did such a fine job that I talked to him again after class, congratulating him on his good work. Then I asked him why he didn't do as well with the class work. At first he hesitated, but then told me he had been running around with juniors and seniors who told him that student teachers "think they know it all," and that he did not have to take any of their "stuff." When he saw how young-looking I was, he thought they were right.

We talked for a long time. I think I finally convinced him that it was worth trying to pass, because it was his future at stake and not that of the other boys to whom he had listened. I pointed out to him that he should seek the companionship of boys his own age, because the others would be leaving school soon anyway. Also, I told him older boys sometimes take advantage of younger boys by egging them on to do things they themselves would not do.

Apparently these thoughts made some impression on him because, I am happy to say, he is now doing his work regularly, and seems to have acquired a liking for at least one student teacher!

### Points for Discussion

- *What can a student teacher do to forestall a false impression such as was formed by the pupil in this case?*

### PROBLEM 15: A TEACHER REALIZES HIS MISTAKE

Three pupils had been absent from a major test I had given the day before, and when they returned I gave each a copy of the test. Two of them I placed in the back of the room, and the third one, Bill, I seated in the front row. I then began teaching the rest of the class. As time went on, Bill's facial expression made it evident that he was having a difficult time concentrating on the test while I was carrying on a discussion with the class.

I realized that my voice was fairly loud, but I could do nothing to remedy the situation. I couldn't lower my voice because the students in the last row wouldn't be able to hear me; yet, at the same time, I couldn't put Bill in the back row because the other students making up the test were there, and I wanted to minimize the chance of their copying from one another.

Fifteen minutes went by. I was aware that Bill was very annoyed, because his face flushed redder every time I said something. Finally, he could contain himself no longer.

"Aw, shut up, will ya?" he moaned in disgust.

I was stunned! I had never dreamed anything like this would happen during my student teaching. I tried to remain calm. I took a deep breath. With my low, steady voice I asked, "What did you say, Bill?"

Bill realized his mistake in blurting out what he did, but he couldn't back down. He repeated, "Aw, shut up, will ya!"

I picked up his test paper, tore it in two, got him by the arm, and sent him from the room. After all, there were thirty-five other students looking on and I had to prove to them I was a disciplinarian.

Bill looked frightened as I ushered him to the door. When he was leaving, he asked in a shaky voice, "What about my test?"

I realized I had to stand firm, and gave no ground. I heroically and loudly replied, "Bill, the only test you'll be taking is a blood test. Get lost!" I was magnificent—I thought.

The rest of the class period proved something to marvel at. There wasn't a sound—not for thirty-five minutes—which must be some sort of record. But I didn't like it; it was *too* still.

I then recognized the fact that I wasn't the hard-boiled, whip-cracker type of teacher by nature. I wanted the class back on my side. I didn't want them to resent me. I would have twenty-four hours to plan my strategy before meeting them again.

When I met them the following day I still had no solution. As the bell rang, I casually walked into the room. Immediate silence reigned. As I faced the class I spotted Bill in his seat, undoubtedly expecting another oust from the room. What was I to do? Then, as though my guardian angel led my hand, I opened my binder, took out a test and gave it to Bill, saying, "Here, Bill. Happy Easter. Do your best."

Bill replied, "Thank you, sir."

I glanced at the rest of the students. When I saw the smiles on their faces, I couldn't help smiling back. I knew my solution was the correct one.

From that time on, I had the class "eating out of my hand." From that time on, too, I was open-minded, for I had learned a lesson.

## Points for Discussion

- *What do you think about giving a make-up test during a recitation?*
- *When may make-up tests be given?*
- *Basically, who was responsible for creating this disciplinary problem? Why?*
- *How would you have handled the problem?*

## PROBLEM 16: AN UNRULY BOY REFUSES TO BE HELPED

Although I tried and failed to help Joe, the facts of his case are interesting enough to be told.

Joe is one of nine children. His father is a professional man who had little time to devote to establish a good relationship with Joe. His mother, on the other hand, truly loves her son, and has shown a genuine interest in his welfare. Joe's older brothers and sisters are well adjusted, and doing well in school—in fact, one older brother is an honor student in college. The younger children, however, seem to be cast in the same mold as Joe. He, himself, commented that the second half of the family "didn't turn out so good."

Joe is sixteen years old and is only a high school freshman. His early school history shows that he was shifted back and forth between four different public and private schools. This may account for his poor reading ability, and for being held back in school.

Sometimes first impressions can be wrong, but not so in Joe's case. The first day I had class, his appearance immediately caught my attention. His hair was long, bushy, dirty, and uncombed. His shirt was unbuttoned to his waist, baring his chest. His trousers looked as if they had been used for football practice, and his shoes apparently were totally resistant to being polished. Obviously then, his total appearance was sloppy.

My first meeting with Joe was on my first day of student teaching, while I was doing cafeteria duty. Joe approached me, was very friendly, and asked me a lot of questions about myself. I thought we were off to a good start, but by the end of the week it became apparent that Joe assumed he had a "buddy" relationship with me. He looked for me each day in the cafeteria, talked to me in a familiar manner, and addressed me by my first name. He followed me around, and if I did not pay attention to him he would become loud and rude. It became necessary for me to tell him that I was his friend, not his buddy. This displeased Joe, because he wanted the other students to think he had an "in" with me.

As time went on, I gathered more information on Joe from other teachers and the guidance counselor. I found that his attendance at school was poor, and that when he does attend he is usually late. His behavior has been erratic and irresponsible. He has a reputation for drinking and using drugs; he was picked up several times by the police because of this. He dates girls of his own age, but prefers older girls. He boasts of having slept with every available girl in town; this has been generally accepted as true. He travels around with a "wild crowd," and has been in several automobile accidents. One day he came to class badly bruised and cut and bandaged. During lunch period he told me about the "great time" the gang had drinking and speeding in a car. I talked to him about the evils of drinking, but he countered by telling me that drinking was fun. As far as school work is concerned, he shows no interest in any subject, his grades are generally poor, and he is currently flunking three major subjects.

## Discussion

- *How would you try to help Joe?*

## PROBLEM 17:  A DELINQUENT GIRL BREAKS DOWN

After two weeks of observation, I took over my class in biology. Everything went smoothly for about a week, and then Lisa, who had been one of the quietest students in class, started to act up. Not a day went by without some sort of disturbance from her. She sat in one of the back seats, from which point she launched paper airplanes; crumpled up pieces of paper and hit other pupils on the back of the head with them; at still other times she drew comical pictures and passed them around the room.

During the first few days I tried to gain her cooperation in a friendly way, but when she became even worse, I changed her seat. This transfer she resented very much. Lisa began humming or whistling softly in the middle of a class recitation. When I reproved her, she would sneer, be quiet for a few minutes, and then think of something else to do.

On the day that we finally had a showdown, Lisa came into class with a midget mouth organ, which she started to play during the part of the period in which we had supervised study. When I took it away, she became very argumentative, so I told her to report to the study hall.

When my cooperating teacher came in a few minutes later, I told him what had happened, and he described the girl's background to me. He said that Lisa had spent the summer in a reform school, but had been released to return to school. At the time of her release she was told that if she was not on her best behavior at school, she would be sent back to the institution. After learning this, I decided to give Lisa a good scare, but I had also made up my mind that I would not do anything that would cause her to be sent back to reform school.

The following day, Lisa came back to class and took her seat, but within ten minutes she had started an argument with her neighbor. When I spoke to her about it, she told me to mind my own business. I again put her out of class, but this time I told her that she would not be readmitted until she had written permission from the principal. Looking immediately very uncomfortable, she started to say something, but I closed the door and resumed teaching class.

In a few minutes, Lisa knocked on the door and asked if I would speak to her in the hall. I stepped out. She told me then about the fact that she would have to keep out of trouble to avoid reform school. She started to cry.

### Discussion

  • *As a teacher, what would you do next in this case?*

### PROBLEM 18: A LANGUAGE LABORATORY CREATES SPECIAL PROBLEMS FOR THE TEACHER

My initial assignment in student teaching was to teach four sections of Spanish I. I began with enthusiasm, but soon became discouraged.

Most of my problems were due to the fact that all my classes were held in the language laboratory. This worked out well when we were working with tapes, but when I tried to carry on other classroom activities, the results were disastrous.

The laboratory had thirty booths, which seemed to swallow the pupils when they sat down. My desk at the front of the room was on a slightly elevated platform, but if I sat down I could not see the pupils, and they could not see me. Even when I was standing I could only see their heads. Also, the booths acted as a sound barrier, or they muffled sound, so that the pupils and I had difficulty hearing each other.

With this type of situation, I had disciplinary problems. Since they were hidden from view unless I was standing near them, many of the pupils occupied themselves with activities that were foreign to Spanish I. They were leaning over to their neighbors, talking, giggling, and passing things around when I was not standing in their vicinity. Many of them were fooling around with their earphones, and I found that some pupils had pulled the wires out of the earphones. I even found pencils stuck into microphones. Some students, too, kept adding to the graffiti in the booths. With all this going on, the pupils tried my patience to the point that I wanted to scream at them, and I sometimes did.

My problems did not end there. We had three chalkboards in the laboratory, one in the front of the room, and one on either side. The pupils in the rear of the room could not see the front board at all, and in order to see the side boards, all of the pupils had to shove their chairs back or stand up in order to see over the sides of the booths. This, of course, created more noise and confusion.

I tried to cope with my problems in several ways. First, I spoke as loudly as I could in order to penetrate the sound barrier. Now the pupils could at least hear me, but if it was necessary for me to lecture for extended periods I started to get hoarse. Next, I asked the pupils to stand when reciting, so that they could be heard by the others. I also made the pupils nearest the chalkboard responsible for correcting the exercises other pupils were writing on the board. During the whole class period, I kept patrolling from one area of the room to another, making certain the pupils were doing their assigned work.

These problems were enough, but my cooperating teacher created more. The tapes we used were correlated with the textbook. Each chapter had a taped story that was related to it. The students listened to the story, then were asked to repeat sentences from it in unison in order to help them learn correct pronunciation. The tape also contained pronunciation drills. As time went on, I found the pupils becoming bored with the taped material. Consequently, I asked my cooperating teacher if I could introduce other types of drills—substitution drills, choral drills, and chain drills—but he preferred that I use the taped ones. I thought peer teaching would be helpful, and I also suggested setting aside a day a week for games and exercises. All of these things, I thought, would add to interest, motivation, and better learning, but my cooperating teacher discouraged their use.

## Discussion

- *What would you have done in this situation?*

## PROBLEM 19: A SENIOR CAUSES TROUBLE IN A SOPHOMORE CLASS

Everything looked rosy during the days I observed my cooperating teacher. The class was running smoothly, perhaps because my cooperating teacher was very strict, a hard-nosed disciplinarian with a "no nonsense" manner. She set the tone for the class, and I remember thinking that it should be a pleasure to take over her classes.

After a few days of observation, I began to teach with my cooperating teacher present. I was a little nervous at first, but I became more relaxed as time went on. Everything was fine; there were no problems.

Then my cooperating teacher started to leave me on my own so that I could get the feel of teaching my own class. It was then that Brian, a huge, handsome fellow, began to come to class late. He would open and shut the door noisily, and would have something to say to everyone along the route to his seat. Then, he would get up in the middle of class to sharpen his pencil, again socializing along the way. At first I was a little frightened, and didn't know what to do. I merely continued with the class as if nothing had happened.

I had hoped that Brian would discontinue his tardiness and his attention-getting tactics, but no such luck. Not knowing what to do, I decided to talk to my cooperating teacher about him. I didn't want to tell her that I had a serious problem, because I didn't want her to think I was ineffective as a teacher. Instead, I implied that the problem was slight, and asked her if she could give me some information about Brian.

What she told me gave me a much better understanding and explanation of Brian's behavior. First, she told me that Brian is the only senior in my sophomore Spanish class, and that very likely he felt that he should show the underclassmen that he could take privileges that they couldn't. Second, his mother and father were members of the faculty; this, too, might have made him feel that he deserved more consideration than other students. Third, Brian was already accepted for admission to college, and therefore lightly regarded his remaining months in high school. Finally, as I discovered from some of the other students, Brian disliked student teachers, and since he was much bigger than I, he felt that if the need arose he could easily whip me.

With all of these explanations, I felt I now understood *why* he acted as he did, but that still left me with the problem of what to *do* about it, because Brian was becoming worse. Besides talking to his neighbors, he kept asking me questions that were irrelevant to the course, such as, "Do you think the Minnesota Vikings will win this week?"

## Discussion

• *What would you do to help Brian?*

### PROBLEM 20: THE STUDENT TEACHER IS UNSUCCESSFUL WITH A DISRUPTIVE PUPIL

Peter caught my attention the first day I began student teaching. His behavior was so unusual that no one would fail to notice it. He continually interrupted class by "volunteering" opinions on any subject at any time. In addition, he seemed to take pride in blurting out profanity, and in displaying obscene books.

The first time he was disruptive, I calmly asked him to be quiet, but his disquieting remarks continued. As they continued, my reprimands became louder and more frequent, but so did Peter's remarks. After a few days of this, I decided to have a private talk with him.

I kept Peter after class, and pointed out to him the ways in which he was distracting the class, and that he was hurting not only his classmates but also himself. I asked him if he had any problems that I could help with. Peter would not volunteer any information about himself, so my talk with him was a waste of time.

Next, I tried to give him a position of responsibility by telling him that he could correct any wrong answers given during a recitation. Either he didn't know what answers were wrong, or he refused to correct them, for he never volunteered.

At this point, I was at my wit's end for a possible solution. My reprimands became stronger and stronger until, one day after class, Peter came up to me and threatened to "beat me up" in front of the class if I continued to pick on him. I told him I would continue to insist that he behave and do his work.

The next day, I gave an assignment in class. When I noticed that Peter was not doing the work, I told him to get busy, and I walked toward him. When Peter saw me coming, he left his seat and headed for the door. I grabbed him by the arm and returned him to his seat, informing him that he would have to do his work. He sat there a minute, then became boisterous and profane. Again, I took him by the arm and told him I was taking him to the office. When he reached· the classroom door, he shook himself loose and ran down the hall.

I reported the incident to the office, and later learned that he was located by the head of detention who dealt with Peter seriously. His parents were notified. His mother visited the school, apologized for Peter's behavior, and promised me that it would not happen again. Peter also apologized to me, but I doubted that he was sincere. After this incident, he became more serious in my class.

A few days later, I returned a test to the students. Immediately, Peter voiced dissatisfaction over the grade I had given him. I told him I would give him the opportunity to come to the front of the room and prove to the class that he deserved a higher grade. Peter accepted the offer, but succeeded only in making a fool of himself amid derisive laughter from his classmates. This embarrassed him, and from that time on he was a quiet student.

When it was time for our next test, Peter tried what I consider to be a desperate act. When I was passing out the tests to my first period class (he was in the second period class), Peter hid behind one of the students in the rear of the room, took a copy of the test, and made his way toward the door when my back was turned. I turned just in time to see him going through the door with a copy of the test.

## Discussion

- *How would you handle this problem?*

**SELECTED READINGS**

Alcorn, Marvin D., Kinder, James S., and Schunert, Jim R. *Better Teaching in Secondary Schools.* New York: Holt, Rinehart and Winston, Inc., 1970, chapters 12–14.

Callahan, Sterling G. *Successful Teaching in Secondary Schools.* Glenview, Illinois: Scott, Foresman and Company, 1971, chapter 13.

Glasser, William. *Schools Without Failure.* New York: Harper and Row, Publishers, 1969, chapters 14, 16.

Hamachek, Don E. *Behavior Dynamics in Teaching, Learning, and Growth.* Boston: Allyn and Bacon, Inc., 1975, chapter 15.

Howard, Alvin W., and Stoumbis, George C. *The Junior High and Middle School: Issues and Practices.* Scranton, Pennsylvania: Intext Educational Publishers, 1970, chapter 16.

Kolesnik, Walter B. *Educational Psychology.* New York: McGraw-Hill Book Company, 1970, chapter 18.

Lindgren, Henry Clay. *Educational Psychology in the Classroom,* pages 349–374. New York: John Wiley and Sons, Inc., 1967.

Noar, Gertrude. *The Junior High School—Today and Tomorrow.* Englewood Cliffs, New Jersey: Prentice-Hall, Inc., 1961, chapters 13, 14.

Oliva, Peter F. *The Secondary School Today.* Scranton, Pennsylvania: Intext Educational Publishers, 1972, chapters 16–17.

Samalonis, Bernice L. *Methods and Materials for Today's High Schools,* pages 103–116. New York: Van Nostrand Reinhold Company, 1970.

Schwartz, Lita Linzer. *Educational Psychology.* Boston: Holbrook Press, Inc., 1977, chapter 13.

Yelon, Stephen L., and Weinstein, Grace W. *A Teacher's World.* New York: McGraw-Hill Book Company, 1977, chapter 11.

# 3

# Problems of Motivation

If it were possible to single out the most important factor in learning, motivation would be a leading candidate for the choice. Motivation is the reason why one acts or is impelled to activity. In school, it would embrace all the reasons why pupils exert themselves to learn, to develop themselves.

We know from our experience that when we have a compelling reason to act, a goal toward which to strive, we act more energetically and with greater continuity of effort than when we have no such purpose. We know that we do not work as willingly when we are merely compelled to do something, or when we do not fully understand the reason for a task. So it is with the pupil in the classroom. If he has a strong will to learn, he will very likely perform at his ability level; if he does not have strong motivation, he will probably never realize his potentialities even though all the other learning conditions are favorable.

Strong motivation sometimes causes a student to perform at a level that might not ordinarily be expected of him. In fact, any experienced teacher will verify that a strongly motivated pupil of average ability may reach a higher achievement level in school work than a moderately motivated pupil of above average ability. In the one case, strong motivation impels the student to work to capacity; in the other case, lack of proper motivation keeps him from actualizing his potentialities. Consequently, all other factors being equal (such as ability level, state of health, and emotional and social adjustment), the degree of motivation will largely account for the difference in degree of achievement among pupils.

Because of differences in endowment, environment, and training, no two pupils are exactly alike; and being different, they are influenced to act for various reasons. What constitutes a strong motive for one pupil may have little or no influence on another. For this reason, it is impossible to conclude that there is one best motive applicable to all students. The best that can be said is that there are some motives more widely appealing than others. It is the task of the teacher to discover and apply motives and incentives that appeal not only to groups but also to individuals who have unique characteristics.

## SUGGESTIONS FOR MOTIVATING PUPILS

The teacher can set in motion some of the motivating forces that stimulate pupils to learn, through the procedures and methods he uses, and through his attitude toward his subject. Following are suggestions on how this might be accomplished.

*Make Your Aims Clear.*   Pupils will work harder if they perceive a goal toward which to strive. Every subject in the curriculum has a definite purpose, and in some way contributes to the development of the student. At the beginning of a course, the teacher should carefully explain the objectives of the subject, setting forth its importance, how it contributes to the growth of the individual, and how it is integrated with other elements of the curriculum. If this explanation is clear enough to show the pupils its value to them as individuals, it provides them with a strong motive to work, and provides direction to their work.

The same procedure should be followed with each lesson taught. The objectives set for each lesson should be explained to the pupils, and the teacher should periodically try to show how the specific aims contribute to general objectives of the subject. The perception of this relationship should provide continuous direction and motivation for the students.

*Be Enthusiastic About Your Subject.*   A teacher cannot hope to generate interest in his subject unless he is convinced that it is exciting and worthwhile. He must regard his subject as alive and indispensable for the proper development of the student. If he feels that way about it, the probability is high that he will convey some of that feeling to his students. Enthusiasm is catching, but it must be transmitted before it can be received.

Most teachers have this desirable type of motivation toward their subjects. A few, however, have an extreme view concerning the importance of their field. They act as if their subject were the *only* really important one in the curriculum. This type of teacher may actually belittle the other subjects students are taking, and may burden the students with so much work in his course that the students do not have sufficient time to devote to their other subjects. It is well for the beginning teacher to remember that every subject in the curriculum is there for a definite purpose, and is therefore important in some phase of the individual's development. Consequently, a teacher should share a pupil's time and interests with other teachers and other activities.

*Teach for Meanings.* Unless a pupil understands the material, he cannot become interested in it; consequently, teaching for understanding is a way of providing motivation to study. While it is true that some things must be learned by rote because they are devoid of meaningful elements, most of the material studied by pupils is meaningful and should be studied to uncover those meanings. The teacher should encourage the pupils to study for understanding rather than for facility in verbal repetition, and should question them carefully to see that they are doing so. If questioning reveals that the pupils do not see the proper meaning, the teacher should explain it to them. The process of teaching for concepts and encouraging pupils to study for meanings should be a continuous one.

*Teach at the Proper Pace.* The pace at which a teacher proceeds has much to do with maintaining the attention of pupils. If he proceeds too rapidly for the pupils to assimilate the material, they cannot be expected to give attention to that which they cannot follow. "Too much, too fast" is a mistake commonly made by beginning teachers. One teacher, who took pride in the rapid pace at which he taught, facetiously remarked: "If a pupil drops his pencil to the floor during my class, he falls a week behind." On the other hand, it sometimes happens that the teacher's pace is too slow. In his anxiety to be sure that pupils thoroughly understand the material, a teacher may sometimes spend too much time with explanations. A high school student recently remarked about one of his teachers: "My teacher wastes a lot of time. He explains something until we know it, and then keeps going over it again and again. It gets boring."

The pace at which a teacher should proceed will depend on the ability level of his class. No two classes are alike. When a teacher has met with a class a few times, he will, with experience, be able to judge the general pace at which he should proceed with a particular group. Through his own questioning of the pupils, through questions from the pupils themselves, and through the results of tests, he will be able to adjust his teaching to a pace consistent with the understanding of a class.

*Use Familiar Examples.* In using explanations and illustrations, familiar examples not only contribute to understanding but also add to interest. Public speakers generally try to learn something about the people and the community in which they are going to speak, knowing that the use of such information immediately captures the attention of the audience. This device also applies in the classroom. If abstract ideas are explained by using familiar or local examples, the pupils will listen more attentively than they would to examples unrelated to their experience. Local government, local points of interest, businesses, terrain, practices, and so on, should be used whenever applicable.

*Use a Variety of Procedures.* In the chapter on discipline, it was noted that a variety of procedures helps to maintain the attention of pupils. It also helps to keep them interested and motivated, because the same routine day after day begets boredom. Although a specific method and procedure may be more appropriate in some courses than in others, there are general methods and procedures that are applicable to all courses. Variations of these are possible, making class work more interesting for the pupils.

Every teacher must spend some time in explaining material. There are many aids which the teacher may use. The chalkboard should be utilized regularly to diagram, illustrate, and work out problems. As he deems appropriate, the teacher may introduce pictures, posters, objects, diagrams, models, specimens, films, tape recordings, phonograph records, television, and the overhead projector. All of these are important as instructional aids and as a means of securing and holding attention.

All subjects lend themselves to the effective use of audio-visual aids. In English grammar, the chalkboard should be used extensively by the teacher and the pupils. In English literature and drama, pictures, motion pictures, phonograph records, and tapes may be used, and the pupils may participate by assuming roles in dramas. In history, maps are indispensable, and pictures, models, and objects of historical interest may be introduced. In languages, movies, records, tape recorders, and pictures and objects of the people add vividness to the study of a language. In the sciences, extensive use may be made of specimens, models, charts, and diagrams. Thus, a great variety of aids and activities are possible in the explanation of material. (See problems 24, 27, 29, 34, and 38.)

In the initial learning of material, the teacher will wish to drill students on important material and on material that is difficult to learn. Drill, involving repetition to fix learning, may be made more interesting by resorting to various devices: competition, flash cards, records and tape recorders, or the use of chain drills or choral drills. One student teacher added interest to drill during football season by dividing the class into two teams and diagraming a football field on the chalkboard. Each time a student answered a question correctly, the ball was moved five yards for his team on the chalkboard diagram.

Most teachers spend some time each period with review. Here again variety is possible. At times the teacher may do the reviewing for the class in the form of a summary; or he may have a cooperative review, in which the pupils also participate. He may appoint a different student to conduct each day's review or summarize the work of the previous day. It is possible to add further variety by occasionally asking for a written review.

The teacher spends considerable time in questioning pupils. Inasmuch as great interest can be aroused by questions that lend themselves to discussion, the teacher should try to prepare in advance a question or two of this type. I have observed classes in which heated discussions, guided by the student teacher, kept the entire class engrossed. It would be well to mention again that attention can be maintained during questioning by the teacher if all pupils are held responsible for the accuracy of answers given to those who are reciting.

Assignments may be made at the beginning of the period, or as the final item of business during a class period. These too can be and should be varied. Variation of the assignment will sustain interest better than if the same kind ("Read the next chapter" or "Read the next ten pages") is made continuously. Following are some of the variations that can be made: reading assignments in the textbook or in sources assigned by the teacher; written assignments, such as exercises in the textbook, or exercises made up by the teacher; answers to questions in a workbook; making up questions on the reading assignment; oral reports on the material in the textbook or on topics assigned by the teacher; drill or review assignments; or special project assignments.

As can be seem from the foregoing discussion, a great variety of procedures is possible in the classroom. There is no justification for the deadly monotony of unchanging routine. The classroom can and should hum with a variety of activities.

The preceding suggestions for motivating students emanate from the teacher's personality and from his methods of teaching. There are many other sources of motivation that come from within the pupil himself, or that are the result of devices used by the teacher for the specific purpose of motivating students to do better work. The following may be placed in those categories.

**OTHER SOURCES OF MOTIVATION**

*Student's Inherent Interests.* A student may have a natural interest and inclination to study certain subjects but at the same time he may abhor other subjects. Although he anxiously gives attention to a subject he likes, it requires great effort for him to concentrate on material he dislikes. Thus, he may be fascinated by the abstract reasoning involved in mathematics, but at the same time consider the study of a foreign language as drudgery. Another student may delight in the prospect of learning to speak a foreign language, but shudder at the thought of mathematics. Although it is sometimes possible for a teacher to arouse interest where none previously existed, the fact remains that for each student there are areas of subject matter which interest him much more than others. (See problems 28 and 32.)

*Perceiving the Value of a Subject.* Even though a student is not interested in a subject, he may exert himself to study it because he recognizes that it has value for him—that it is necessary and useful in his daily life, or that it is prerequisite to some larger or more remote goal. Thus, a pupil who may dislike the study of English grammar will apply himself if he recognizes its utility in his school work and future life, and will learn it even though it does not appeal to him. (See problem 33.)

*Desire for Recognition.* Everyone wishes to be recognized in some way. Some pupils are motivated to study to win the approval of teachers, parents, or friends. This does not necessarily mean that the pupil must excel in order to win approval. If he discovers that making good progress, or showing improvement, brings a word of commendation, he will ordinarily strive to perform at a level that will bring him approval.

*Desire to Excel.* Since a relatively small proportion of the school population has the ability to excel (achieve honors, qualify for scholarships, rank in the top tenth of the class), this incentive appeals only to those who have the ability to reach that type of goal. Yet it cannot be overlooked as a source of motivation even among pupils of lesser ability who may have an interest and talent in a certain subject in which they may strive to excel. Needless to say, not all pupils of high ability or exceptional talents have a desire to excel.

*Desire to Avoid Failure.* This is a negative type of motivation which nevertheless sometimes works to the pupil's advantage. Assuming that he has not been adequately motivated, and that he has not been working as much as he should, the realization that there is a possibility he might fail the subject will often stimulate the pupil to great effort in order to avoid failure. Too often, pupils exert themselves only enough to "get by." Sometimes they misjudge the amount of work necessary for them to meet minimum standards, and they slip into a borderline category. Not wishing to fail, they then apply pressure on themselves to get a passing grade.

*Knowledge of Progress.* Supplying the pupil with information concerning his individual progress, and his progress in relation to the entire class, has been found to be an incentive to learning. The teacher may provide this type of information by individual conferences with pupils, by keeping individual and class progress charts, by posting distributions of test grades, by displaying good work on the bulletin board, or by orally commending pupils who are making progress. If pupils know their rank in class, those at the lower level may strive to improve their position, while those in the upper rank may work hard to stay there.

*Competition.* Competition has been used in the classroom to motivate students and stimulate them to greater effort. There has been considerable controversy over the advisability of its use. Those who favor it hold that competition in life is a fact, and that using it in school not only simulates later life situations, but it helps pupils to learn to live with failure as well as enjoy success. The opponents of competition, on the other hand, state that it causes pupils to draw comparisons between themselves, that some students appear in an unfavorable light because there are always losers, that the losers may develop feelings of frustration and inferiority, and that it produces great emotional stress in some children.

If the teacher uses competition to increase the motivation and achievement of his pupils, he can minimize its purported dangers by trying to equate the competing groups, so that each group will have its share of victories and defeats. If, in the process of competition, the teacher sees that it causes undue emotional stress in some students, they should be excluded from further competition. (See problem 29.)

*Praise.* A pat on the back, figuratively speaking, for a job well done will invariably motivate the student to continue to do good work. Praise should not be limited to good students, but should be given to any student who shows improvement in his work. In fact, judicious praise sometimes makes a good student out of a poor one who for some reason has not been working up to his capacity.

*Reproof.* The effectiveness of reproof varies with the individual. Some pupils, for whom a reproof from the teacher is akin to a tragedy, will work very hard to avoid a repetition of it, especially if the teacher is one they like and respect. Other pupils simply shrug off a reprimand, and seem little affected by it. In general, however, the effect of a reprimand is to stimulate pupils to overcome the conditions which brought it about. A reprimand, of course, should be given only when it is deserved, and it is effective only if the pupil recognizes that he deserved it.

*Reward.* Some teachers have found rewards to be effective incentives. This type of incentive may be related to praise, for praise is a form of reward. Similarly, it may be associated with desire for approval or recognition, since a reward is an outward manifestation of the recognition of good work. Various forms of reward have been used by teachers. Excusing excellent students from taking a major test may stimulate more pupils to strive to reach that level. Rewarding above average improvement with achievement citations or pins may drive some students to show great improvement. Granting special privileges for noteworthy achievement may also produce beneficial results.

*Punishment.* The various forms of punishment and their effectiveness were discussed in the chapter on discipline. Punishment is another incentive that motivates pupils in a negative way, because it acts as a deterrent. Although many pupils work to avoid punishment, it is not a good source of motivation because it is based on fear. Nevertheless, it serves a purpose when other sources of motivation are not accepted by the pupil.

*Parental Influence.* Whether or not parents act as a motivating force in study depends on the parents themselves. Parents who have a respect for learning, who continuously encourage their children to do their work, who make certain that homework is done, and who take an interest in the affairs of the school, are motivating their children by example and direction to form proper attitudes toward school work. On the other hand, parents who give little or no attention to the child's school work and activities are at least indirectly minimizing the importance of education, and are fostering similar attitudes in their child.

Another type of motivation emanating from parents rests on the child's fear of parental disapproval if his school progress is inadequate. The amount of motivation will depend on the degree to which the child seeks parental approval, or fears disapproval.

*Tests.*   Tests have several purposes, such as measuring achievement, diagnosing weaknesses, and classifying students. Their usefulness as an incentive to study is sometimes questioned, because some educators feel (and rightly so) that students should not study simply to pass tests. Yet, tests are used, and must be used, to obtain the semblance of an objective evaluation of a student's progress. The student knows this, and exerts extra effort in order to make a good grade on a test. Thus, even though he may be studying to pass a test, there are favorable concomitant outcomes in that he is drilling, reviewing, and making an attempt to understand and organize his material. It would seem, then, that even though pupils should have a better reason to study than merely to pass tests, tests *do* give them a reason if they have no other. Frequent minor tests and occasional major tests will serve the purpose of producing continuity of effort on the part of the pupil.

● ● ●

Many of the problems previously cited to illustrate how student teachers handled disciplinary problems also contain elements of problems of motivation. The cases which follow are more exclusively problems of motivation, although in a few instances it will be recognized that disciplinary difficulties are also involved. The cases presented show that there are many ways to convert an apathetic student into an interested one. In most cases, this change was brought about by a teacher who recognized an individual problem and was conscientious enough to try to do something about it.

## PROBLEM 21: VOCATIONAL STUDENTS DISLIKE ENGLISH GRAMMAR

During the second week of my student teaching, I asked my junior vocational class to write a paragraph on the value of studying English. The following paragraph was turned in by Joe.

> English is to me as Greek is to you. It is a disgusting, horrible, and stupid subject. What is the sense in learning definitions and examples of nouns, predicates, objects and what have you? After I graduate, people will not expect me to know all these definitions because I'm not even going to college. English may be all-right for those "College-Joes," but not for us vocational boys. We can be doing something more useful than studying this awful English. English is too cut and dry. Therefore it puts me to sleep. By the way, I hope I am not marked down for giving my honest opinion. In conclusion, I still dislike English.

Judging by this paragraph, and some of the others turned in, I could see I had my work cut out for me. Joe and the other vocational students had an extreme dislike for English grammar and composition. How could I, an inexperienced teacher, do something to motivate them?

Although my problem included the whole class, I gave particular attention to Joe because he seemed like a sincere boy. He was rather colorless, both in appearance and personality. Basically, he was a follower, not a leader. Clues to his character are found in a paragraph in which I asked the class to list good and bad things to do. As good things to do, Joe listed: "Help at home, work and give your family some board, be obedient, and don't be always borrowing money." Under bad things, he said: "Don't be disobedient to anybody, don't run around at nights too much, don't go with boys and girls you know that are bad, don't do things you're not supposed to do at work."

I had several conversations with Joe which revealed that he thought highly of his family, admired but did not resent successful people, and that he had very little confidence in himself. Regarding school, he said: "I'm disappointed in school this year. Things just don't pan out like you want them to." Scholastically, he was in the bottom half of his class, but he was not seriously concerned about his achievement because, as he said, high marks are only for "College-Joes."

Joe had two problems I wanted to help him with: an inferiority complex, and a dislike for English (although the latter problem was common to the whole class).

First of all, I knew I had to make the class more interesting and stimulating by putting life and enthusiasm into my teaching. I started to bring examples of everyday life into our discussions and drills, and make use of hobbies and other things the class was interested in. The illustrations I used are too many to mention, but the following example is representative. In teaching independent and dependent clauses, I illustrated with musical instruments. "Would you say an accordian is a band in itself? Would you consider a drum to be a band in itself? An accordian player can play independently; he does not always need accompaniment. A drummer needs accompaniment; therefore he is dependent on someone else." These questions and comments had nothing to do with English grammar, but they started the class on the way to an understanding of independent and dependent clauses. I tried very hard to keep using interesting and vivid examples, and, as time went on, I think Joe and the class showed interest in spite of their prejudices against English. Another thing that helped a great deal was instead of using drill material from the textbook, I selected material from the daily newspaper or current periodicals.

At the same time, as the class progressed, I tried to give Joe special attention. Since he was reluctant to recite, I directed more questions to him than the others. Also, I assigned paragraphs for the class to write for homework, and then I would have students read in class what they had written. Each time I called on Joe to read his, he would say that he was not ready, even though he always turned in a paragraph when I collected them. I talked to him about it, inquiring why he was never ready to read. He said he thought his paragraphs were not good enough to read in front of the class. My next step was to have him read aloud from the text whenever the opportunity presented itself. That broke the ice, and he finally started reading the paragraphs *he* had written. One day he came up to me after class and said: "You know, it's not as hard as I thought it was to speak before the class. I always thought the class would laugh if I made a mistake up there. They don't laugh. This really surprised me."

When it was time for me to leave student teaching, I think Joe knew a little more about his capabilities than he did before, and I feel that his feelings of inferiority have diminished. Before I left he told me: "It seems that English is not as boring as it used to be. I'll have to admit you made it more interesting, but I'm still keeping my same opinion of English."

## Points for Discussion

- *Making use of the knowledge you gained in your theory courses, what would you do to try to show your pupils the value of the subject or subjects you hope to teach?*

- *How did the student teacher's use of newspapers and periodicals contribute to motivation?*

- *Comment on the techniques used to bring Joe "out of his shell."*

## PROBLEM 22: A POTENTIAL DROP-OUT IS SAVED

Of all the pupils I had while student teaching, I shall always remember Nancy. She was a student in my tenth grade biology class.

Nancy was a rather short but attractive girl. She showed average intelligence, and was well-liked by her classmates. However, during my first week of teaching, I discovered she hated school.

While most of the other students were interested and attentive, Nancy would either be talking to one of her friends or she would be off sailing on "cloud nine."

At the end of my first week, I gave the class a test. As I expected, Nancy was the only one in the class who failed, and she failed miserably. That same day, I talked to her during free period, asking her what had happened on the test. She told me she did not study or take notes in any of her classes. It was then she told me she hated school.

Nancy said she wanted to quit school at the end of the year, but her father would not permit it. I knew her father did not graduate from high school. Since I had the same type of problem when I was in high school, I thought it might help to tell her about it.

I told Nancy that my father never graduated from high school, and the only thing he wanted for me was that I get as much education as possible. I had never taken school seriously, and at the time I thought he was "talking through his hat." I'll never forget the day I graduated. With tears in his eyes, my father said: "You accomplished what I never had an opportunity to do. Don't stop here, go on while you can." I did go on, and have never felt sorry. I told Nancy that when I look back and see what happened to some of my friends who dropped out of school, it makes me thankful to that smart father of mine. I told her that my drop-out friends went from job to job, never finding satisfaction in what they were doing. Finally, I told her that although there are exceptions, the person with a diploma gets much more out of life than a drop-out.

After a long discussion, Nancy told me she was interested in becoming a teacher, but her marks were too low for her to be accepted in college. I told her most colleges based their acceptances on the grades of the last two years, and on entrance examinations. I assured her she could get good grades if she paid attention in class and did her homework. Also, I told her my door would always be open to her if she had problems of any kind that she wanted to discuss with me.

I did all I could to help Nancy. I changed her seat, putting her between two above-average students who were not prone to talking in class. I kept her attention through frequent questioning. If she did not know an answer, I gave her hints until she literally tripped over the answer. I praised her frequently when she gave correct answers. In the weeks that followed, I could see Nancy improving beautifully, so much so that I hated to see my student teaching drawing to an end.

Without any doubt, I can say dealing with Nancy has made me aware of the true teacher-student relationship that I have read about in many books but never realized or cared about until now. It made me feel *so good* just to have a minor role in wiping out a student's defeatist attitude and putting her back on the right track.

It would not surprise me at all to hear of or see another father with tears in his eyes when it is time for Nancy's class to graduate.

### Points for Discussion

- *In general, how much do you think high school students value the advice of their parents?*

- *What were the sources of motivation that put Nancy back on the "right track"?*

### PROBLEM 23:  A SENSE OF PRIDE IS RESTORED
####          TO AN ECONOMICALLY DEPRIVED STUDENT

When I first began my student teaching experience, I tried to come into contact with and understand each of my students during the relatively short period I was with them. During this process, one girl in particular caught my interest and concern. She had no interest in my Spanish course, and never volunteered to participate in class. Her name was Rose.

My cooperating teacher told me Rose had been equally indifferent in her class. Looking into the school records, I found that Rose had an I.Q. of 125, and that she had scored at the 98th percentile on another national mental ability test. Her earlier records showed that in elementary school she had received A's in all of her subjects. Then, to my surprise, her grades dropped progressively from grades 7 through 11, although she did not fail any of her subjects.

Rose was pretty as well as bright. I did notice, though, that she did not socialize at all. One day, I observed a handsome boy making overtures to Rose, but she reacted as if she wanted nothing to do with him.

In the meantime, I gathered some information on her family background. Her mother, a housewife, had finished high school, and her father, also a high school graduate, was employed by the city as a garbage collector. There were six other children.

Things about Rose now began to fall into place in my mind. While in the seventh grade, Rose worked part-time at school in a program which was designed to help low-income families. While all students knew of this program, and many worked in it, Rose apparently became self-conscious about being identified with a poverty program, and may have been ashamed of being in it. She was aware of her low socio-economic status within her peer group, and from the seventh grade on she started to become anti-social. Her economic level was further emphasized by a meager wardrobe, in sharp contrast to the latest styles worn by the other girls.

I wanted desperately to show Rose that in spite of her economic status she was equal to anyone else, and in some areas, she had talent superior to others. Although she was doing acceptable work in all her subjects, there was one in which she always received superior grades—music. The thought occurred to me that I might make use of her talent in music in my course in Spanish.

In teaching Spanish, I make use of music one day each week. I asked Rose if she would be interested in helping me prepare materials for this weekly presentation. She reacted positively. We worked together, during which time she showed greater interest and asked many questions. She was happy to accept additional responsibility. Although she could not type well, she struggled through the task of typing lyrics for a song I intended to use in class. During our singing in class, I discovered she was endowed with a fine singing voice, so I asked her to lead the class in singing Spanish songs. At first she did this hesitantly, but as time went on she did it proudly. Her classmates enjoyed and admired her singing.

I feel that my plan to help Rose was successful. Not only did she do very well in the weekly music classes we had, but her achievement also rose in the regular Spanish classes. My greatest satisfaction came when she joined the Spanish Club and started to participate in extracurricular activities.

I don't think I have changed this young lady's personality, or even solved her problems. I do think, however, that I have helped give her a feeling of pride and dignity among her peers, a feeling which had been slipping away from her.

## Points for Discussion

- *How would you deal with Rose's problem if you could not capitalize on her musical ability in the course you will teach?*

- *In general, how does economic status influence acceptance by peers?*

**PROBLEM 24:  STUDENT PARTICIPATION IN EXPERIMENTS
              AROUSES A PREVIOUSLY UNINTERESTED STUDENT**

Once I began my student teaching it did not take me much time to
realize that Rick was not at all interested in general science. My cooperating teacher confirmed this observation, stating that Rick was
simply biding time until he was old enough to leave school. He did
not cause any disturbance in class; he was just indifferent to school
work.

When I decided to have a little talk with Rick, he told me he did
not care whether or not he passed. I asked him why he was so uninterested in science, since it could be so interesting. He had no
particular reason for disliking it, he said, but he could see no benefits to be derived from studying it. In a way I was glad to hear this,
because I was sure I could show him how useful it could be.

Since we were studying magnetism and electricity, I decided to
have Rick assist me in making an electromagnet during our next
class. Under my supervision, he made the electromagnet on his own,
and it appeared to me that he enjoyed what he was doing. Also, it
showed him a practical application of what we were studying in
class. He immediately showed interest in magnetism, asked questions, took an active part in class activities, and began to turn in his
assignments willingly.

The next time we were going to perform an experiment in class,
I appointed Rick and three other students to prepare a telegraph
with equipment we obtained from the physics laboratory. For the
next four days, they worked under my supervision during the activity period to prepare the telegraph. Rick's attitude toward science
was improving all the time. The experiments we performed also
seemed to create more interest in the other pupils in class, as indicated by the increased number of questions, their willingness to do
work, and the improvement they showed in tests.

I must say it was very gratifying to me to be able to instill an interest in science in a pupil who was previously uninterested, and, at
times, even belligerent in his attitude toward school work.

## Points for Discussion

- *There are many pupils like Rick, waiting to become old
  enough to be able to leave school. What kind of approach
  would you use with them?*

- *What procedures will you use to keep your pupils active in
  the subjects you will be teaching?*

### PROBLEM 25: ENCOURAGEMENT AND OUTSIDE INTERESTS HELP MOTIVATE AN UNRULY BOY

I had been assigned to teach a tenth grade biology class, all the members of which were below average. On the first day I became aware of a problem child. From the reports I had on him, I gathered he was a trouble-maker, a known truant, and that he rebelled against school work.

He proved to be everything his advance notices said he would be. He caused disturbances, would not open a book, and was occasionally absent without sufficient reason. He was a typical Huck Finn type of boy, with unruly hair, wearing dungarees that had seen plenty of outside action. His home was near a river in the country. The one contribution he made to class was to bring in specimens of salamanders, tadpoles, and garter snakes. I must say he looked more at ease with a snake in his hand than with a pencil.

Huck seemed to have an attitude of resentment toward teachers and toward all authority. I felt that my first job would be to gain his confidence by showing an interest in him. I made a practice of speaking to all students when passing them in the halls, or when they were getting on or off the bus, and I made a special effort to speak to Huck.

One day, I tried having the pupils ask each other questions on the subject matter. If a student answered a question correctly, he was entitled to ask a question of another student. Huck surprised me by taking an active part in the questioning. Whenever he answered, I would encourage him with a word of praise. It was not long after that he began to take more interest in the subject. Knowing that he liked hunting, fishing, and everything pertaining to the outdoors, when any question came up on the outdoors I would ask him his opinion on the matter. By thus correlating his favorite sports with the functionings of biology, I increased his interest in the subject greatly. Whenever we had slides to be shown, or made preparations for the use of microscopes, he was more than willing to help.

All during the semester he showed slow but steady progress. His truancy ceased, and he even took it upon himself to check others who were starting to be disorderly. My greatest thrill came near the end of the semester, when my master teacher questioned the whole class and was very pleased with the progress it had made.

### Points for Discussion

- *How would you have tried to motivate Huck if you were teaching a subject other than biology?*

- *What outside materials (aids, models, specimens, etc.) can you utilize in your subject field?*

## PROBLEM 26: A PRIVATE TALK STIMULATES A GIRL TO DO BETTER WORK

Susan is a fifteen-year-old sophomore in my history class who refuses to do any studying. When I checked her grades, I discovered she did not have a passing grade in any of her subjects during the current year. I decided to see if I could help her.

One day I went to the office and looked through her personal record. When I found that both her parents were well educated, I assumed that her home conditions and environment were conducive to study and learning. Also, she had two sisters, both of whom were very good students when they attended high school. Susan had taken three I.Q. tests, on which her score ranged from 97 to 108, an indication that she was capable of passing her high-school subjects. Her record showed she was friendly but that she was easily led by others, that she liked attention, and that she was easily distracted.

With this knowledge I felt I was in a better position to help Susan. First of all, I called on her more often in class and tried to work up a friendly relationship with her. Giving her this personal attention helped some, because she began to respond in class.

After I felt that she knew I was interested in her welfare, I decided to have a private talk with her. We discussed her low grades for a short time, and then I said: "Susan, you owe it to yourself, your parents, and society to try for better grades. Everyone can't be a genius. Each one of us has just so much to work with. Nobody expects or asks for the impossible. Don't be ashamed of what you have, and don't feel discouraged because others have more. Just do the best with what you have. No one can ask for anything more."

After that talk, Susan began to work. It seemed to me that she really did try to do her best. I know she at least tried to do a lot better than she had before, because when the next report card came out, she received a passing mark in history.

## Points for Discussion

- *What unwarranted assumption was made concerning this student's home conditions?*

- *Do you think this student's performance might have been affected by the high school performance of her sisters? Why?*

- *What should a teacher guard against in having private talks with students?*

## PROBLEM 27: AN ENTIRE CLASS IS MOTIVATED TO WORK

When I received my assignment as a student teacher, I was given two freshman and two junior classes. The freshman and one of the junior classes were well disciplined, but the other junior class consisted of a "slow college prep" group that turned out to be a problem for me. During my period of observation, I honestly admit I was afraid to take over that class.

When I first started to teach the class the students weren't bad, but they were definitely far from good. Gradually they became wilder, until finally I realized I had to do something.

The class was made up of thirty-six students. After questioning my cooperating teacher, I found out that most of the students were in the college prep course because of parental pressure, and that very few of them had the desire to continue their education after high school. This was unfortunate because the curriculum was structured for those who actually intended to go to college.

One of the first things I did to try to motivate them was to make extensive use of audio-visual aids. The students enjoyed these very much. It made the work more interesting and understandable for them. However, there were still five trouble-makers who showed no interest in the work at all.

Gradually, I began to get some ideas on how to control the trouble-makers. At first I used the demerit system. This worked very well in the case of one girl. The others just ignored the demerits because they didn't care about school; for them in a sense, getting demerits was great, because they regarded suspension as a "vacation" from school.

The second step, which I was advised to take, was the use of physical force. This I didn't want to do. I just couldn't imagine myself having a physical encounter with any student, so I avoided this advice. I believe in treating students as ladies and gentlemen, and I know that physical action is an improper way to treat any person.

My third plan worked. It consisted of keeping the students so active that there was no time for playing around in the classroom. This meant that the students and I had to work harder. It was not hard work, but it was continuous work. One of the biggest trouble-makers offered to give an oral report before the class. Then, after we started to read the play *Macbeth*, all the students were begging for individual parts to read. They enjoyed being actors and actresses, especially the students who had caused disciplinary problems. Now they had a new and constructive way of displaying their qualities before the class. It also gave them the attention they had been striving for when they were upsetting the class.

I was finally convinced that my third plan had worked when one day, as I was writing notes on the board, one of the loudest talkers in the class turned around to one of his friends and told him to shut up. And you know what—his friend did! This made me feel better than you can imagine.

As I said, this "work policy" put a lot more pressure on me in the way of preparing and presenting lessons, but in all honesty and sincerity, it was worth every ounce of effort to see the former trouble-makers turning into sincere, interested, and respectful students.

## Points for Discussion

* *The student teacher made use of participation to motivate his class. Besides adding to motivation, what other benefits does participation have in learning?*

* *In your theory courses, what recommendations were made regarding keeping pupils active in class?*

### PROBLEM 28:  AN ENGLISH TEACHER CAPITALIZES ON A TROUBLESOME STUDENT'S ART ABILITY

If there was one word that could best typify Tony's personal history, it would definitely have to be *troublesome*. His entire life was a series of turbulent problems and difficulties, all of which had an extremely negative effect upon him.

Some of these difficulties stemmed from his home life. Tony's parents had an unhappy marriage, and lived together for just a few years before the father died, leaving Tony and his mother penniless. Unable to provide for Tony, his mother left him with a step-grand-mother who was neither responsible nor capable as a guardian for the child.

As a result of this lack of attention and love, Tony began to develop feelings of insecurity and frustration, accompanied by an aggressive and hostile attitude. This attitude, coupled with an urge to cover up his family's problems, expressed itself in rebellion against authority. Although his personal attitude was very negative, he nevertheless did acceptable work as a student. But he lacked the desire or incentive to really develop his potentialities. His primary problem, then, seemed to be one of motivation.

On consulting with several faculty members who had previously taught Tony, I obtained many different accounts and opinions regarding his personal and scholastic problems. Several teachers had tried talking with the boy in an effort to change his indifferent attitude toward school work. Others held conferences with his guardian, and some even altered their lesson plans to accommodate Tony's problems. None of these attempts produced positive results. Consequently, the majority of the faculty, and even some of the students, labeled Tony as a misfit whose mere name suggested bad news.

Although Tony's position was grim, I was hesitant to accept these discouraging reports as being final and decisive. I soon found out the reports were well substantiated. I started to experience a countless number of difficulties and problems with his personal attitude and his work in class. At times, he disrupted the entire class during a recitation by standing up just to tuck his shirt in his trousers. He ignored my questions, without even attempting an answer. His test papers were poor; often, he wouldn't even put his name on the paper. Reprimands made him more hostile. Sarcasm only increased his contempt for authority. Approaching him as a friend tended to arouse feelings of suspicion and mistrust.

I, too, was about to give up on Tony when one day I learned from the art teacher that Tony had superior ability in art projects, such as sketching and drawing. I knew if I could utilize his art talent in my English class it might motivate him to study English. At the time, we were discussing the tales of the knights in class. I asked Tony if he thought he was good enough to draw a poster of a knight that I could use as an illustration for the rest of the class. By doing this, I challenged him to prove himself in his own area of interest and talent. It took a few days of coaxing, but he finally agreed to do it. The sketch he brought in took him only a short time but it was excellent, superbly distinct and precise in every detail.

Thereafter, I asked Tony to bring a little sketch or drawing that would illustrate our daily lessons. I knew he would have to study the material in order to do this. At first, Tony produced mediocre work, but as time went on he began to take pride in producing better illustrations. At the same time, his work in English and his class participation improved considerably. It seemed strange, but as Tony became more involved in his work, disciplinary problems with him became non-existent. He became more friendly and congenial toward his classmates, not to mention a more trusting and sincere attitude toward his English teacher!

## Points for Discussion

- Do you agree with the student teacher's analysis of the causes of Tony's problems? Why?

- Outline several courses of action for motivating students like Tony.

## PROBLEM 29: A BOWL CONTEST GENERATES INTEREST IN ENGLISH GRAMMAR

On the whole, my seventh grade group in English grammar consisted of youngsters who were above average in mental ability. As we discussed various elements of English grammar, we moved along rather easily and smoothly. I sensed, however, that an intangible something was missing; the pupils were not as well motivated as I would have liked them to be. Also, there was a girl in class who was doing B work, which was good, but she had the ability to do outstanding work.

For days I tried to think of some way to stimulate more enthusiasm in class. Finally, while I was watching television, I came upon what proved to be the perfect solution to the whole problem. The program which attracted me was a "bowl" contest in which points were awarded to opposing teams for answering questions correctly. I became intrigued with its format, feeling that I could adapt it to my class. After thinking and planning, I came up with my own "Seventh Grade Bowl," with the format based on the television show but geared to the level of my seventh graders.

When I announced the plan to the class, there were cries of excitement and enthusiasm. The class and I began to formulate plans for our contest, and even this preliminary work caused a stir of excitement. First, we chose two panels of four students, each panel consisting of two boys and two girls, with one student chosen as captain and spokesperson for each team. Next we chose a moderator, two scorekeepers, and three judges. It was decided that I would act as the final authority in the event of a tie or controversy. The game was to be played with questions concerning English grammar, this being decided by a near-unanimous vote of the class.

The procedure was fully explained to the class. The moderator was to ask a question worth ten points, which was to be answered by the first panel to signify knowledge of the answer. If the panel answered the question correctly, they scored ten points and were given the opportunity to answer a bonus question worth from twenty to fifty points depending on its difficulty and complexity of wording. Thus, if Panel A answered the ten-point question, and correctly answered a bonus question of twenty points, the members would have posted a score of thirty at the end of the first round. If Panel A missed the ten-point question, however, the members forfeited their chance to answer the bonus question, and both questions would be offered to the opposing panel. A definite time limit was set for the game, and the winning panel was to return the following week to meet a panel of challengers.

It took us a few minutes of the first contest to iron out the kinks, but then the game proceeded smoothly and rapidly. It was an instant success with the pupils. In order to maintain discipline, the remainder of the class was told to look up the answers to the questions as they were asked. As it turned out, the competitive spirit of the youngsters came to the fore, and they were busily engaged in rooting for their favorites, checking the answers to see that their favorites received a fair deal.

After the game was over, excitement rose to a fever pitch in choosing the panel of challengers for the next week. During the week, interest was high in the regular work because the present week's work was to be included in the questions for the next contest.

The contest also solved the problem of the girl who was not working up to capacity. She was chosen as a member of one of the first panels, and encouraged by me and her rooters, she actually led her team to three successive victories. The impact on her was so great that she shook off her lethargy and excelled in every phase of the work thereafter.

As a result of our contests, the interest of the class became so intense that it even pervaded our daily work. However, my biggest thrill came after I had asked the class if they would like to include questions from other subjects in the contest. Almost in one voice they cried out: "No! Let's stick to English grammar."

In view of the fact that English grammar is usually considered to be dry and boring, their response was very gratifying to me. It was the attitude of the students, their ability, and their imagination that actually gave impetus to the revitalized interest. Consequently, the students, my cooperating teacher, and a popular television program all combined to make my student teaching an exhilarating experience.

## Points for Discussion

- *Would a contest such as this be suitable for average or below average pupils? Why?*

- *Explain the ways in which this student teacher safeguarded performance on daily work.*

- *Evaluate competition as an incentive to learning.*

## PROBLEM 30:  A CLASS CLOWN TURNS INTO A SOURCE OF MOTIVATION

During my period of observation, I immediately noticed Jim, a fifteen-year-old sophomore. Jim seemed to be a class "cut-up," always disrupting the class with untimely remarks and observations. He was the prime aggravation of my cooperating teacher, and paid no heed to her many threats of detention. To him, everything was a joke. He never seemed able to sit still, and he had a short attention span. I dreaded the thought of having to cope with him.

My cooperating teacher clued me in on his behavior. She called him immature and lazy, although she admitted he learned very easily. Jim craved and demanded attention, all kinds of attention. He was equally satisfied with praise or punishment. The more attention he received from the teacher and the class, the happier he seemed to be.

A conference with the guidance counselor revealed that Jim's achievement was erratic, his grades ranging from 66 to 92. This told me that Jim could perform well if he really wanted to. His I.Q. of 113 confirmed he had the ability to do successful work in school. I asked the counselor if Jim could be classified as a hyperactive child, but he maintained that Jim's records showed no such hyperactivity. "He's very much a boy," he said, referring to Jim's classroom antics.

Further delving into Jim's background revealed that both parents worked, so that as a child, Jim was put into the care of an aging grandmother who could not speak a word of English. Perhaps this contributed to his subsequent lack of disciplined behavior in the school situation. In fact, Jim had been a discipline problem ever since his kindergarten days. He attended a private parochial elementary school, and was asked to withdraw because of his poor behavior. The parents acted highly insulted, and placed Jim in a public school. They insisted Jim's behavior was normal, since "boys will be boys." The parents' defense of Jim's "boyishness" may have been a contributing factor to his classroom clowning.

As time went on in my student teaching, I tried to establish a rapport with Jim, being careful not to give him an excessive amount of attention. In my dealings with him, I found that Jim, for all his clowning and fooling around, was never sarcastic or disrespectful. There was a great deal of innocence and good nature in him. In fact, it became very easy to love him.

I decided I would try to turn his clowning to advantage by using him as a motivational force in the classroom. For example, if there was a dialogue to read, I'd call on Jim to come up to the front of the class to read i  He always readily obliged, and would put a lot of dramatic expression into his reading. The students enjoyed his dramatics so much that they became increasingly interested in the material to be learned. My discipline problem was actually motivating the class! Later I learned Jim and his parents had spent the previous summer traveling abroad, so I got Jim to relate his experiences to the class. He loved the attention, and the class enjoyed hearing his dramatic explanations.

I have come to the conclusion that idle threats of detention are useless in dealing with "class cut-ups" like Jim. By giving Jim positive, constructive attention instead of threatening him, he became more interested in his work. Equally important, his interest and dramatics boosted the spirits of the other students, and helped greatly to stimulate their interest and participation. Whoever would have guessed that Jim, my discipline problem, could become a paragon of motivation!

## Points for Discussion

- *Do you believe that "boys will be boys"? What kind of conduct does the statement imply?*

- *What might be the danger of giving a "class clown" extra attention?*

## PROBLEM 31: THE STUDENT TEACHER'S PERSISTENCE FINALLY MOTIVATES A BOY

After my first few days in class, I began to realize the great difference in attitudes and personalities I had before me. There were those who seemed to grasp for knowledge, and those who shut their minds to it. One of the latter was Eddie who was in my ninth grade biology class.

I did not really notice Eddie until my second week of teaching. He was a quiet boy until one day he began to annoy the girl sitting behind him. Even though I reprimanded him several times, he continued to be obnoxious. So I finally asked him to see me after class.

When I asked Eddie why he insisted on being such an annoyance, he said he didn't care about biology because he was going to join the army after graduation. The only reason he was taking biology, he said, was because it was mandatory. Anyway, he had decided not to do anything because he felt that it was useless.

This little discussion momentarily stunned me. I couldn't believe that a student would actually tell a teacher that he wouldn't do any work in class. I made up my mind to find out more about Eddie.

The next day, I spoke to a few of his teachers. They were also having trouble with him, and advised me to "shut him up early." No one seemed to want to help him, so I thought I would at least try.

From the guidance counselor, I found that Eddie's I.Q. was 104, that his reading ability was a little below average, that as a person he wanted to be a leader, and he could not tolerate being led. I found it very interesting that he had not failed any of his subjects, and that his main interests were English and science. Why, then, was he not interested in biology?

For the next two weeks, I gave more attention to Eddie, not only in class but also in the halls and around the school. He seemed to respond to me personally, but he still refused to show an interest in class. When called on to recite, he either refused to answer, or answered in a joking way. In spite of his jokes, I kept drawing answers out of him. Finally, I thought I had it made, because he was actually raising his hand and giving good answers. This continued for about a week, until hunting season was opened. Eddie was absent for an entire week. When he returned, he reverted to his old ways of being silent and disinterested.

I had another talk with him. He told me he thought he would fail because of the material he had missed during his week's absence—so, why do anything? I told him it would be necessary for me to repeat the material, because over half the boys were absent and several other students had been out because they were stricken with the flu. So, he had as good a chance of passing as the others. This seemed to encourage him and he promised to try.

The next week was encouraging. Eddie was interested, answered when called on, and even remained after class to ask questions about the material. I decided to keep his interest alive by placing him in charge of lab specimens, a shipment of which was due within a short time. I was pleased to find that Eddie not only read the book I gave him but also did some library research on his own. When the shipment arrived, he was ready and eager to take care of the organisms. He did an excellent job of it, and was proud of his work. From that time on, I had no problems with Eddie.

Eddie never became an A student, but he did do his best. He seemed to shine in lab periods, and also took an active part in class. He was always willing to help, and never again caused a commotion.

Giving a student a chance instead of judging him by his reputation, trying to interest him instead of confronting him, being a guide instead of being a tyrant—all of these definitely helped Eddie to change his attitude toward learning. Perhaps this form of treatment may not work with every student, but in this case it helped someone, and indeed it helped me.

### Points for Discussion

- *Discuss the pros and cons of having required courses in the curriculum.*

- *What do you think was responsible for Eddie's change of attitude toward learning?*

### PROBLEM 32: MAKING USE OF TELEVISION PROGRAMS WATCHED BY PUPILS

A particularly interesting lesson I had in my American history class had to do with the Cattle Kingdom. Before class, I drew on the blackboard a map of the Cattle Kingdom, containing a picture of the three important cattle trails that started in Texas and ended at railroad sites.

I explained to the class that this was the region over which most of the cattle roamed at the time. Then I described the trails and the famous cattle towns along them, pointing out that these towns are the ones that appear in the movies and on television shows. Among them were Cheyenne, Dodge City, Kansas City, Topeka, Atchison, Omaha, Denver, and Abilene. Questions were then raised by the class on the importance of railroads. They asked how labor was obtained to build the railroads, where the railroad ties came from, where the cattle were taken to be slaughtered, and so on.

I pointed out that at Abilene order was maintained by "Judge Colt" in the person of Marshal James B. (Wild Bill) Hickok, who unerringly fired from the hip and who was felled by a shot in the back.

This discussion led to an outline of the five forces that brought an end to the Cattle Kingdom: the Indians, the farmers, the sheep raisers, intervention of state governments, and finally, the invention of barbed wire, which enabled the farmers and sheep raisers to fence in their land, and forced the ranchers to do the same, thus preventing the cattle from roaming over the Cattle Kingdom.

The class followed the whole lesson attentively and asked questions spontaneously. I think their interest was heightened by the fact that they felt they almost knew the territory and some of the historical characters when we correlated the material with movies and television programs they had seen.

### Points for Discussion

- *Think of some motion pictures and television programs that would provide useful material for the subject you intend to teach. How would they be useful?*

- *What are the common interests of the age group you will be teaching?*

### PROBLEM 33: A DISINTERESTED STUDENT IS SHOWN THE VALUE OF EDUCATION

The school records showed that Ray was a bright student through the seventh grade, but that he was now repeating the eighth grade. He had absolutely no desire to apply himself to academic work, and was doing poorly in his second bout with eighth grade. Around the school, I heard him branded by various teachers as retarded, a delinquent, a no-good, and many other discouraging terms, and they told me that talking to Ray was just a waste of time. I decided to talk to him anyway.

I asked Ray to see me after class. When he came, it appeared that he was resentful that I had summoned him, because he was cynical and rude. I maintained my "cool," and tried to act more like a friend than a teacher, with the result that Ray started to talk about himself.

He told me he did well in school until he reached the eighth grade. At that point, he started to wonder what it was all about, and

questioned the value of an education, especially the academic subjects. So he stopped studying. He told me he hated school, and was
just waiting to be old enough to quit so that he could go to work in a
gas station. I asked him how much he knew about cars. He replied
he did not know much, but that cars fascinated him. I used that as a
starting point, asking Ray how he expected to be a good mechanic if
he didn't study motor manuals, shop manuals, go to factory schools,
and so on. He countered by saying he would join the army if he
failed as a mechanic.

I then told him about a friend of mine who joined the army after
doing very badly in high school. In the army, my friend decided to
apply himself by studying electronics, did very well, and had a profitable job waiting for him when he was discharged. But, I emphasized, he succeeded only by studying. I also told him I had read that
even garbage collectors were required to have a high school diploma
before some cities would hire them.

Finally, I offered Ray a challenge. I told him if he could think of
five situations in life in which education would be of no help, I would
not bother him in class, and I would give him a passing grade for the
semester. Ray was surprised to find he could not think of one such
situation.

The talk with him apparently did some good. Ray studied more,
and his grades began to improve. His average rose 20 points in my
class. There was also considerable improvement in his behavior. Ray
told me I was the only one who had ever shown an interest in him.
As time went on, he became one of the leading students in my class.

Unfortunately, it seems that the improvement in Ray took place
only in my class. His other teachers told me that he was the same
old Ray in their classes. Nevertheless, I feel quite proud of myself
for getting this problem child and so-called juvenile delinquent to
become a good student, even if it was only in my class.

## Points for Discussion

- *How would you answer a student who told you there was no
  value in getting an education?*

- *What do you think of the student teacher's challenge to Ray?*

- *Why was there no improvement in Ray's work in other
  classes?*

### PROBLEM 34: A HISTORY CLASS MAKES USE OF RELATIVES' WAR EXPERIENCES

This is the case of a student who, to all outward appearances, disliked the study of history. Her test marks were average, but her work in daily recitations was unsatisfactory because she remained silent most of the time. My problem was to get her interested enough to participate in the daily work.

We were about to begin the study of the Korean war, which in itself was more interesting than the material preceding it. I felt it was a case of now or never, as far as arousing her interest was concerned. Looking into her background, I came up with the fact that her father was a veteran of the Korean War. I decided to try to use this as a wedge.

When we began to study the war, I asked each pupil to write a brief paper on it, telling them that they could get much helpful information from their fathers, relatives, or neighbors who had been in the war. I explained to them that first-hand information from a person who had been in actual combat or who had lived during that time might sometimes be better than just reading about the event in a history book. The response was encouraging. The following classes were marked by zealous discussions of battles and events in which the parents or relatives of the students had taken part. Leading the discussions was my problem child. She not only had the names of battles and places but also had pictures to back up her statements.

Open praise for her good work was in order. Then, to prevent her from slipping back into the proverbial rut, I kept her busy doing research work on the subsequent treaties and peace proposals. Her daily recitation mark rose sharply, and her interval mark increased greatly. The marks, however, are incidental. The important thing is that this student now knows that history can be alive and interesting.

### Points for Discussion

- *What measures might have been taken to motivate this student if her father had not been a veteran?*

### PROBLEM 35: THE STUDENT TEACHER'S PERSONAL INTEREST MOTIVATES A BOY

John is a pleasant boy, a little plump, and always ready to emit a smile. He has many good qualities, but one gift he does not possess is high intelligence. His I.Q. test scores ranged between 83–90. He is hampered in school work by his inability to spell and his very poor penmanship which, I believe, is an attempt to obscure his poor spelling.

As far as discipline was concerned, John and I had no trouble whatsoever. He sat in the last seat in the second row, and remained silent and disinterested. It seemed to me that because of his poor work in school, he had feelings of inferiority, and that he compensated by resisting learning in order to "save face" with his unscholarly friends. He did, however, do his homework, and he came to school every day. His records showed that he was failing in every subject except gym, shop, and music.

John was such a nonentity in class that I could have been oblivious to him. However, he interested me because he was a pleasant boy, and, although his intelligence bordered on the slow-normal, I felt he could do passing work. I decided to have a talk with him at an opportune time.

The opportunity presented itself in a gym class that I had taken over for the coach. John came over to me, asking advice on how to shoot a set-shot in basketball. I worked with him for about ten minutes, doing my best to show him how to do it. Later, we talked together. He told me of his interest in fishing and hunting, giving me a great deal of information about those hobbies. When we parted, he told me that this was the first time he had ever talked to a teacher on such an informal basis.

The next day I went over a test I had given. I called each pupil to my desk to examine his or her paper, and to answer their individual questions regarding the test. When John's turn came, he learned he had a failing grade. In the course of our conference, I remarked, "Well, John, you can't catch trout without bait, and you can't pass a test without studying." I then told him I had checked his I.Q. and found it high, and that I knew he could do good work in history. I felt this little "white lie" might give him the incentive needed to launch him on a new course.

After this episode, a new John emerged. He was attentive, and startled his classmates by asking questions. One boy came up to me and told me that this was the first time in three years he could remember John asking a question. But that was not all. Besides asking questions, John also volunteered answers—*right* answers! Whenever I asked a question, the hand in the last seat in the second row was usually up and waving. Somehow, with the change in John, there came a change in the other students. They showed greater interest and participation, perhaps not to be outdone by him. Also, a new attitude of respect for John was developing in the class. You could see the feeling of pride reflected in his eyes.

In our next history test, John came through with an 87, the fourth highest grade in the class. I took time out to commend him publicly, giving him another boost in the eyes of his peers. John was now respected as a student, as shown in the next test I gave. As a precaution against cheating, I asked the class to spread out over the classroom. Two students moved to the back of the room, within viewing distance of John's paper. I am sure that this made John feel twelve feet high.

John's work improved in other classes too, but not as much as in mine. At least he was doing passing work. My only hope is that his motivation will continue, and that he will graduate to become a responsible citizen in our society. I hope I have been instrumental in helping this fine young man find his way.

### Points for Discussion

- *The student teacher identified with John because of their common interest in sports. If you had no interest in sports, how would you have tried to motivate him?*

- *After John's work improved, why did the work of other students improve?*

- *What are the pros and cons of telling a student that his I.Q. is higher than it is?*

### PROBLEM 36:  CONSIDERATION HELPS TO MOTIVATE AN UNRULY PUPIL

Amos was an attention-getter in my eleventh grade American history class. While I was observing the class prior to student teaching, I noticed that he paid little attention to the lesson. Instead, he would periodically do something to gain attention. My cooperating teacher punished him each time, after which he would quiet down. Amos was not a really serious problem. He was an annoyance. He simply seemed to want attention. After he got it, he seemed satisfied for a while, and then would crave attention again.

I inquired into his background, and found he had been expelled from a private school before coming here. He was enrolled in an academic program, which caused me to wonder about his ability to learn. My cooperating teacher assured me that Amos had the ability to succeed in the academic program, but that, like so many other boys, he lacked motivation. The cooperating teacher informed me that during the week prior to my student teaching, Amos had been sent home and was told not to come back unless he was accompanied by his father. The father came with Amos, but in this case it turned out that Amos was innocent of wrong-doing. He had been blamed because of his reputation. The cooperating teacher told me that the father's behavior during this episode led the school personnel to believe that Amos' problems had their origins at home.

Before taking over the class, I had a talk with Amos about his behavior. I told him that I would meet him half-way in trying to help him after I took over the class. He promised he would try to do better than he had been.

Apparently he was sincere in his promise. Occasionally, he would get off the track, but he would right himself quickly. On one occasion shortly after I began to teach, he gave concrete evidence that he was really trying. I had assigned oral reports in preparation for Washington's birthday. On the day of the reports, some of the boys I called on had failed to prepare one. I was fearful that Amos might be one of these. I called his name and then held my breath. Amos rose from his seat and came to the front of the room. With his head bowed he began to read his report. As he read, he seemed to gain confidence, his head gradually came up, and he put all the emphasis he could in his reading. The class seemed amazed, for here was the class joker in front of the class, giving a good serious presentation.

The change in Amos caused a change in the other boys. Their attitude improved greatly. I think they felt that if school was acceptable to Amos, it was acceptable to them. Besides, I think they did not want to be outdone by Amos.

There was one more incident that could have caused trouble between me and Amos. During preparation for a test, I put questions and answers on the board, to be copied by the class. These would be helpful in studying for the test. I gave the class time to copy the material, and then, before erasing it, I asked if everyone had finished copying. Since no one answered, I began to erase. As I did, a voice from the back of the room boomed: "You erase that board and I'll knock your block off." I recognized the voice as of Amos.

The eyes of the class were on me to see how I was going to react. Amos was looking straight at me too.

## Discussion

- *How would you handle the threat made by Amos?*

## PROBLEM 37:  A SLOW STUDENT FEELS CHEATED ON A TEST

Betty is small for her age group and slightly below average in intelligence. She gave me the impression that she felt physically and mentally inferior to her classmates. She would perform various acts
merely to get attention, and when called upon to recite she would
either remain silent or make a ridiculous reply.

Before I started teaching this class, I sounded out some of the
other teachers on Betty. They all regarded her as difficult to handle,
though they felt that she could do better work than she was doing.
One teacher told me she had some success with Betty by praising
her for anything she did. She recommended that I try that approach.

The first few days I taught the class I called on her several
times, but only received giggles and sarcasm in return. She showed
no interest in her work. Finally, I decided to ignore her for a while,
thus depriving her of some of the attention she was getting. I did this
for three days, after which I noticed her hand going up once in a
while to answer a question.

The greatest step forward with Betty came after a quiz I gave
the class. It was an objective test, with each question counting five
points, and the passing mark was sixty-five. Betty received a sixty.
After class she approached me with tears rolling down her face.

"You cheated me," she said.

When I asked her what she meant, she showed me her paper.
One answer that was marked wrong she felt was correct. Because
she had badly misspelled the correct word, I had marked it wrong.
She told me she knew the answer but didn't know how to spell it.


## Discussion

- *How would you handle this situation?*


## PROBLEM 38:  SPECIAL PROJECTS AND A
               PUPIL-CONDUCTED CLASS ADD INTEREST

I had been teaching my classes a week without being able to arouse
anything more than a polite interest on the part of the pupils. I
therefore decided to try a new approach.

Since we were to start a new unit which was quite interesting, I
decided to have the students conduct a few classes under my supervision. The material we were about to take up incorporated a discussion of knights, castles, and feudalism—a subject which I felt would
prove interesting because most students like to read about the deeds

of great knights. I assigned each student a topic to look up on his own, and told them that they would be expected to report to the class on their respective topics and answer questions asked by their classmates. As a visual aid, I asked them to see a movie which was playing at the local theater. The movie would be helpful in giving them concrete images of castles, castle life, clothing, and warfare. I also asked for a few volunteers to build a castle out of cardboard.

When the day for the reports came, I was surprised to see how well prepared the students were. They seemed happy to have the assignments. When the class started, I gave a brief summary of what we would discuss in the chapter and then turned over the class to the students. They gave their reports, and each one was asked many questions by the class. We also discussed various aspects of the movie I had asked them to see. The whole thing was clearly a success and enjoyed very much by the pupils.

## Discussion

- *Describe a special class project that could be incorporated into the subject you will be teaching.*

### PROBLEM 39: A SUPERIOR STUDENT WITH FAILING GRADES NEEDS MOTIVATION

This is a case of a student who was continuously the lowest in performance in the entire class. Because it was an accelerated class, I knew his I.Q. was above average; placement in that class was dependent on past achievement and on I.Q. Yet the highest mark made by this student in any of the tests I gave was 66.

I arranged a talk with him, during which my approach was direct and simple, but friendly. In return, he was just as frank with me. He said basketball practice and rehearsal for the school play were taking a great deal of his time, but that was not the real reason for his poor performance in class. Indeed, this fact was obvious, because other students in the class were just as busy with other activities and yet were doing excellent work. The true reason, he said, was so much emphasis was being placed on science and mathematics these days that he could not see the value of studying civics. He felt almost an annoyance at having to take it. He liked math and science and was doing well in them.

My next step, obviously, was to try to show him that a course in civics was important to him. I explained the need for civics to help him find his place in society and its place in providing a student with a well-rounded education. I simply asked him what science and mathematics would avail him if he could not learn to live properly in society with other people. He frankly admitted he had never had the question put to him in that light. I made another appeal to him on the basis of his ability as an athlete. I told him that competition in future life would be severe, and that here, in civics, he would find the basic elements that would help him meet that challenge. He admitted he had never considered this either; he simply never had thought in terms of the future. I did not press our talk any further. He promised to think about what I had said.

### Discussion

- *What would you say to a student who told you he could see no value in studying the subject you will be teaching?*

### PROBLEM 40: USE OF IMPROPER SOURCES OF MOTIVATION CAUSES TROUBLE

"We grow old too soon, and smart too late." I suppose I made a lot of mistakes during student teaching that I wouldn't make again. My biggest problem was trying to motivate one of my classes to study.

My cooperating teacher had told me that my seventh period class was intelligent and easy to get along with. Things went well the first few days while the cooperating teacher was in the room. When she left me alone, however, the class became a little noisy. I mentioned this to my cooperating teacher who suggested that I give them a short quiz every time they became noisy.

The trouble immediately started on my first day alone with the class. I guess they were testing me to see how far I would let them go. I asked a question. While a student was answering the question, the rest of the class wasn't paying attention at all. I got some paper from the desk, distributed it, and gave them a quiz. They didn't take it seriously. There was a great deal of copying, and they were still talking, so I told them they would have another test the next day.

To put it mildly, the class wasn't pleased when I gave them the second test, but they were quiet, and remained quiet for a few days. Then one day, they started throwing chalk around the room. I gave them a little lecture on the kind of behavior I expected from them.

Then they started talking again. I told them to keep the noise down, but they paid no attention to me. I passed out some paper, made them outline a section of the chapter in class, and told them that this material would be in their next test. This seemed to settle them down.

Later on in the course, I had the students giving oral reports. During one of these reports, two boys were talking. As I was walking toward the front of the room after the report was completed, these two boys decided to play a game of tossing a paper wad between them. That was the last straw. I decided if I was going to get any work done in this class I would have to stop threatening and start acting. I put one of the boys on detention, and told the other boy he would get double detention if he made one wrong move.

## Discussion

* *What would you have done to motivate this class?*

**SELECTED READINGS**

Callahan, Sterling G. *Successful Teaching in Secondary Schools.* Glenville, Illinois: Scott, Foresman and Company, 1971, chapter 14.

DeCecco, John P. *The Psychology of Learning and Instruction: Educational Psychology.* Englewood Cliffs, New Jersey: Prentice-Hall, Inc., 1968, chapter 5.

Gage, N. L., and Berliner, David C. *Educational Psychology.* Chicago: Rand McNally College Publishing Company, 1975, units 14–17.

Gibson, Janice C. *Psychology for the Classroom.* Englewood Cliffs, New Jersey: Prentice-Hall, Inc., 1976, chapter 6.

Goodwin, William L., and Klausmeier, Herbert J. *Facilitating Student Learning.* New York: Harper and Row, Publishers, 1975, chapter 11.

Hoover, Kenneth H. *The Professional Teacher's Handbook.* Boston: Allyn and Bacon, Inc., 1976, chapter 4.

Mouly, George J. *Psychology for Effective Teaching,* 3rd ed. New York: Holt, Rinehart and Winston, Inc., 1973, chapter 13.

Smith, M. Daniel. *Learning and its Classroom Applications.* Boston: Allyn and Bacon, Inc., 1975, chapter 7.

# 4

# Problems of Emotional Adjustment

Emotions, being a very complex state, defy definition. Yet each of us is continually experiencing a variety of emotions—joy, sadness, anger, fear, or anxiety. We know what they are through experience, but because emotions transcend our whole being we cannot capture all the elements of an emotion in a single capsule-like group of words. When we experience an emotion, it is accompanied by a feeling of pleasantness or unpleasantness; by sensations, images, ideas; by a tendency to overt action; and all of these are directed toward a particular person or thing. Thus, if we are insulted or humiliated by another person, we may experience tingling sensations of the body, we may have flights of imagination, we may think of various ways of handling the situation, and we have a tendency to protect ourselves or to commit a retaliatory act.

Emotions are very important because they permeate so many of our activities. They can stimulate us to great effort, or they can cause us to grow miserable and inefficient, to the point of affecting our physical and mental health. A student with serious emotional problems cannot work up to his capacity and is ineffectual in his work. In fact, if the emotion is strong enough, it may cause mental blocks to the point that the student is not able to think rationally at all. Since this is so, it is important that a teacher be able to recognize symptoms of emotional maladjustment so that these blocks to the student's progress can be noticed, recognized for what they are, and, if possible, removed.

There are many causes contributing to emotional maladjustment. Many of them may be traced to the home, the school, or to various phases of the individual's environment.

The home represents to the growing child or adolescent the gratification of his needs. Among his basic needs are the need for security and the need for love. Anything which threatens or deprives him of these basic needs may lead to insecurity and chronic uncertainty on his part, which in turn may lead to a predisposition for emotional maladjustment.

One of the more serious negative situations is the broken home. A home may be considered broken when one of the parents is dead, or if the parents are separated or divorced, or if the occupation of a parent keeps him away from home for prolonged periods of time. Or, in a psychological sense, a home may be considered to be broken if family relationships are not harmonious, or if parents are continuously quarreling or bickering. In homes such as these, the individual feels insecure and he is deprived of the love which he craves. He may become anxious or resentful, or both, and he may resort to abnormal forms of reaction to discharge his tensions and frustrations.

Home training may have an influence on emotional adjustment. Overprotecting an individual and gratifying his every desire is not conducive to a realistic adjustment to life's problems on his part. Expecting too much of the individual, on the other hand, serves to build up tensions within him because he cannot attain the unreasonable goals set for him. Depriving the individual of attention because of the birth of another child, imposing heavy responsibilities on the oldest child, allowing the youngest child to be ordered around by all the other children, applying pressure on the adolescent to go into an occupation he dislikes, showing favoritism among children, not allowing them the freedom they think they deserve, and many other home situations, may contribute to emotional problems.

There are many anxiety-provoking situations in school to which most individuals gradually make a satisfactory adjustment. Occasionally, however, a student meets a situation with which he finds it difficult to cope. Each year the student is called upon to make adjustments to new teachers, new methods of teaching, new subjects, new companions, and perhaps new regulations. Most students who have had normal upbringing and who have normal ability make the transition more or less smoothly. In some few cases, however, there may be a personality clash with the teacher, or dislike for a subject, or resentment against regulations—any one of which results in painful emotional conflicts. One may find, for example, an above-average student doing poor work for a particular teacher. Or one may find a below-average student hopelessly floundering because he does not have the ability to cope with a new level of schooling. There may be a student here and there who dreads reciting. Some students who are held back in school may develop feelings of inadequacy. Others, rejected by the group, may withdraw from normal relationships, or they may go to the other extreme and become obnoxiously belligerent. There are then, in school, many experiences which may cause humiliation, resentment, anxiety, or inferiority, because the individual could not make a normal adjustment to them.

Outside of the home and the school there are other influences which affect an individual's adjustment. The most prominent among these would be the adequacy of recreational facilities. Playgrounds, athletic fields, civic and church recreation centers, and youth centers permit children and adolescents to discharge their energies and explore their interests in wholesome activities. Lacking such facilities, some adolescents, either individually or in groups, vent their energies, frustrations, and resentment through unlawful activities such as vandalism, theft, street fights, alcoholism, or drug use. Once apprehended, the individual acquires a stigma which is sometimes difficult to heal, and which is never completely erased.

This is but a brief sketch of a few of the situations that may cause emotional problems for the student. A beginning teacher has usually gained some knowledge of this type in the psychology courses which are part of his training program, but has had little time to experience them. The following suggestions, therefore, may prove useful to the beginning teacher in recognizing and dealing with emotional problems that he is sure to find among some of his pupils.

## SYMPTOMS OF EMOTIONAL PROBLEMS

All of us like to think well of ourselves, and have others think well of us. Consequently, when we make a mistake, or when we find ourselves in an embarrassing or anxiety-provoking situation, we often unconsciously resort to several forms of reaction to protect our self-esteem or to discharge anxiety or frustration. No harm results from the occasional use of these reactions. It is only when they are *overused* that harm may result. The teacher, therefore, should be alert to discover pupils who habitually react in the following ways.

*Rationalization.*   "I didn't want it anyway," is symptomatic of rationalization. The student who was unable to achieve a desired goal excuses himself by claiming that the goal was not a desirable one anyway. In rationalization, the excuses given are plausible, but they are not the *true* reasons. Thus, a pupil who fails to win a class office may state that he did not try very hard to get it because the office would involve too much work on his part. In reality, he *did* want the office, but failing to get it, he deceives and consoles himself by stating otherwise. The teacher will find students continuously giving excuses for their conduct, tardiness, lack of preparation, etc. If this happens with any one pupil on rare occasions, the teacher may dismiss it with tongue in cheek. However, if the teacher suspects frequent rationalizations on the part of the pupil, that pupil should receive help in seeing things realistically. Rationalization has sometimes been described as "making excuses instead of making good."

*Projection.* When a student is at fault for something, and he shifts the blame to someone else or something else, he is using projection. Indifferent or lazy students who are doing poor work may blame the teacher's methods for their lack of progress. A good student who failed a test because he did not prepare well may say that the test questions were unfair. Another student who holds a part-time job may blame the job for his lack of progress, even though he has adequate time for his school work. In all such cases, the individual is at fault, but he peddles the blame elsewhere.

*Daydreaming.* At times, a student tries to escape from a problem through daydreaming. He resorts to flights of imagination in which he pictures himself successfully handling situations which he did not solve adequately in reality. The boy who conducted himself awkwardly when he met a girl may later have a daydream in which he enchanted her with his brilliant conversation and charming manner. The failing student may imagine himself doing excellent work, receiving commendation instead of criticism. The pupil who is having trouble with his parents may picture himself running away from home, with repentant parents running after him and begging his forgiveness. In such cases, the individual experiences some emotional relief from his problem, but the relief is temporary. When he returns to reality, his problem is still there, facing him.

*Compensation.* There are some students who have a real defect or shortcoming, while there are others who do not have a shortcoming but think they do. Because of this real or imagined shortcoming, they may develop feelings of inadequacy or inferiority. Through compensation, the individual tries to overcome his handicap by developing a strength in some other area. The short, underdeveloped boy, unable to participate in athletics successfully, may concentrate on achieving success in academic work to obtain the recognition he desires. A girl who has not been endowed with an attractive physical appearance may strive to develop an engaging personality. A crippled child may seek recognition by trying to excel in some field for which he has talent, such as art, music, or writing. Quite often, therefore, a feeling of inadequacy may stimulate a student to unusual effort to achieve a desirable goal. There are times, however, when compensation leads to undesirable results. For example, an individual who feels inferior may try to appear self-confident to the point that he becomes obnoxious. He may boast excessively, talk in a loud manner, and may even become belligerent. Although he may hide his feeling of inferiority by this extreme aggressiveness, he is creating additional problems for himself in his relationship with others.

*Identification.* In identification, the student who has been unable to achieve success in his own experience may identify himself with other persons or organizations from whose successes or prestige he receives emotional satisfaction. A girl interested in dramatics, but having little talent for it, may attach herself to the heroine of school productions to the point of almost becoming her lady-in-waiting; she basks in the reflected glory of the heroines, and receives emotional satisfaction from it. Almost all students identify themselves with their school, and receive satisfaction from its achievements even though they may not have contributed to them. Perhaps we all identify ourselves to some degree with friends, relatives, and heroes of one type or another. A common reaction experienced by many of us when we hear someone praise an achievement of a friend is to exclaim: "I know him well. He is a good friend of mine!" Some people are "name droppers," pointing out that they have ties with prominent people. Somehow they feel that their status is improved simply because they know successful people. There is no harm in these identifications, provided the individual still strives for success on his own. It contributes little to the student's development and adjustment to "rest on the laurels" of someone else. Moreover, identification can become a serious problem if the student submerges his own personality and tries to assume the traits and characteristics of his hero.

*Withdrawal.* Another reaction to problems and frustrations is to retreat from them through the mechanism of withdrawal. Even though the individual may have a strong desire to approach the situation or problem, he withdraws because of fear of failure. Or, if he has repeatedly failed to solve a problem, he may finally retreat from it completely. Withdrawal may manifest itself by avoidance of situations in which the individual has experienced failure. Thus, a student who has failed in a position of responsibility may avoid accepting responsibility in the future. A boy who has been jilted by a girl may avoid emotional involvement with other girls. Or, a student who has set inordinately high standards for himself may delay in turning in his project, or may not turn it in at all because he thinks it is not good enough. There are other ways of escaping from problems, such as overeating, or resorting to alcohol or drugs. Withdrawal does not solve problems, but it may give the individual temporary relief from the pressure of facing them. Temporary withdrawal may be beneficial to the individual in providing him emotional relief while mustering or regrouping his forces for another frontal attack on his problem. If, however, he retreats from one fray after another, he needs help to make him realize that he cannot continually run away from life's problems. (See problems 48, 52, and 54.)

*Attention-getting.* As a reaction to the lack of recognition that the individual feels he should be getting from the home, the school, or his peers, he may resort to attention-getting, using a variety of activities to draw attention to himself. Sometimes these activities are compensatory in nature, as in the case of an individual who is boisterous and excessively aggressive, or one who seeks recognition through trying to excel. At other times, the acts bear no semblance to compensatory activities. The student simply seeks attention—by throwing paper wads or sailing paper airplanes through the classroom, by pulling hair or starting arguments with students, by making supposedly humorous remarks during a recitation or in answer to a question, or by any one of a host of sometimes bizarre activities which would draw to him the attention of the teacher and pupils. These attention-getting devices are so familiar that they need no elaboration. An occasional act of this type may be explained away in terms of normal mischief, or a symptom of the growing-up process. However, in the case of any one pupil, chronic activities of this type would be symptomatic of poor adjustment. (See problem 43.)

*Repression.* Finally, as a way of avoiding painful thoughts, the individual may unconsciously push them from consciousness through repression. Since these thoughts keep trying to revive themselves in consciousness, but at the same time are being repressed, the use of this mechanism increases tensions and anxieties instead of reducing them. However, if the individual is able to release his repressed feelings or needs in some other direction, no harm may result. For example, a student may have built up feelings of resentment and hostility against a teacher he hates, but he represses those feelings because of his fear of the consequences if he did not. If he could vent his hostility against the teacher in another way, it would relieve his tensions. Thus, talking it over with someone else, or even yelling at someone else, might provide relief for him. Or, if he went to the gymnasium and pictured his teacher's face on a punching bag he was punching, he would undoubtedly experience considerable relief.

The preceding reactions are known as defense mechanisms or protective devices. As noted previously, they may serve to relieve anxiety or to protect our self-esteem, and no harm results from their occasional use. If used habitually, however, it would mean that we are not facing life's problems realistically.

Reactions to problems can be more serious than those just described. If an individual has a severely traumatic emotional experience, or if he is in a chronic state of anxiety and cannot solve his problem, cannot run away from it, and cannot adjust to it, he may develop a *neurosis*. In a neurosis, there is usually irregularity of conduct in some particular area, but normal conduct in most other areas. The individual may be aware of the irregularity of his conduct, but does not seem to be able to do anything about it. Examples of neuroses are: neurathenia, phobia, obsessions, compulsions, hysteria, and psychosomatic disorders. The most serious reaction that can result from emotional problems is a *psychosis*. In this reaction, the individual fails to distinguish between the world of reality and the world of imagination, or he may misinterpret reality. The most common psychoses are schizophrenia and paranoia. Some recent studies have theorized that at least some cases of psychosis originate from physiological rather than emotional causes.

The beginning teacher will find relatively frequent use of defense mechanisms by his students, but he will seldom encounter a student with symptoms of a true neurosis. Since a person with a psychosis is usually institutionalized or is receiving intensive therapy, it is highly unlikely that the teacher will encounter a psychotic student. For these reasons, together with the fact that neuroses and psychoses require the attention of specialists, the discussion in this chapter has been limited to defense mechanisms.

### SUGGESTIONS FOR HANDLING EMOTIONAL PROBLEMS

*Do Not Jump to Conclusions.* In his anxiety to help pupils, the beginning teacher should not jump to conclusions concerning emotional maladjustment. A pupil who misbehaves occasionally may be simply working off some of the excess energy of youth, or another student who seeks attention may be manifesting a normal desire for recognition. Many pupils who fail to do their work on time will give the teacher excuses for failing to do so; some of these excuses will be legitimate ones, others will be false. In any such case, the beginning teacher should not immediately conclude that this is a case of attention-getting, or rationalization, or projection. Instead, the teacher should observe the future activities and reactions of these pupils. If certain reactions are chronic in a particular case, the teacher can start to suspect that this pupil has a problem requiring attention.

*Look for Extremes of Behavior.*  The beginning teacher should be alert for abnormal behavior patterns. At one extreme, there may be the pupil who is shy, retiring, withdrawn, or who does not mingle with other students. At the other extreme is the individual who is loud, bois- terous, or belligerent, making himself a nuisance to the teacher and the other pupils. The probability is high that students exhibiting either of these extremes of behavior have a problem that needs attention. (See problems 46 and 55.)

*Have a Private Talk.*  If the beginning teacher notices a student who definitely appears to be disturbed, he should have a private talk with him. Under no circumstances should the teacher question a student publicly in class about a personal matter, because it would embarrass the student, make him resentful, and he certainly would not volunteer any information of a personal nature. Instead, having a private talk with the student shows him that the teacher is interested in him and his problem, and the student is more likely to discuss his problem openly under these circumstances. Many students have minor problems that a teacher can help them solve. It may be that there is illness in the family, or that there has been a quarrel with a member of the opposite sex, or that the student is disturbed over a poor grade. A talk with the student will reveal the problem, and a sympathetic discussion, together with suggestions for constructive action, may be all that is necessary to solve the problem. A private talk may also benefit the student by reliev- ing some of his tensions. Talking a problem over with someone else seems to act as a release valve for built-up pressure. (See problems 44, 45, 49, and 51.)

*Seek Information From Other Sources.*  Sometimes the nature of the student's problem is not readily identified in a private talk. In such case, enlightening information may be obtained from other teachers who have the student in class, or have had dealings with him in the past. Or, a visit to the school counselor may reveal that he has knowl- edge related to the student and his difficulty. Also, if the situation calls for it, the teacher can try to enlist the aid of the student's parents.

Should the student teacher wish to consult the pupil's school records for information, he is cautioned that legally he needs the parent's permission to do so. After obtaining information through a private talk, and correlating it with information from other teachers, the counselor, and the parents, the teacher is in a better position to understand the student's problem and to help him with it. (See problems 41, 43, and 45.)

*Be Objective.* The teacher should not permit himself to get emotionally involved with the student's problem. Unless he remains objective, he will not be able to see the problem in its true perspective. Under such circumstances, obviously, he would not be able to help the student solve his problem because he would be dealing with it on an emotional rather than rational basis.

*Try to Find and Eliminate the Cause.* There is always a reason for an emotional problem. In order to help the individual, the cause must be surfaced, the individual must see it on a rational basis, and must be willing to take realistic action to overcome it. Sometimes symptoms may be suppressed, but this does not really help solve the problem if the cause still remains. Thus, a teacher with a strong personality may be able to suppress the outbreaks of a boisterous, belligerent student in his class, but unless the cause for those outbreaks has been removed, the student's hostility may break out in the classrooms of less forceful teachers, or in the corridors, or in the neighborhood. In order to help this student, one would have to find and eliminate the *cause* of his hostility. (See problems 44, 45, and 46.)

*Refer Serious Cases.* Emotional problems may have deep-seated causes which are difficult to uncover. If an untrained person attempts to help a person who is deeply emotionally disturbed, he will very likely aggravate, rather than relieve, the problem. If the teacher tries to help a student with an emotional problem, and finds it to be more serious than he thought, he should refer the student to the school psychologist, psychiatrist, or counselor. Unless he does, he will do more harm than good. (See problem 55.)

● ● ●

Many of the problems which follow are not very complex in nature and were generally handled successfully by the student teacher. However, it will be seen that a few of the problems were so serious that the teacher was unable to do anything constructive about them.

### PROBLEM 41: A GIRL TRIES TO ESCAPE FROM POOR HOME CONDITIONS

One evening I entered a local dress shop to pick up a dress my girl-friend had ordered. I saw three girls there who were in one of the classes I had just begun to teach. Much to my surprise, they were looking at bridal gowns. Cindy was trying one on, so I assumed she was the one who was getting married. Although the other two girls were talking excitedly about the gown, Cindy appeared to be disinterested, even unhappy, with the whole process. On my way out, I stopped to ask Cindy when she was getting married. She said she wasn't sure. I left the store feeling a little disturbed over Cindy's apparent indifference about her forthcoming marriage.

Since it appeared that Cindy had a problem, I decided to look into her background. I found her academic achievement was above average throughout her schooling, her adjustment was good, and her attendance was excellent up to the eighth grade. In the eighth, ninth, and tenth grades, there were an excessive number of absences. The records showed her parents were divorced while she was in the eighth grade. Apparently the divorce had affected Cindy greatly, and may have been responsible for her absences from school.

Cindy did what was expected of her in my class, but she seemed lifeless. While the other students were typically active, chattering, or socializing, she sat inactive, alone with her thoughts. I kept wondering what was bothering her. Then, one day when I was standing in the hall, I learned the answer. Cindy was carrying on an animated conversation with a group of girls. "What happened?" asked the girls. "I left, and I'm never going back home," she answered. "My stepfather got mad and beat me again, so I left. I can't take him anymore. Last night really did it." The bell rang for the next period and ended the conversation.

I went to see the counselor as soon as I had free time. He had already been informed of the incident by Cindy's mother. The mother had phoned that morning, stating that Cindy went to an aunt's home and refused to return. The counselor told me such incidents had occurred previously. The stepfather drinks heavily and, when he gets angry, he beats Cindy.

I received additional information from Cindy's friends and faculty members that enabled me to piece together more of her background. Cindy is very fond of her natural father, and misses him terribly. She writes to him often, which makes Cindy's mother very angry because she thinks her ex-husband is worthless. When her mother remarried, Cindy was resentful and turned against her mother. At the same time, she refused to accept her stepfather, and refused to call him "father." Cindy's friends told me she refuses to consider her stepfather as a member of the family, and calls him a stranger (which may be a contributing factor to the beatings).

I tried to talk to Cindy many times to see if I could do anything to alleviate her problems. I broke the ice by asking about her wedding gown—whether she had chosen one, what style, and so on. She told me she was very disappointed that her mother didn't come with her to select the gown, and that her aunt will be paying most of the wedding expenses. At first Cindy was shy and reluctant to speak. However, as time went on, she began to regard me as sort of a confidant. I had to be careful of this relationship, because she asked my advice on personal questions that I tactfully avoided answering. I felt it was not my place as a student teacher to get too personal.

I wish I could have done more for Cindy. She is a sweet girl who wants and needs love and understanding. She feels insecure because her parents are divorced. Perhaps in time she will come to accept her parents and their relationship with one another. I am sure when she is able to do this her life will be much happier.

In the meantime, while only a sophomore in high school, she is planning to be married. Why is she getting married? I never really learned the reason before I left. Perhaps she thinks marriage will give her the love, security, and understanding that she so desperately needs.

## Points for Discussion

- As a teacher, how do you think you could have helped Cindy?
- What other sources of help are available for problems of this type?
- In handling students' problems, what degree of personal involvement should a teacher allow?

## PROBLEM 42: A STUTTERER IS HELPED TO RELAX

When I first started student teaching, I was unaware of Dick's problem. During my period of observation, I noticed he was always interested and alert. Whenever he noticed that I was looking in his direction, he would make known to me through a wide range of facial expressions just how he was reacting to my cooperating teacher's lesson. It seemed strange to me that, in spite of his strong interest, he never raised his hand to answer a question when it was posed to the class.

Two or three days after I started teaching, I asked Dick to summarize orally what I had just been teaching. It was then I discovered his problem. He stuttered very badly. I was momentarily caught off guard, and didn't know what to do. After what seemed like an eternity, he finished the summary.

After class, I asked my cooperating teacher about Dick. She apologized for not letting me know about his problem, and informed me that Dick's problem was of long duration. His parents had done everything possible for him, including sending him to a noted speech clinic in a nearby city. But Dick continued to stutter.

I knew that if specialists had failed to cure him, I certainly couldn't hope to do so. However, I could do something to make him less conspicuous and more comfortable than I did when I first called on him to recite. These are the things I tried:

1. Whenever I asked a question in class that would require only a one-word response, I called on Dick to answer it.

2. I always gave him as much praise as possible after he answered a question correctly, but I tried not to overdo the praise.

3. If I happened to see him outside of class, I would approach him, say a few words, and try to make him feel at ease when talking.

4. I made him the class time-keeper, It was his responsibility to inform us when there were two minutes of class time left.

I had reasons for taking these measures. First of all, I didn't want to cause Dick the embarrassment of stumbling through long oral answers, and felt that if he became at ease with short answers, he might attempt longer ones. Then I praised him and talked with him to bolster his self-confidence and to put him at ease; I had learned in my theory courses that many stutterers do not stutter when they are relaxed. Also, I thought that making him time-keeper might bolster his self-confidence.

As my student teaching progressed, Dick did appear to be more at ease in my class. He even raised his hand to answer questions that required more than single-word answers! Whenever he was relaxed, he spoke without any problem, so I tried to keep him as relaxed as possible.

There are many problems that we as teachers cannot solve, but we certainly can do something to alleviate them. I think that Dick will eventually overcome his stuttering because he has great motivation and a desire to succeed in life.

As a postscript, I might add that Dick advised me to do some of the things I was trying to do for him! Following is an evaluation he wrote of me as a student teacher:

> When you first came here, you seemed very uneasy and nervous, but after a while you seemed to loosen up. If you continue at the rate you are now, some day you'll be a real good teacher. Just be more relaxed, try to be funny, listen to your students, try to be their friend, don't be too strict, and if the students want to or don't want to do something they should vote on it. Be democratic. Let everybody have their say. The students will like you. Not that they don't like you now (ha, ha) but they will really like you. Good luck. Peace.
>
> Dick

It all goes to show that as teachers we can learn things from our students.

## Points for Discussion

- *Evaluate the advice given in Dick's letter.*

- *What are the causes of stuttering?*

## PROBLEM 43: A BOY'S DESIRE FOR ATTENTION IS CHANNELED IN THE PROPER DIRECTION

This is the case of John, a seventh-grade student. While I was observing the class he caught my attention, and I discussed him with my cooperating teacher. It seems everyone had given up on John. According to my cooperating teacher, he was scarcely doing enough work to pass. He also said John was known as the clown of the class, and that he was the butt of many of the jokes of his classmates. Yet he seemed to enjoy this. Apparently he wanted attention so much that he did not care in what form it came to him.

I decided to try to see what I could do with him during my sixteen weeks of student teaching. First of all, I noticed John's handwriting was extremely neat. Also, I noticed when I called on him, he usually did not know the answer, or at least claimed not to know it. Yet from his manner of speech it seemed that the boy had much higher intelligence than he displayed in the classroom. My next step was to talk to the other teachers; in all of his other classes he was also doing barely passing work.

Next, I decided to delve into his personal records. I found two things which I thought were significant and important. First, his I.Q. was above average, which indicated he was capable of much better work. Second, and I thought this was very important, John came from a broken home. I concluded that more than likely, if he was not getting attention and recognition at home, he was trying to compensate for that by seeking attention in school by whatever means possible.

My next job was to motivate John. I had to try to reach him to make him realize his potential was much higher than his accomplishment. I tried a few things to bring about that realization, but there was no noticeable improvement for the first few weeks.

Finally, I decided on a private conference. Evidently I had a good relationship with him because his attitude was one of interest and cooperation. Perhaps the fact that he found somebody he thought was really interested in helping him was the turning point.

I explained to John just what his capacity was, and pointed out to him how far away he was from what he was capable of doing. He seemed to like the fact that I recognized he had ability, and that I was sincere in what I told him. We talked for about twenty minutes, after which he promised he would try to change his attitude.

In the weeks that followed, John really made an effort to improve. It wasn't easy for him, but I tried to keep him going by praising everything he did well. I gave him little special jobs in the classroom; this he liked very much. I also assigned a special project to six students, with John in charge. All of these signs of improvement brought favorable comments from his classmates. John finally realized he could get approval and attention through achievement rather than through clowning.

His marks steadily improved, from which I received as much satisfaction as John did. For the fourth interval, his mark rose to seventy-three; for the fifth interval it went to seventy-six; and for the sixth period it jumped to eighty. That ten-point gain may not seem like much, but to me (and I'm sure to John) it seemed like a hundred!

## Points for Discussion

- *How could John have been started on the road to improvement sooner than he was?*

- *Do you agree with the student teacher's explanation of John's behavior? Why?*

- *Distinguish between a student's natural desire for recognition and the use of attention-getting devices.*

## PROBLEM 44: A BRIGHT STUDENT WORRIES ABOUT HIS PARENTS

When I took over my first class in history, I was worried that I would not be as effective as my cooperating teacher, and that the students would judge me as a poor teacher. Because of this, I made every effort to think of methods and procedures that would stimulate interest and participation. Some of the sources I used were books, teachers, and television. In class I used an electric map, I gathered local materials and examples, and most important, I used a variation of the contests that appear on television. In the contests, I matched poor students against each other, then good students, followed by mixed groups, and finally, interclass participation. The results were positive. I was surprised at the high degree of interest shown by the students.

After starting a group contest one day, I noticed a boy who refused to answer any questions. I then noticed he would not participate during our regular classroom discussions. When I questioned him about it after class, he said he liked my methods of teaching, but that he just didn't feel like answering any questions. During subsequent classes, I kept questioning him but he did not answer. I decided to provoke him a bit. When he refused to answer, I told him that apparently he was not listening and did not know the answer. This pricked his pride, because he gave me a detailed and logical answer, for which I praised him. Yet, it was only when I "needled" him that he would participate. The question was: Why would a boy of high ability refuse to recite?

In my mind, I ran through many of the causes of problems experienced by adolescents: physical, social, sex, peer group relationships, progress in school, etc. I had several talks with him to try to identify his problem. Weeks went by before I was able to do so, and I found the cause of the problem only because I had built up a good relationship with him.

His problem was one experienced by many children, including me: a mother and father who live under the same roof but do not get along together, causing anxiety and division among the children. The boy had difficulty doing his school work because of the constant tension at home. He told me if he unconsciously showed any partiality, he was condemned by one or the other parent. He got the feeling he could not rely on either parent, and his chief worry was that of bringing about a reconciliation between them. He hated to go home because of the violent quarrels that took place. Instead, he said, "I just hang around the pizza parlor, and steal hub caps off cars."

I told him that I had had an identical problem, and that there was only one way to solve it. His parents probably did not realize the deadly effects of their behavior in the presence of their children. I told him to try to have a talk with his parents, telling them how ashamed and insecure he felt because of their conduct.

He later told me that he took my advice. His parents listened, and thanked him for talking to them. In the days that followed he was surprised and gratified to find that, although he did not completely unite his parents, they were deeply concerned about his future and would do everything in their power to see him succeed in life.

I am happy to say that he is a completely different person now, and that next year he is looking forward to entering college.

## Points for Discussion

- *What is the danger in following the advice given by the student teacher?*

- *What other kinds of problems may result from lack of harmony in the home?*

## PROBLEM 45: UNEXPLAINED ILLNESSES
##                 ARE DEVELOPED BY A STUDENT

I shall always remember Doris as the most unusual student I had during student teaching. She was a freshman, and a very attractive one at that. She did not possess the gawky frame and baby face that is characteristic of many girls her age. She was past the transition stage, and was more a woman in her development than the other girls. My first contacts with her showed her to be a carefree, happy-go-lucky type of girl. At the same time, she was a dedicated and hard-working student. Her fine personality contributed to her acceptance by her peers and by the faculty.

During my first two weeks of student teaching, Doris was a delightful student to have in class. She participated voluntarily, and her carefree manner added to the rapport of the class. Her marks were above average on the first two tests I gave.

Doris failed the third test I gave, but I was not overly surprised at this because she had been absent three days that week, so I assumed the failure was due to lack of preparation. The next week she had two absences, and this was followed by three absences the following week. When she did come to class, I had her make up the tests that she missed, but she scored no higher than 20 percent on any of them.

It was not consistent with her past performance to be failing tests so badly. This caused me to be concerned. Besides that, she became an introvert overnight, silent, sad, and retiring. What was wrong?

I went to the principal's office to inquire about her absences, and was told that she was absent because of illness. Next, I stopped at the school nurse's office. The nurse told me that Doris was a very sick girl, having been in and out of the hospital where she was treated for stomach pains and nervousness. However, the doctors reported that they could find nothing medically wrong to account for her illness. This continued for three weeks.

In the meantime, Doris came to class sporadically, still remaining in her shell. If I had not seen her other side when I started student teaching, I might have thought she was an exceptional child of some sort. Having seen her bright side, I knew there had to be some emotional basis for this radical change in her personality.

After consulting with the school nurse again, I now found that the doctors felt her problem was a psychological one, and I found out why they thought so. Doris' father is a career officer in the armed forces. He had just been transferred overseas to serve with a combat-ready unit which could be shipped to a trouble-spot at a moment's notice. Doris was very close to her father. The fact that he was transferred overseas was bad enough for Doris, but his placement in a combat-ready unit nearly made her hysterical. Not only would she be separated from her father, but also his life would be endangered if his unit were sent into combat. Her change in personality coincided exactly with the news of the transfer, and from that point on her attendance and grades declined.

I had several talks with Doris after I learned what the real problem was. I tried to encourage her by pointing out that we were not at war, and that the chances were excellent that her father would never get into combat. I also told her that his tour of overseas duty would probably be short, and that he would soon be home again.

Before I finished student teaching, Doris had begun to come out of her shell. There was improvement in her work and attendance, but she was not as carefree as she was before. Everybody had a part in trying to bring her back to normal; I did a little, and so did the counselor, doctor, and her classmates. I think she will be all right.

**Points for Discussion**

- *What are psychosomatic disorders? How do they differ from actual physical disorders?*

- *How do emotional problems interfere with performance?*

## PROBLEM 46: AN ONLY CHILD CREATES DISTURBANCES

As the novelty of having a strange teacher wore off, the students in my freshman class regained their normal composure—or perhaps I should say they tried to make their student teacher lose his composure. I soon pinpointed the disorder to Jim. Numerous disturbances began to emanate from the students around him. A hue and cry would arise every time he took something from another student's desk, or when he pulled the hair of the girl in front of him.

When I changed his seat to the front of the room, he began a series of attention-getting actions. He brought into class a group of extraneous objects, such as fishing flies, rubber toys, pipes, and comic books. Each time I confiscated one of these articles he seemed pleased with himself, and drank in the response of the class. Finally, when his attitude bordered on the insolent by a refusal to recite, I told him to write out fifty times the material that he should have recited. I warned him he would not be permitted to enter the classroom unless the assignment was completed.

As I expected, he returned to class without his work. In keeping with my threat, I dismissed him from class. The following day he again returned without his work, and I again dismissed him from class. Finally, on the third day, he returned with the assignment completed and took his place. The treatment seemed to have been effective, because Jim caused no trouble for a while.

My problem was far from solved, however, for after one week there were signs that he was reverting to his old antics. This time I was determined to nip it in the bud. Since I thought he wanted to attract the attention of the class to himself, I decided to isolate him from his fellow students by assigning him a seat in the rear of the room. Apparently this was one solution to the problem because since then, he has been behaving himself admirably.

In inquiring about Jim shortly after I met him, I found out he was an only child who had apparently been spoiled by his parents. He had been dismissed from classes other than mine; indeed, on one day he must have been in rare form, because he was dismissed from three classes. His parents took an interest in what he was doing and frequently talked to the teacher and to the principal about him. I believe his parents were too solicitous of him and that his antics were in some way a reaction to his home conditions.

## Points for Discussion

- *Was this problem really solved, or was it merely deferred? Why?*

- *Discuss the potential problems of being an only child.*

## PROBLEM 47: UNFAVORABLE HOME CONDITIONS AFFECT A BOY'S WORK

Mike was in a slow group in my English class. Even under ordinary conditions it is difficult to hold the attention of slow students, but Mike contributed some extraordinary distractions which made matters still more difficult.

The day I started to teach, Mike kept tapping his fingers or feet, or talked to the boys around him. I reprimanded him, and thought he would behave himself; but that first week of teaching consisted of 90 percent disciplinary action and 10 percent teaching.

Mike was overactive. I discovered from his record that he made good marks, but was considered a real disciplinary problem. In my classes he would have his work done, and would answer most of my questions, but it seemed that there was always need to correct him for something. One day I asked him why he wasn't behaving himself. His reply was: "I hate English, and I hate teachers!"

I let his remark pass, but checked with the principal on the problem. The principal told me Mike had a very poor home background. His father was an alcoholic, who seemed to get relief by punishing the children unjustly. The principal also told me Mike had been placed in an advanced class in English because he had high ability, but that he had refused to work, probably because most of the pupils in the advanced class were on a higher social level. It had become necessary to send Mike back to the slow group.

The following day I had a talk with Mike, one that turned out to be very profitable. I explained to him that we all have problems to meet in life, and that he actually had an advantage over the other pupils in his age group because he was meeting his problems early in life. I told him if he learned to face them now, he would be stronger in the future. I also pointed out that to get along in the world, people have to trust each other, and he would have to begin this trust somewhere. Mike listened to all this attentively.

Slowly I could see a change coming over him in class. He recited and he cooperated. He was happy to be called on in class, to be recognized, to feel important. Mike and I became very good friends. He would often stop to talk to me after class, and sometimes very seriously.

At present, Mike is relieving his nervous tension by tapping his fingers and feet on the bass drum in the school band, of which he became a member. I didn't change Mike, but I may have reassured him.

### Points for Discussion

- *What other kind of help might have been given Mike earlier?*

- *Do you think he belonged in the slow group after he refused to work? Why?*

- *How does being confronted with problems help maturation?*

### PROBLEM 48: A WITHDRAWN BOY COMES OUT OF HIS SHELL

Jack was a student in my English class. Before I started to teach, I observed him as being sulky, moody, and withdrawn. He never paid attention in class, never did his assignments, and did below-average work on his tests. I thought his case was worth looking into.

Looking into his records, I found that during his early life he lived in an impoverished home. It was interesting to note that when he first entered school, the school nurse singled him out for a daily inspection before he was permitted to enter the classroom. Because of his unsanitary appearance, his coat and sweater were hung in a room separate from the other pupils' clothing. He remained in these conditions for several years before he was put in a foster home. Psychological tests and interviews showed that he felt deprived, destitute, helpless, and defeated. After he was placed in a foster home he was better cared for physically and emotionally, but some of the old scars still remained.

As a student, I found Jack lacked motivation of any kind. He was listless and appeared to be brooding constantly. He never turned in his homework; when asked why he didn't, he always responded with, "I don't know." He was a "loner," having little to do with the rest of the class.

After he repeatedly neglected his assignments, I had a talk with him in which I was very firm. The next day he brought in his work. There was no repeat performance on his part, for he lapsed right back into his daydreaming. On occasion, I noticed Jack pantomiming to himself, with the students around him paying absolutely no attention to him.

After about five weeks of this, I set up an interview with Jack in the guidance room. I think I was more scared than Jack. What was I going to say to him? Perhaps I had bit off more than I could chew. Jack came in, and for the first five minutes it was as I feared it would be. He simply sat there answering my questions with a yes or no. Then I asked him about Christmas, which was coming up soon. Well, that opened him up, and I hardly had an opportunity to say anything after that. He told me that now his family was good to him, that he deeply loved his foster mother, and he was making her a Christmas present in shop. He said he had enough money to buy her something, but he felt that she would appreciate it more if he made it. He asked my opinion on this and I concurred. Then he talked at length about how religious his foster mother was, and how they go to church together on Sunday. It was quite a conversation! After it was over, we parted on good terms.

There is not much more to say. From that point on, our relationship was a good one. Jack often approached me with questions that he had. I gave him extra help with his assignments, showed him that literature can be interesting and fun, accepted him for what he was, pointed out to him his mistakes, and was firm in expecting him to conform. He developed positive behavioral patterns, such as:

1. He showed more interest in class.
2. He completed most of his assignments, or at least made an effort to do so.
3. He actually smiled in class.
4. He answered my questions about 50 percent of the time, instead of the previous "I don't know" answers.
5. He actually went out of his way to speak to me in the halls.

So, I think the personal interest I showed in Jack produced good results, for right before my eyes I saw a change take place that I didn't think was possible. For me personally, my efforts were rewarded many times over with a feeling of deep satisfaction and personal fulfillment.

## Points for Discussion

- *Discuss the impact of poverty on Jack's personality.*

- *What was the key to the good relationship between Jack and the student teacher?*

## PROBLEM 49: A SHY GIRL IS HELPED TO RECITE

Joan was a girl of average intelligence, but was extremely shy in the classroom. Whenever I questioned her she would simply remain silent, not even indicating whether or not she knew the answer.

I tried in several ways to draw a response from her. At first I asked her questions in the same way as I did others, but when she failed to respond, I tried rephrasing the questions. This did not help. Next, after she failed to answer a question I called on another pupil to give the answer, and would ask Joan to repeat the answer. She repeated it very timidly, but I could see she was embarrassed over the fact that she had to repeat answers given by someone else.

Finally, I decided to have a private talk with her. I asked her whether she knew the answers to my questions and when she replied in the affirmative, I asked her why she didn't answer the questions in class. She told me that since she was not sure of herself and her answers, she remained silent to avoid embarrassment in front of the class. I pointed out to her that she was as good as any student in the class, but she would never be able to prove it to herself unless she started to answer my questions. All she was doing now, I said, was to lower herself in the eyes of her classmates, thus simply adding to her feeling of inferiority. I told her to keep in mind that her answers were as good as those of any other student in class, and that she was in no way inferior to them.

Our little talk seemed to be the solution. She began to answer my questions, at first hesitantly, and then confidently. It was good to see her whole manner and attitude changing from meekness to confidence.

### Points for Discussion

- *Evaluate the comments made by the student teacher during the private talk.*

- *What would you have told this pupil if you were having a private talk with her on her problem?*

## PROBLEM 50: A BOY IS HELPED TO OVERCOME HIS STUTTERING

After teaching Barney for about a week, I noticed he had a slight impediment. It took me that long to notice it because he refused to take part in reading and recitation. He became very ill at ease when called upon to recite.

I stopped him after class one day and jokingly asked him why he would not take part in recitations. He stammered a bit, and would not give a direct answer. It was evident that he was self-conscious about his speech defect.

Checking his file in the office, I found that he had been doing acceptable work, but that he had the same problem in other class recitations. His file showed he had an average I.Q., he wanted to go to college, and he eventually hoped to get into the F.B.I.

During the next few days, I had several talks with Barney during his study periods. I asked him about his future plans; his answer corroborated the office file. I then pointed out to him that to get through college and through law school he would have to do a great deal of oral work. During our private talks he seemed at ease and his impediment scarcely showed itself. He did admit he was very self-consious about stuttering, and for that reason did not want to recite in class.

I tried to tell him he did not have anything to fear in class recitations, and that if he would at least try, it would be a step in the right direction. To help him along, I told him that for a while I would indicate to him beforehand what he would be called upon to read in class. He agreed, and seemed anxious to try it.

His first attempt at recitation was only fair. He showed marked self-consciousness, but he got through it. During his recitation some of the pupils showed impatience with him, and at the end of the period I told them I would not tolerate ridicule of anyone who was reciting. Most of them, I pointed out, had some difficulty or other in pronunciation, and all should strive to correct their own errors rather than ridicule others.

After a few days of this type of recitation, Barney became more relaxed and there was a steady improvement. At the end of two weeks, I told him his improvement was so great that I would no longer tell him beforehand what he would be expected to recite. I am happy to report that he continued to improve. By the end of the term he had lost most of his self-consiousness, and his stutter was not nearly so marked as it had been.

## Points for Discussion

- *Why do pupils with speech defects sometimes become worse while they are in school?*

- *What do you think of telling the pupil beforehand what he will be asked to recite?*

## PROBLEM 51: A CHANGE OF HOME ENVIRONMENT HELPS A GIRL

Vicki was a student in one of my eighth grade history classes. She was a problem, not in the sense of causing any disorder, but rather because of her indifference to what was going on in class. I learned from her friends that she intends to quit school when she becomes sixteen years old.

On the first two tests I gave, Vicki received a D and an F. Since her cumulative record showed she had an I.Q. of 119, I knew she was capable of better work so I decided to have a talk with her. The things she told me pointed to problems at home. She said she could not get along with her father which made her so tense that she was not able to sleep at night. Indirectly, she told me she was using drugs.

Next, I stopped to see the guidance counselor who shed more light on Vicki's home situation. The counselor informed me that her mother was dead, and her father was a retired army man who drank excessively. The father had recently been arrested for beating Vicki, and at the moment, the authorities were seeking his permission to allow Vicki to live with her aunt.

A few days later, I was fortunate to be able to speak with Vicki's aunt at a Parents' Day meeting. She told me she was very concerned about Vicki's future, and that she had received permission for Vicki to live with her. She assured me Vicki would now receive the love and care her father failed to give her. In parting, the aunt asked me to try to convince Vicki that she now had a worthwhile future to look forward to.

Just after the Christmas holidays, I spoke with Vicki again. She was a changed person. There was a sparkle in her eyes that had not been there before. She told me she had moved in with her aunt, and that for the first time in a long time she had an enjoyable Christmas. She especially emphasized being happy about not seeing her drunken father, and not being beaten by him. I told her I was happy for her, and that I was sure she would spend many happy years with her aunt, because her aunt really wanted to help her and make life enjoyable for her. At the same time, I pointed out to her that she should try to help her aunt in every way possible to show her appreciation for being given a home that was truly a home. Also, I encouraged her to take schooling more seriously. Finally, I pointed out that she no longer needed to resort to drugs to escape her misery because she would be able to enjoy life and develop her potentialities through education.

Now that Vicki's basic problem was solved, she no longer lived in a state of fear and anxiety. Her aunt made sure she received proper food and rest, and that she did the right things. Vicki's attitude toward school improved. In my class, she showed an interest she never had before, and she actively participated in our work. I was almost as happy as she when she received a B on my last history test. I was even happier when during my last few days of student teaching, Vicki came to me and said: "You know, Mr.—, you're the greatest! You tell it like it is. For the first time in my life, I really like school, and my marks are showing it. Thanks for everything."

That, I know, was the greatest moment of satisfaction I had in student teaching. Vicki no longer wanted to quit school, she was no longer using drugs, and she had a bright future ahead of her. The whole thing brought home to me how important home life can be in a child's school work, relationships, and outlook on life in general.

## Points for Discussion

- *What does research show about the effects of drugs?*

- *What could have been done for Vicki if she had not been able to move in with her aunt?*

## PROBLEM 52: A GIRL HAS NO FRIENDS

Janet is a girl of average intelligence whose grades for the past two years have been in the seventies. After getting to know her, I concluded that her main problem did not concern her studies. Her greatest need was to have some friends.

She lives in an average home in which there are no financial problems. Her father is a skilled craftsman who provides well. Her mother evidently takes an interest in school affairs, because she attends P.T.A. meetings regularly. It seemed to me, however, that Janet's mother was the one who could very easily have done something more about her problem.

To me it seemed Janet's problem stemmed from her appearance. She wore dresses inappropriate for school, always with saddle shoes, and combed her hair straight back in severe fashion. She was clean and neat in appearance, but never in style. I found out that even though she is seventeen, her mother had never allowed her to choose her own clothes, nor even permitted her to choose her own hair style.

Since she did not dress like the others, she seemed to avoid their company; and, because she was different, the others made no attempt to be friendly with her. Janet seldom talked to anyone unless on a matter of necessity. When she was called on to recite, her voice seemed very shaky and low, as if she were afraid to speak.

I wasn't sure exactly how to go about it, but I wanted to get Janet to feel that I was her friend. I tried greeting her on every occasion when I saw her, but my "Hello, Janet," only resulted in her lowering her head. Then I tried encouraging her in class by complimenting her on every possible occasion, but I still couldn't reach her. Finally, I directed comments in class to her in such a way that it would appear she was my friend and advisor, comments such as, "Isn't that right, Janet?" and "We know that to be true, don't we, Janet?" After a while, the ice started to break, and she would occasionally answer in a clear voice, without being nervous. This improvement continued gradually.

Janet now talks to a few of her classmates who are seated in her vicinity. What really pleased me, though, was that near the close of the school year she took part in a skit during a school assembly. The skit was in charge of one of the girls with whom Janet had become friendly.

I don't know how many others were trying to help Janet at the same time that I was, but I like to feel I contributed my small share in bringing her out of her shell. The problem will not be solved completely, however, until her mother permits her to change her style of dressing and doing her hair.

### Points for Discussion

- *Do you think it would have been advisable for the student teacher to speak to Janet's mother? If so, when and where? If not, what else could have been done for Janet?*

- *Discuss the importance of being a member of "the group" during adolescence.*

### PROBLEM 53: AN UNRESOLVED PERSONALITY PROBLEM

Tonie was a girl in the ninth grade, enrolled in my first year French class. She had a problem about which I could do nothing. The only think I did to help her was to identify the problem, and then point it out to the counselor so that she might receive the professional help I was sure she needed.

The thing that particularly attracted my attention to her was her general appearance of disorder and her lack of organization. Three weeks after I had taken over the class, Tonie informed me she had lost her French book. Furthermore, she told me not to trouble myself by trying to locate another book for her, because she would have no further use for one. Perplexed, I asked why she wouldn't want another book if I could find one for her. She shrugged her shoulders and said, "That stupid book can't teach me anything anyway." Such an outright statement virtually floored me at the moment. So, for the last six weeks, Tonie has had no book, has not borrowed one from anyone else, and has been frequently truant.

From other teachers I found out that our little miss came from a broken home located "across the tracks." Her parents separated five years ago, and she is now living with her mother and three brothers. Other teachers who had her in class said she had a poor attitude, was generally disheveled in appearance, a poor student, difficult if not impossible to motivate, was always losing her books as well as other things, and she was a constant daydreamer.

Her records showed that ever since fifth grade, teachers made comments about her having a problem which they felt stemmed from her home life. Her fifth grade teacher characterized her as "a daydreamer, disoriented, disorganized, and having no friends." In the sixth grade, her teacher described Tonie as "a sad child, seemingly friendly but without friends, disheveled, a poor student who constantly loses everything, and has great difficulty in self-expression." A battery of tests she took while in the sixth grade showed her to be about a year behind in her achievement. Her I.Q. test scores were average, ranging between 97 and 104. Her expressed vocational goals changed each year. In the seventh grade, she expressed a strong desire to become a nurse. The following year, she wanted to become a horse trainer, and this year she was leaning toward completing high school, after which she hoped to attend a business college.

This information shows that she has remained basically the same in personality and attitude ever since the fifth grade. We can only hypothesize about the cause of Tonie's problem. Everyone who has come to know her over the past few years has felt that her problem is related to her home life, about which very little is known.

The guidance counselor had been unaware of Tonie's problem until I came in and asked for specific information about Tonie. He was surprised that no one had brought it to his attention before. He promised me he would arrange a consultation with Tonie in the near future, and see what, if anything, can be done for her. I personally believe she needs psychiatric help of some sort.

What do I think is the cause of Tonie's problem? In looking over her record, I found that her problems began shortly after her parents separated. You can draw your own conclusion.

### Points for Discussion

- *What do you think of the counselor's statement that no one had brought Tonie's problem to his attention?*

- *What facilities are available to help students like Tonie?*

### PROBLEM 54:  A PUPIL CHANGES FROM AN INTROVERT TO AN EXTROVERT

I had little or nothing to do with the change in David, but his case was an interesting one. My first contact with him was in a drama class that I had been assigned to teach. He appeared to be a very outgoing person with a pleasant sense of humor. The only problem was his sense of humor sometimes had to be checked because it disrupted the class. I soon learned that this was not the David who entered high school just two or three years ago.

From my cooperating teacher I learned that when David entered our high school he was a very shy and reserved person. As time went on, it was apparent that he was becoming so introverted that he was almost totally unresponsive to normal student social life.

The counseling office provided more details. David was a transfer from a school in another state. He was brought up by an overbearing and overprotective mother whom he loved, but he expressed a dislike for his father who was a tavern keeper. His first year as a transfer student was marked by frequent absences resulting from visits to the hospital. It was believed he had some sort of nervous disorder. In class, he displayed nervous tendencies, such as biting his fingernails, and unrestrained hysterical laughter for no good reason. Being somewhat effeminate in his mannerisms, he was sensitive to the whispers and giggles of other students that were directed toward his actions. He began to associate with boys younger than he, or with girls near his own age. His shyness became so profound that he refused to ride the school bus in the morning.

David's records showed him to have average mental ability, but his performance was very erratic. One semester his grades were up, the next they were down—in the same subject. He asked for frequent course changes which were prompted by his mother. It appeared that his mother was the root of his problems; it was she who made all the decisions for David. Because of this, and because of his mannerisms, he was known throughout the school community as a "mama's boy."

Fortunately for David, someone took a personal interest in his problem. That someone was my cooperating teacher. Last year she got him to join the Drama Club, which put on a play toward the end of the year. As scared and as shy as he was, David performed his role well. The play was a hit with the students and, for the first time since he entered the school, he felt that he was a part of it.

To my cooperating teacher's surprise, David enrolled in her drama course this year. By continual encouragement she got him to participate in more plays, so that gradually he came out of his shell, to the point that he was demanding starring roles. His quiet manner melted away, and in its place there reared a proud, boisterous "monster" (which my cooperating teacher jokingly referred to as her creation).

My only real accomplishment with David was to make him feel at ease when he talked to me. This was quite an achievement, because for weeks he avoided even looking at me. I did this by talking to him during seminars, but by not giving him too much attention. He finally lost his feelings of suspicion, and talked to me in a relaxed manner.

I did make one suggestion that may have helped David along. I suggested to my cooperating teacher that David be put on the closed circuit T.V. news broadcast of the school. This idea nearly induced panic in David, but my cooperating teacher told him he would have to do it "or else." After the program, David said he was terribly nervous but that he would do much better if he were allowed to do it again.

David has come a long way since entering this school, but there is still a great deal to be done with him. This will be attempted by other teachers, who are now noticing his potentialities.

## Points for Discussion

- *What are the implications of the student teacher's last statement?*

- *Discuss the problems of a child who is dominated by his mother.*

## PROBLEM 55:  A STUDENT TEACHER IS EXPOSED TO A SERIOUS CASE OF EMOTIONAL MALADJUSTMENT

John was a pupil I had in class, a transfer from another school district because his father's change in employment made it necessary for the family to move. When John entered our school, he was twelve years old and was placed in the sixth grade. Before long, it was noticed that John did not make friends in his own age group, but that he behaved like a bully with children who were smaller than he.

In the meantime, he had been given a few aptitude and mental ability tests which showed him to be below average in mentality. Subsequent investigation also revealed he had received psychiatric treatment from time to time over a period of three years. It was found that he was completely dependent on his mother; she had to remain in his room with him until he fell asleep, and she answered his calls frequently during the night. The psychiatrist's report stated that he had a fear of darkness. His psychiatric treatment had been progressing well, but had to be stopped when the family moved.

His attendance record had been poor in the school from which he transferred, and continued so in our school. His assignments were only partially completed. His class recitations were also poor, and he stuttered while trying to recite. His reading ability was average, and he prided himself on the neatness of his writing. His appearance was also always neat.

John was dismissed from class regularly for reasons such as talking aloud, disrupting the class, annoying other students, being defiant, and threatening the teacher. In addition, he had numerous fights with boys, all of whom were smaller than he. In the midst of these disturbances, school officials tried to arrange conferences with the parents, but both of them worked and always made some excuse to avoid the meeting. Though his mother did appear on one occasion, she sided with her son, saying that everyone was "picking on him."

Our school psychologist has been seeing John regularly. Lately he has been attending classes, and his behavior has improved, but everyone is wondering how long it will last.

## Points for Discussion

- *What defense mechanisms are exhibited by John?*

- *On the basis of the facts given, what would you suspect to be the cause of his emotional maladjustment?*

## PROBLEM 56: A GIRL SEEMS TO FEIGN ILLNESSES

Susan had a poor attendance record throughout her years of schooling. She had to repeat the first grade because of rheumatic fever which caused her to be absent a great deal. From then on she missed an average of fifty school days a year. However, even though absent a great deal, her records showed she had always been a hard worker, and she maintained average grades. She attained especially good grades in creative subjects, such as writing, art, and music. Her average on I.Q. tests was 99.

Now in the tenth grade, Susan continued her absenteeism. She did not involve herself in any school activities, and seemed to have difficulty in getting along with others. She had no friends. In fact, she annoyed students sitting around her to the point that they requested a seat change. During the current year, her teachers found her to be irresponsible and lacking in integrity. Her character and her grades seemed to be deteriorating.

When I took over Susan's class, I discovered she was claiming a back injury which prevented her from attending school for more than an hour or two a day. Yet, I noticed when she was in school she appeared to be physically well and lively, without any evidence of a back injury. She had no trouble walking, bending, or getting in and out of her seat. I even saw her running down the corridor! Strangely enough, her mother accompanied her to school, asked the teachers about the assignments she missed, and even pleaded with the teachers to pass Susan. In the meantime, Susan put forth little or no effort.

On several occasions, I asked Susan to see me so that I could give her extra help with the class work because she was in danger of failing the course. When she came to the help sessions, she was unprepared, expected me to do all the work, asked for my class notes, and even wanted a summary of the readings I had assigned. When I asked her why she couldn't get the class notes from other students, she claimed she was not friendly enough with anyone to ask for them. I helped Susan as much as I could, but I certainly could not do her learning *for* her. I told her on many occasions that she would have to put forth some effort herself if she expected to make progress in school, but my admonitions made no impression on her. Instead, she seemed to be pleading for a good grade without doing anything to earn it.

Susan's mother didn't help the situation. Instead of encouraging her daughter to be self-reliant and to do her work, the mother pampered and sympathized with Susan, and continually interceded with the teachers on Susan's behalf.

## Discussion

- *What seems to be the cause of Susan's problems? What can be done for her?*

## PROBLEM 57: AN EIGHTH-GRADE BOY FEELS LOST AFTER HIS MOTHER DIES

Although I did not participate to any great extent in Tom's problem, I became very interested in him because he was a pupil in one of my classes.

Tom is a healthy boy with an I.Q. of 115. In class he was inattentive and indulged in considerable daydreaming, with the result that his school work was suffering. His health record was satisfactory, thus eliminating the possibility that some physical defect might be interfering with the learning process. His parents were college graduates.

Tom's mother was very solicitous over the welfare of her child. Although she had trouble with her heart, she escorted him to and from school everyday. When the weather called for a raincoat, she was always at the door of the school waiting to put it on him. She allowed him to do very little for himself. One day she kissed him good-bye at the door of the school as usual, and that was the last time Tom saw her alive, for when she returned home she suffered a heart attack and died.

Tom's aunt came to stay with the family. During this time, he and his father became inseparable. When it was necessary for the father to be away from home, Tom was very sad. He was especially sad when it became necessary for him to walk to school alone.

Before long, Tom's father remarried. Tom never accepted his stepmother, and was resentful of the attention his father gave her. Though she was interested in Tom, trying very hard to help him, he would not accept her help. He became depressed and his school work suffered. In an effort to try to bring his marks up, his parents arranged for him to be tutored. This did not help much.

## Discussion

- *What could be done to help Tom?*

## PROBLEM 58: A BROKEN HOME LEAVES A GIRL WITHOUT SUPERVISION OF HER HOME STUDY

In my freshman class a girl attracted my attention because she made the lowest mark on every test I gave. When I had a talk with her, I was impressed with her good manners, friendliness, and facility of expression. I questioned her in an indirect way to try to find out the reason for her poor marks, but I obtained nothing concrete to go on. Our talk ended with an invitation to come to see me if there was any way in which I could help her.

During the next few weeks, I tried hard to help her in class, but to no avail. She missed the simplest items on tests. I then discussed her with my cooperating teacher, who told me that her trouble was due to the well-known malady: a broken home. Her parents were separated. She received little time from her mother, who was operating a small store, and she rarely saw her father. She and her mother were now living with her grandmother, who was quite old.

I knew she was a very intelligent girl. The only answer I could think of to explain her poor work was that she did no homework, since there was no one at home to see that she did do it. I was sure if she gave some time to study, she would pass easily.

### Discussion

- *Offer other explanations for this girl's poor work.*

### PROBLEM 59:  LITTLE PROGRESS IS MADE
###              WITH A JUVENILE DELINQUENT

We know very little about people until we look into their background. I discovered this when I decided to help Chuck, who was a student in my World Cultures class. Chuck showed no interest in the subject. He was a clean, neat individual who caused me no trouble, but it troubled me that he was so indifferent. I decided to try to change his attitude, but before doing anything else I checked several sources about his background. What I found out amazed me.

Chuck's home environment was not conducive to study. His father was deceased, so it became necessary for him to work after school and on Saturdays, leaving him little time for study. His mother was an irresponsible, shiftless person who had no control over him, and on several occasions, Chuck used physical force to quiet her. She was known to keep company with men, single and married, who came to the house for long periods of time. Because of this, she was reputed to be a "hooker." With lack of discipline, and home conditions as they were, Chuck spent whatever free time he had drinking. Confidential records further revealed that Chuck had been found guilty on two counts of burglary for which he was institutionalized for a time.

With knowledge of his background, I felt in a better position to try to help him. My first step was to try to achieve a friendly relationship with him, which I did by talking to him in the presence of other students before class, in the halls, and in the study hall. Then I arranged a private talk with him, questioning him about his home, hobbies, and his general attitude toward education. He told me he had no interest in my subject, or any other subject, and that after he graduated he would join the army and learn a trade. I pointed out to him that the army preferred men who were successful in high school because success in high school work, along with tests they administer, enable them to predict success in learning a trade in the army. I further told him that he owed it to himself to try to make the best of every situation, even though he disliked it. This, I said, was part of "growing up," and would help him to overcome obstacles in later life. Finally, I tried to show him the benefits of studying World Cultures, especially since army life might take him to different parts of the world.

Following this talk, Chuck did take a more active part in classroom discussions. His answers were not always logical or correct, but he did try. Also, he told me he was going to do a research paper on military life. I was very pleased about his improved attitude. Even my cooperating teacher told me: "For some reason, in the past few weeks his interest and cooperation has increased."

Christmas vacation came. One day while reading the newspaper, I noticed a story about a store that had been burglarized. Chuck's name appeared as that of the person who was apprehended for the crime.

## Discussion

- *What approach would you take with Chuck when he returned to school after vacation?*

## PROBLEM 60: WORRY CAUSES A BOY'S WORK TO SUFFER

Jerry was a senior who was failing my course in science. Though he was a good-looking, neat, intelligent individual, he always appeared to be abstracted in class, thinking of something else. When I called on him, he would simply say he did not understand the work.

In checking his past marks, I found that he had never failed a subject before. It was obvious something was wrong, but I could not determine exactly what it was. This situation went on for several weeks, until shortly before report cards were due for a marking period.

At that point Jerry came up to me and asked me if there was anything he could do to bring his mark up to passing before report cards came out. I told him I could not change his mark because it would be unfair to the rest of the class. He then explained to me that he had been in serious trouble a short time ago, and that he would be expelled from high school if his grades were not passing. He said it was the first time he ever got into trouble, and he was worrying so much about it he could not concentrate on his work.

I checked his story with my cooperating teacher, and found he was telling the truth. I decided to help him in any way I could.

## Discussion

- *If Jerry were your pupil, what would you do?*

## SELECTED READINGS

Blair, Glenn Myers; Jones, R. Steward; and Simpson, Ray H. *Educational Psychology.* New York: Macmillan Publishing Co., Inc., 1975, chapter 15.

Bricklin, Barry, and Bricklin, Patricia M. *Bright Child—Poor Grades.* New York: Delacorte Press, 1967.

Cruickshank, William M., ed. *Psychology of Exceptional Children.* Englewood Cliffs, New Jersey: Prentice-Hall, Inc., 1971, chapter 12.

Donahue, George T., and Nichtern, Sol. *Teaching the Troubled Child.* New York: The Free Press, 1965.

Dupont, Henry. *Educating Emotionally Disturbed Children.* New York: Holt, Rinehart and Winston, Inc., 1969, chapters 3–4.

Garrison, Karl C., and Force, Dewey G., Jr. *The Psychology of Exceptional Children.* New York: The Ronald Press, 1965, chapters 16–19.

Gibson, Janice T. *Psychology for the Classroom.* Englewood Cliffs, New Jersey: Prentice-Hall, Inc., 1976, chapter 12.

Harshman, Hardwick W. *Educating the Emotionally Disturbed.* New York: Thomas Y. Crowell Company, 1969, chapters III–IV.

Hewett, Frank M. *The Emotionally Disturbed Child in the Classroom.* Boston: Allyn and Bacon, Inc., 1968, chapters V–IX.

# 5

# Problems Related to Individual Differences

The fact that there are differences among students needs no corroboration. Observation of any group of pupils all in the same grade will reveal wide differences in height, weight, and other physical characteristics. Varying degrees of emotional and social adjustment will become evident from their behavior, and their performance in learning activities will show a considerable range of difference in mental endowment. Many other types of differences might be listed, but physical, emotional-social, and mental differences are the ones that receive the greatest attention from educators. Since social-emotional differences were discussed in the preceding chapter, this chapter will be limited to a necessarily brief discussion of problems related to students who are physically and/or mentally exceptional.

## SOME COMMON PHYSICAL DEFECTS

There is a relationship between bodily efficiency and mental efficiency. Defects of the senses and other bodily defects interfere with the learning process, preventing the student from doing as well as he might do otherwise. Although physical defects are a medical problem, the teacher has certain responsibilities in the matter. It is the duty of a teacher to familiarize himself with at least the more common physical defects found among pupils, and to know some of their general symptoms, in order to identify danger signals when they appear. Lack of this type of knowledge could lead to a misinterpretation of the pupil's conduct and learning performance, and could needlessly impair his progress.

Most of the defects described will be found periodically by every teacher who is familiar with their symptoms. Excluded from this discussion are the blind, the deaf, and the severely crippled because they require special education. Recently, some educators have advocated "mainstreaming" for these exceptional students, but this procedure is in an experimental stage, and its merits are being strongly debated.

*Visual Defects.* Since a great percentage of all sensory impressions come through the sense of sight, a pupil with defective vision is greatly handicapped in the learning process. Faulty vision presents the mind with erroneous data, leading in turn to the formation of inaccurate concepts. It is highly important, therefore, to be able to recognize these disorders. Following are some of the symptoms of visual defects:

1. Holding reading material or objects at a greater than average distance from the eyes.
2. Holding reading material or objects at less than average distance from the eyes.
3. Turning the head to one side or the other while looking ahead at reading material or objects.
4. Becoming restless or irritable during sustained reading.
5. Watering or redness of the eyes.
6. Mispronunciation of words that look alike.
7. Complaints of headache, dizziness, nausea, or blurred vision.

Should a pupil have one or more of these symptoms, he may have one of four common visual defects: hyperopia, myopia, astigmatism, or strabismus.

A pupil with hyperopia (farsightedness) is able to see distant objects, but has difficulty seeing things at close range. Thus, the farsighted pupil may not be able to read printed material held at a normal distance, but he will be able to read from the chalkboard. Holding books or objects away from the eyes at greater than normal distance is an obvious symptom.

Myopia is the opposite of hyperopia. The student is nearsighted, unable to see well at a distance. If there is a fairly high degree of myopia, it will be necessary for the individual to hold things abnormally close to the eyes in order to see them. When writing, for example, he will bring his eyes close to his work. Another obvious symptom is a complaint of being unable to read material on the chalkboard.

An astigmatism is an irregular curvature of the lens or cornea of the eye, resulting in blurred vision. An individual with this defect may turn his head to one side or the other in order to obtain a better focus than he might by looking straight ahead. Besides blurred vision, therefore, turning the head to one side while reading might be symptomatic of astigmatism.

Strabismus is a defect in which there is lack of coordination of the muscles of the eye. When this condition is pronounced, the individual is "cross-eyed." However, not all cases are obvious to visual inspection. In some cases, it occurs only after a period of eyestrain, at which time there is a noticeable deviation in the eye coordination.

*Auditory Defects.*   Because they do not hear well, pupils with auditory defects may develop several types of problems. Since the defect may limit his hearing in the classroom, he may not make normal progress in school and this, in turn, may lead to feelings of inadequacy. Also, if the defect is serious enough to interfere with normal conversation and normal activities with his peers, it may affect the student's social-emotional adjustment. He may begin to feel "left out," or think others are talking about him (when they are not), and as a result, he may have a tendency to become retiring and withdrawn. Defective hearing, then, not only impedes learning progress, but also may result in serious problems of adjustment.

The symptoms of defective hearing are relatively obvious. The pupil may frequently state that he did not hear the teacher's question or other pupils' answers. If the hearing of only one ear is affected, he may turn his head so that the normal ear is in the direction of the speaker; or the pupil may cup his ear with his hand in order to hear better. Sometimes the individual is not able to hear certain pitches of sound at all, which might manifest itself in mispronunciation of words incorporating those sounds. Other possible symptoms of defective hearing are: the pupil may talk louder than average; he may watch the lips of the speaker; he may speak in a monotone; or he may complain of an earache, dizziness, or nausea.

*Malnutrition.*   A malnourished pupil has a body that has not been properly nourished because of lack of food, improper diet, or inability of the body to assimilate food properly. The individual who is malnourished need not necessarily be underweight. Actually, he may be fat and flabby, but may be classified as malnourished if his diet has not included a sufficient amount of some nutrient that is essential to good health, such as lack of sufficient protein.

The symptoms of malnutrition vary with its degree. Besides being underweight or possibly overweight, his skin may be pale or sallow. His muscles may be underdeveloped, and he may be round-shouldered and flat chested. He may be listless and he may fatigue readily, or on the other hand, he may be hyperactive, restless, and irritable.

The malnourished pupil lacks the energy to carry on sustained activities. His general efficiency in both physical and mental tasks is reduced, he is easily distracted, and lacks interest in things around him. Consequently, a malnourished child, being less efficient, does not do the level of work that he could if this defect were removed.

*Chronic Infections.*　These are infections that are located in such a place that the toxins do not drain out of the body. Common locations are the tonsils, teeth, sinuses, appendix, and ears. If such an infection persists, the individual may develop symptoms such as irritability, restlessness, headaches, indigestion, and chronic fatigue. As in the case of malnutrition, such a pupil would not work up to his capacity.

*Epilepsy.*　Although epilepsy is not as common as some of the other physical defects mentioned, the beginning teacher should know something about it. If he has not witnessed an attack of epilepsy, it can be a frightening experience for him.

The two most common forms of epilepsy are *petit mal* and *grand mal*. Petit mal is a mild attack, which is characterized by dizziness or momentary loss of consciousness. The individual may have a vacant stare for a few seconds. There are no convulsions, but sometimes there may be slight tremors. After regaining consciousness, the individual resumes activity without knowing that anything happened. Grand mal, on the other hand, is a severe attack in which the individual loses consciousness and falls to the floor in convulsions which may last up to a few minutes. While thrashing around during the convulsions, there is danger that the individual might injure himself by striking objects near him. Consequently, the teacher should immediately remove such objects from the vicinity of the epileptic, and put something soft under his head to prevent head injuries which might result from beating the head against the floor. Also, to prevent choking if he vomits, the individual should be turned on his side as soon as it is possible to do so. Finally, a wooden object (such as a ruler) should be used to pry his teeth apart to prevent injury to the tongue or to determine if the individual might have swallowed his tongue. In the meantime, at the onset of the attack, the teacher should immediately send a pupil to the office for medical help.

*Physical Deformities.*　These, in themselves, may not interfere with a student's health or learning ability, but they may affect a pupil's adjustment and personality, which in turn, may interfere with learning efficiency. The deformities can be minor or serious. They may range from pimples on the face, or a scar or birthmark, to a misshapen facial feature or limb, or the loss of a limb. Individuals with deformities often become self-conscious about them, and may develop feelings of inferiority. If the condition cannot be corrected, it would be beneficial to help him develop some potential strength or a special talent he has. If he is able to do this, it compensates for his defect, and may restore to him a measure of self-confidence. (Compensation was discussed in the previous chapter on emotions.)

## SUGGESTIONS FOR DEALING WITH PHYSICAL DEFECTS

*Become Familiar With Symptoms.* It can be stated as a general principle that the teacher has no other responsibility in dealing with pupils' physical defects than to be familiar with symptoms and to make medical referral when symptoms are noted. Needless to say, the teacher's suspicion that a child has a physical defect will not always be confirmed. However, it is far better for him to refer a pupil and find nothing wrong than to try to judge a case for himself, only to discover later that the pupil *does* have a physical defect which should have been given attention.

*Do Not Jump to Conclusions.* Although the teacher should be alert for symptoms of physical defects, he should try to be fairly certain that a defect actually exists before making a referral. The symptoms could be due to causes other than a physical defect. If a student complains of not being able to read the chalkboard, it might be due to myopia, but it also might be due to the fact that the writing on the board is too small, or even illegible. The fact that a pupil does not respond to the teacher's questions may suggest a hearing problem, but in fact might be due to inattention. Again, the teacher may observe that a particular pupil always appears to be listless and fatigued; instead of being due to a physical defect, the student's chronic fatigue may be due to spending late hours with a part-time job or other activities, or it may even be due to an emotional problem that has exhausted him. And so on. If the teacher weighs and sifts out the various possibilities, and still feels that a physical defect is involved, then a referral should be made.

*Make Some Adjustments Pending Diagnosis.* While a suspected physical defect is being diagnosed and/or corrected, the teacher should take measures to alleviate the student's handicap. In the case of a suspected visual or auditory disorder, a change of seating arrangement would be advisable, bringing to the front of the room pupils who might be myopic, or who might have a hearing disorder. In dealing with other physical defects, the teacher should be patient and understanding, but not over-solicitous.

*Follow Up on the Results of Your Referral.* In cases of medical referral, the teacher should try to obtain the results. He should consult with
the school doctor or school nurse to discover the full implications of the
disorder, so as to know what limitations are to be placed on the pupil's
activities. It is quite likely that medical personnel will have constructive suggestions on how the teacher can cooperate in handling the
pupil's case. (See problems 63, 67, 70, 72, and 74.)

### DIFFERENCES IN MENTAL ABILITY

Although no two pupils have exactly the same mental endowment,
classifications of mental ability have been evolved which permit cate-
gorization of pupils into general ability levels. These classifications
have been expressed in terms of the intelligence quotient (I.Q.), which
shows the relationship of a pupil's mental age (M.A.) to his chronological age (C.A.). If a pupil's mental age, as measured by tests, is high
compared with that of average students of his own chronological age,
he has a high I.Q. If it is low for his chronological age, he has a low I.Q.
The formula for computing the I.Q. is:

$$\frac{M.A.}{C.A.} \times 100.$$

In trying to adapt school programs to differences in mental ability,
pupils are usually classified by I.Q. into four general categories:

1.  Mentally superior, with an I.Q. of 110 and above. Depend-
    ing on how high the I.Q. score is, students in this category
    have been variously classified as superior (110–119), very
    superior (120–139), and genius or gifted (140 and above.)

2.  Average, I.Q. 90–109.

3.  Below average, I.Q. 70–89. In this category are the
    mentally slow (80–89) and those of borderline intelligence
    (70–79).

4.  Mentally retarded, I.Q. below 70. Whereas once these
    pupils were classified as feeble-minded, they are now
    classified as educable (approximately 50–69), trainable
    (approximately 25–49), and custodial (below 25).

The main stream of the school program is directed to the average,
since the largest number of students fall into this category. Special provisions are then made for the above average, the below average, and
the mentally retarded students. The discussion of individual differences in mental ability, therefore, centers around pupils who deviate
from the average in either direction.

*Homogeneous Versus Heterogeneous Grouping.* The beginning teacher will find considerable controversy over procedures for taking care of individual differences in mental ability. One of the major questions debated is whether or not pupils of like mental ability should be segregated. Some educators strongly oppose homogeneous grouping, claiming that it is undemocratic, that it deprives superior students of the opportunity of mingling with and understanding pupils of other ability levels, and that it deprives the below average and average pupils of the stimulus provided by superior students in classroom activities. Opponents of homogeneous grouping think it is better to have pupils of all ability levels represented in each classroom because it is representative of society as it exists, and because it does not create those difficulties just mentioned. An additional disadvantage claimed by opponents of ability grouping is that segregation may result in intellectual snobbery on the part of superior students, and feelings of inferiority in the below average pupils.

Proponents of homogeneous grouping, on the other hand, have their own set of arguments. They claim that the undemocratic argument has been overworked, for although our democratic society tries to guarantee equality of opportunity in education, it cannot guarantee that everyone has the ability to profit from it equally. Segregation into ability levels *is* democratic, they say, because it provides opportunities for all to develop according to their capacity, inasmuch as all the activities, materials, and procedures used by the teacher during the entire class period are directed to their level, and their level alone. Regarding the argument that pupils in a homogeneous group may develop feelings of superiority or inferiority, they reply that pupils are discriminating enough to recognize their ability level in relation to others whether they are in a heterogeneous group or a homogeneous group. Moreover, they say, it is unrealistic to try to delude pupils into thinking that there are no ability levels in school, and then to thrust them into a society in which there are various strata of occupations and responsibilities to which they must adjust.

From this discussion, it can be seen that there is room for argument on the relative merits of the two forms of grouping. Both have been used, and are being used in schools. It is beyond the scope of this book to describe in detail the many procedures that have been used in each type of grouping. Only a short summary for each category follows.

In heterogeneous grouping, where the superior, the average, and the below average mingle in one graded class, it becomes necessary for the teacher to adapt his instruction to the different levels of ability in his classroom. He must find ways of challenging the few superior students, must modify the work for the few slow students, and at the same time prepare his instructional activities for the large group of average students. In effect, then, the teacher must make three preparations for each heterogeneous class (the mentally retarded are usually instructed separately). A further difficulty lies in the fact that the teacher must share his instructional time with the three groups, and therefore cannot give his full attention to any one group for the entire class period. In recent years, new procedures have been developed which largely eliminate the aforementioned problems. These procedures permit each pupil to work at his own rate of speed, so that each pupil in the heterogeneous class could conceivably be working on a different phase of the instructional activities that have been planned into the program. Among the procedures that permit this type of individual progress are: Programmed Instruction, Individually Prescribed Instruction, Personalized System of Instruction, Computer-Assisted Instruction, and the open classroom. Most of these procedures are still being operated on an experimental basis.

Homogeneous grouping has also taken several forms. In larger population areas there are special schools for exceptional children. The more frequent practice has been to have special classes for them within the same school that is serving all other pupils. The superior pupil may be required to take special classes in all his subjects; or, as a variation of this, he may take special classes only in the subjects for which he shows special talent. Similarly, there are special classes for the mentally slow pupils. Modification of the curriculum usually accompanies ability grouping, each group following a different curriculum or "track." Thus, superior children who may be college-bound follow an enriched "honors" or "college preparatory" track. Those who are not college-bound may take a "general" track. For the below average student, a modified "basic" curriculum would be available.

*Acceleration.*   Another way of meeting the needs of superior students is through acceleration. In this type of program, superior pupils are permitted to complete their schooling in a shorter period of time than usual. Acceleration may or may not be combined with enrichment, and may be used within the framework of either homogeneous or heterogeneous grouping.

Many forms of acceleration have been in use. A child of superior mental ability may be permitted to begin school at an earlier age than usual. Once in school, it is possible for him to advance more rapidly than the average student. Skipping a grade was practiced in the past, but is seldom done now. Other procedures that have been used are promotion by subject, more frequent promotions, permitting special groups to advance more rapidly, taking tests on subjects without formally taking the courses, or carrying an extra course load in order to finish school sooner. Other previously mentioned plans which also permit acceleration are Individually Prescribed Instruction (IPI), Personalized System of Instruction (PSI), Computer-Assisted Instruction (CAI), and programmed instruction.

Although acceleration has the advantage of permitting superior students to advance faster than the average student, this plan is opposed by some educators. The chief argument against its use is that even though a pupil may be several years advanced intellectually over children of his chronological age, other phases of his development may have lagged behind, so that the pupil may be only average in his physical, social, and emotional development. Thus, an intellectual giant who has been accelerated three or four years, and who has been placed with children that are several years older than he, may appear to be a physical dwarf in relation to the others. This presents problems of adjustment for such a pupil, especially if his social and emotional development have not kept pace with his intellectual advancement. It is for this reason that some educators frown upon acceleration, holding that it is better to keep the student in his proper chronological age group, while enriching the program to take care of his intellectual development. However, other educators maintain that accelerating a superior pupil by one or two years will not create any special problems of adjustment.

The preceding discussion shows that there are various school settings in which the beginning teacher may be dealing with differences in mental ability. He will have to adjust his teaching techniques to the plan or plans adopted by the school system in which he is teaching. It is beyond the scope of this book to describe specific techniques and methods that might be used in conjunction with the many plans mentioned. However, it is possible, and it may prove useful, to offer a few brief general comments on dealing with mentally exceptional children.

## SUGGESTIONS FOR DEALING WITH MENTALLY SUPERIOR STUDENTS

Effective instruction of superior students depends on accurate knowledge and understanding of their characteristics. As one might expect, they are better able to deal with abstractions, and are able to reason more logically than pupils of lesser mental ability. It follows, then, that the teacher can expect them to see meanings and relationships more quickly and more clearly than other pupils. It also means that, given premises, they will be able to draw more valid conclusions. Consequently, in dealing with superior students, the teacher should have to do less actual instructing than with average pupils. He should permit them to do more work independently, and should try to confine himself to setting the stage while they enact the drama of learning. The questions "Why?" and "How?" should be directed to them frequently. They should be asked to analyze, synthesize, criticize, generalize, and to solve problems, so as to challenge their superior cognitive powers. The teacher can reasonably expect them to give correct answers and solutions most of the time. If they are unable to do so, they can be more easily led to logical conclusions than can other pupils.

Other characteristics of superior students include the following: they have broader interests, are more capable of sustained attention, are imaginative, and assume responsibility more readily than other pupils. This combination of characteristics, together with their better reasoning ability, makes it possible for the teacher to assign them challenging individual or group projects, and to expect excellent results. They can present the results of their research in written or oral form, the latter being advantageous because it can result in stimulating classroom discussions.

In general, then, the teacher should adjust his methods and techniques to the fact that learning activities can be more intensive and extensive with superior students. He can proceed faster, probe deeper into meanings and relationships, spend less time drilling and reviewing, use fewer illustrations, and expect more initiative and activity from his pupils. He will find that teaching superior students can be a pleasure as well as a challenge.

Some student teachers are apprehensive about teaching mentally superior children. They are fearful that they may be dealing with pupils who are of higher intelligence than they, and that the pupils may ask questions that they will not be able to answer. Both of these fears are sometimes well founded, but the beginning teacher should not develop anxiety over it. Experienced teachers encounter the same situation, but they have learned to adjust to the fact that all teachers, at some time or another, will meet pupils of higher mental capacity than theirs. Right from the beginning, it would be advisable for the student teacher to tell all his pupils that he encourages questions from them. He should point out, however, that there will be times when he will be unable to answer a question, because no one really knows all there is to be known in any field. Depending on the type of unanswered question, the teacher can offer to look up the answer, or he may refer the pupil to sources that would provide it. The beginning teacher can save himself embarrassment and apprehension by following this procedure. (See problems 61, 64, 65, 71, 73, and 77.)

## SUGGESTIONS FOR DEALING WITH MENTALLY SLOW STUDENTS

It might be said that the mental traits of the mentally slow student are the opposite of those of the mentally superior. The mentally slow pupil has more limited ability to abstract, generalize, and reason. He has difficulty in seeing relationships and in forming logical associations; for that reason, his rote memory is better than his logical memory. His attention span is relatively short, he is more difficult to motivate, and he needs considerably more direction in his work.

Because of these limitations, it is necessary for the teacher to proceed more deliberately and slowly in unfolding a lesson. There is a need for frequent drill and review. The teacher must use many more examples and illustrations to establish meanings, and can expect the pupil to see only the simpler relationships. Problem-solving activities must be adjusted to his more limited capacity. Because the mentally slow child is not so easily motivated and is not so capable of sustained attention, the teacher must try to vary his procedures at shorter intervals, and must try to make the material as interesting and attractive as possible. The teacher should frequently check the progress of slow students in order to determine whether they are learning what is expected of them. If they are not, the material should be reviewed or re-taught until they achieve an acceptable level of proficiency. Many slow students make limited progress in reading and reasoning. Lack of progress in these two areas has caused some of these students to be held back in school a year or more.

Unless a beginning teacher knows these things in advance, he may become discouraged with the lack of progress made by slow students. A typical reaction is: "I went over and over the material with them, but they still didn't know it." The beginning teacher must accept the fact that with slow students he cannot expect to treat as much material nor treat it as thoroughly. He will have to exercise his ingenuity to think of appropriate examples and to vary his procedures in order to hold their attention. If he does, he will find that his patience and painstaking efforts will be rewarded by the understanding he sees mirrored in the eyes of his pupils.

As a final note, it should be pointed out that some beginning teachers mistakenly identify lack of mental ability with laziness. Since they think these pupils are not working up to capacity (when actually they are), the teacher prods them, coaxes them, or even criticizes them, in order to stimulate them to do better work. This, of course, is discouraging for the student. He may come to feel: "I'm doing the best that I can and I still get criticized, so why try?" Similarly, other teachers, even though they recognize the students' limited capacity, impatiently try to move along with the material at a faster pace than the pupils can take. This type of situation prompted one mentally slow student to remark: "I get so tired of being hurried up all the time." The teacher should set a reasonable standard and pace for his slow students. He should be understanding and supportive, not critical. If he is not, the results will be as discouraging for him as they are for the students. (See problems 62, 66, 69, 76, 79, and 80.)

## LEARNING DISABILITIES

There is much to be learned about learning disabilities. Although a proliferation of terminology has caused confusion in the discussion of the topic, the beginning teacher should at least be aware of the existence of this type of handicap.

A pupil with a learning disability has difficulty with a particular learning process, such as reading, writing, numeration, verbal expression, or formation of ideas or associations. He may not be able to function normally in one skill, such as numeration, but may be able to learn normally in others. The particular impairment, it is thought, is not due to an identifiable physical defect, emotional problems, or mental deficiency. Many types of learning impairment have been classified as learning disabilities: visual or auditory dyslexia, minimal brain dysfunction, hyperactivity, perceptual handicap, aphasia, and others. Depending on the type of impairment, the pupil may exhibit symptoms such as: inability to distinguish between letters, numbers, or words that look alike, or between sounds that are similar in spoken words; visualizing things in reverse; difficulty in ordering things in sequence; impaired language development; poor eye-hand coordination; difficulty in recalling words; short or erratic attention span; poor reaction and interaction in class; and hyperactivity, sometimes manifested by aimless wandering. Because information on these disorders has come to light only recently, many of these pupils were, in the past, designated as mentally retarded or emotionally disturbed, yet intelligence tests showed them to have at least average mental ability.

Pupils with learning disabilities are not likely to be encountered by the high school teacher unless the disability was undiagnosed or untreated in the elementary school. Alert and knowledgeable elementary teachers can identify such cases within the first two years of schooling. In dealing with these pupils, it is first necessary to identify the specific area in which the pupil is handicapped. Once the disability has been identified, students can be given a special program of educational, medical, psychological, and social services.

• • •

The problems which follow represent some of the more general ways in which student teachers have attempted to provide for physical and mental differences they found among their pupils. It will be noted that even among student teachers, there is a difference of opinion concerning the relative merits of some of the procedures they used.

## PROBLEM 61: A BRIGHT GIRL IS NOT CHALLENGED SUFFICIENTLY

Mabel is a student in my senior English class. She is an attractive, healthy, intelligent girl, with an I.Q. of 121. The academic work is no problem to her, but she is a problem to herself and others because she is continually getting into trouble with the school officials. The only thing keeping her from being on the honor roll is her bad behavior. Several of the teachers punish her by deducting points from her grade.

Mabel's mother is dead and her father is a drunk who has no control over her. In my conversations with her, I learned that she has no respect for her father. She has seven brothers and sisters, three of whom have completed college. For a while, she became such a problem at home that she was sent to live with a sister in New York, but she remained a problem, so they sent her back home after two months.

Smoking on the premises is one of her main infractions of rules; for this she has been put on report at least once a week. In class, she seemed bored all the time, and spent most of her time whispering or reading magazines. If a teacher put her on report, she further aggravated the teacher by arguing the point. She has told several teachers that she does not care if she is expelled from school. As an example of her indifference, one day she went to the movies instead of going to school, and wrote out her own excuse, as follows: "Mabel was absent from school yesterday because she went to the movies." She signed her own name to the excuse. For this, she was suspended from school for three days.

When I started teaching, I had the same trouble with Mabel— lack of attention, whispering, and reading magazines. Instead of scolding her, I had a personal conference with her, during which I asked for her attention and cooperation in class. She said her main problem was that she was bored with her classes, and that she could obtain good grades without paying attention. I then realized she was not being challenged enough.

From that point on, I kept her busy with extra work. She gave oral reports in class that were excellent. During class, I asked her the more difficult questions. I found by doing this she became more interested in our daily work. Then I made arrangements for Mabel to work on the yearbook. This showed excellent results because she devoted much of her spare time at home and in school to working on it. The teacher in charge of the yearbook gave her additional responsibilities, all of which she shouldered very well.

Before I left student teaching, Mabel ceased to be a problem in school. In her study hall and free activity periods, she was always busy with work for the yearbook. In my English class, she paid attention, made excellent class contributions, and volunteered for difficult assignments.

The moral of the story is that we very often overlook the obvious. We know that every student should be challenged to work to his individual capacity, but sometimes we don't bother to find out what that capacity is. Once Mabel was kept busy with work at her level, she didn't have any time or inclination to get into trouble.

## Points for Discussion

- *What do you think of deducting credit as a form of punishment?*

- *How would you try to challenge a superior student in your class?*

## PROBLEM 62:  A SLOW STUDENT IS GIVEN SOME PRIDE

Sixteen-year-old Sam was a student in my English class. About a year ago, he was transferred to this school from a school located in the ghetto area of a large city. He came as a seventh grader, and is still in the seventh grade. If he returns to school next year, he will spend another year in the same grade. However, Sam has other plans. He is already looking into job possibilities, and is just waiting for school to end so he can take advantage of one of them.

Before coming here, Sam grew up in a tough neighborhood, so he did not bring with him an inferiority complex even though he had below average learning ability. He knew how to handle himself in physical encounters, but he was not a rough student. Of sixteen boys in the class, he was among the best disciplined. He was not at all shy in expressing himself, and he did it well even though his grammar was poor and he used many slang expressions.

Sam spent two years in the seventh grade of the school he was transferred from. He had been placed in a "special" class—special in the sense that he would not "hold back" other students of higher mental ability. There, he and his classmates read comic books or looked through magazines. It seems there was very little supervision other than discipline.

Shortly after being assigned to teach the class in which Sam was a pupil, I noticed he was absent one morning. The following day I learned he was being expelled for playing hooky. Later that day, Sam's father came to see the principal, and told the principal that if Sam were absent again, he would "kick the hell out of him."

The following day Sam was back in class. I assigned a composition: "Write about any interesting experience you have had." A few days later I collected them, and was greatly impressed by Sam's. His spelling and punctuation were atrocious, but his account was vividly descriptive. He wrote about an automobile accident in which he and his friends were involved. It was both humorous and interesting.

Before returning the compositions, I told the class that they were all good, but that there was one that was especially so because I could picture all the things that happened. Then, I asked Sam if he would mind if I read his composition aloud. He nodded his consent. All the students turned and looked at Sam with awe. While I was reading it (with corrected grammar, of course), Sam had a proud look on his face. After I finished reading, the class agreed that they too could picture everything as it happened. Sam couldn't have been prouder.

On the back of Sam's composition, I wrote a few notes telling him to use a capital "I" when referring to himself in writing, and noted a few examples. However, the next composition showed no improvement; he still used a small "i" in referring to himself. So, one day during activities period, I sat down with him and taught him to use a capital "I." I also was able to get him to place a period after one thought, and to begin the next thought with a capital letter.

We continued having compositions two or three time a week. As time went on, Sam seldom used a small "i" when referring to himself. He even began new sentences with a capital letter, and often used periods correctly.

This wasn't much, but he became more interested in our English class. With a little special attention, he got the feeling that someone was interested in him. He felt even more important when one day he fixed a jammed lock on a cabinet door in the secretary's office. He explained to the secretary just how every part worked. Even the janitor had been unable to fix the lock. (I could not help wondering where Sam learned to pick locks.)

In the last issue of the school newspaper, one section was devoted to a questionnaire asking "What do you like best about school?" I noticed Sam's name among the others, and his reply was "I got used to it."

### Points for Discussion

- *What do you think of special classes for students like Sam?*

- *How was it possible for sixteen-year-old Sam to spend so many years in school without learning basic punctuation?*

### PROBLEM 63:  EYEGLASSES MAKE A DIFFERENCE

Esther was a sixteen-year-old sophomore in my slow-learner biology class. She was doing barely passing work in all her classes. She sat in the last seat of the third row, and seldom raised her hand to volunteer an answer. When I called on her, she was shy in giving an answer and mispronounced words. In her written work, I noticed she made frequent spelling errors.

One day I turned around after having finished writing on the chalkboard, and I noticed Esther leaning forward in her seat, straining to see what was written on the chalkboard. After class, I called her to my desk, and asked if she was having difficulty seeing the chalkboard. She admitted that she was. The next day I changed her seat to the front of the row. I thought this would settle her problem, but I found her still squinting and straining to see the board.

I then went to the school nurse, explaining the situation to her. She told me that Esther was myopic, that glasses had been prescribed for her but that she never wore them.

The next day I arranged for Esther to be excused from study hall, and we had a long chat. I asked her how long she had worn her newly prescribed glasses. "Two days," she replied. She contended that they bothered her. I then explained to her that some things take a little while to become accustomed to, and glasses were no exception. She admitted two days wasn't much time on which to base such a decision. She then told me her girlfriends said the glasses were unbecoming to her. I asked her to put them on, which she did. I told her they looked quite nice on her, and did not at all detract from her appearance. I reminded her that not wearing them was bad for her eyes, and interfered with not only her schoolwork but also hampered her in any activity requiring normal vision. I assured her that if her girlfriends were in her position they would be wearing the glasses instead of jeopardizing their activities. I smiled and told her that her friends might even be a little jealous of how nice her glasses do look. Esther seemed buoyed by our conversation, thanked me, and went back to her study hall.

From then on, Esther was a different student. She raised her hand to answer questions, her spelling and pronunciation improved, and most important, she wore her glasses. Previously, she had misspelled and mispronounced words because she could not see them correctly. Now that she could, the whole learning process improved.

At the end of the quarter, I was very pleased to inform her that her average had jumped thirteen points, to an eighty-five. There was similar improvement in her other subjects. Now Esther appears to be quite happy with herself, her work, and her glasses.

## Points for Discussion

- *Was Esther's reaction to her girlfriends' comments a normal one? Explain.*

- *Regarding their appearance, what things make adolescents self-conscious?*

## PROBLEM 64: THE STUDENT TEACHER ENJOYS A WELL-ROUNDED SUPERIOR STUDENT

The greatest pleasure I had in student teaching was in dealing with an exceptional "exceptional child." Mary Beth has an I.Q. of 144, and is truly a classroom magician. She is always ready with a response, and rarely misses a correct answer.

Neither of her parents is exceptional, and neither went to college. However, all their children are doing extremely well in school. In fact, one of her brothers, except for one B, is just finishing high school as a straight A student.

Mary Beth has to be motivated occasionally, but not often. She values education highly, and becomes annoyed at the lack of interest and initiative in other students. All subjects come easily to her, but her favorites are English and history. Her least-liked subjects are math and natural sciences. When she reads in class she does so rapidly, with fervor in her voice. Her exuberance and tone are a refreshing relief after listening to the monotone of other students. It is the reading and various writing styles that make English and history particularly interesting to her. On the other hand, she finds the systematic solving of math problems boring.

For these reasons, she prefers to be grouped homogeneously in English and history, so that she can study them in depth. For math and science, she prefers heterogeneous grouping because she is not as sure of her intellectual competence in those areas.

One of her biggest thrills in the classroom is to challenge the teacher. In doing so, she is neither arrogant nor overbearing—she is simply seeking knowledge and intellectual challenge. On many occasions she was responsible for starting stimulating classroom discussions. On some occasions, her questions were so provocative I simply had to say "I don't know."

So far, her high school record is excellent. In her freshman year she had all A's; in the sophomore year, 4 A's and 1 B; and so far this year she has registered 4 A's and 1 B. Her career plans include college and hopefully graduate school. In my opinion, she definitely is graduate school material, and it would be a pity if she would not be able to pursue that goal.

Mary Beth not only is superior intellectually but she also has a well-rounded personality. She is effervescent, speaks beautifully, and always has a ready smile and cheerful greeting. All her classmates like her, probably because she never flaunts her superior intelligence. She is magnificent both as a student and a person. It was a privilege for me to have her as a student.

### Points for Discussion

- *Compare Mary Beth's traits with those of superior children.*

- *Do you agree with Mary Beth's decision to be in heterogeneous groups for math and science? Why?*

### PROBLEM 65: SUPERIOR STUDENTS STUMP THE STUDENT TEACHER

When I began my period of student teaching, one of the things I feared most was that I would not be able to answer the questions raised by the students. I was assured that although every teacher is unable to answer a question occasionally, it would not happen very often. It was just my luck to run into the exception, and the exception came in the form of two exceptional students.

The two students in question had I.Q.'s of 133 and 139. I had not been teaching long before I felt the weight of their wisdom. I thought I knew biology pretty well, but very soon was humbled by their questions.

Since it sometimes happens that students try to parade their knowledge, or try to trap a new teacher, I thought I would give them a dose of their own medicine. I began asking them questions about the lesson, and beyond the lesson; but they were as ready with the answers as they were with questions. I was amazed at the extent of the reading they had done. Through it all, they behaved like gentlemen, and at no time did they act superior. I came to the conclusion that they were sincerely seeking knowledge through their questions.

Convinced of their sincerity, I always tried to find the answers to their questions. Sometimes this meant I had to spend as much time for that purpose as I did for preparing my lesson in general. As time went on, and as they continued to bring up these questions, I began to doubt the quality of my own preparation. I even began to doubt that I should be a teacher.

I kept the problem to myself for about three weeks, feeling that it was a reflection on me to admit I was not able to go through a period without saying "I don't know," or "I'm not sure." My co-operating teacher was in and out of the room for daily observation, but she did not make any comments about the two students. Finally, I bluntly told her that these two students had me at my wit's end because they appeared to know as much about the subject as I.

She laughed, and said, "I wondered how long it would take you to mention it. Don't worry. Every teacher in the building has had the same problem with them, so don't think that you are doing something wrong. Your preparations are very good."

It did continue to worry me, even though I was relieved to know the other teachers were having the same difficulty. For the rest of my student teaching I continued to work and prepare as I had never done before. I am not sure who profited more from these preparations—my two exceptional students, or I.

### Point for Discussion

- *This student teacher did a conscientious job of teaching, but he made a major error in method in handling the exceptional students. What was the error, and what should he have done?*

- *Do you think the cooperating teacher acted wisely in not saying anything to the student teacher? Why?*

- *What provisions can be made for superior students who are in a heterogeneous group?*

## PROBLEM 66:  A SLOW GROUP "MAKES GOOD" BY PUTTING ON A PLAY

The school in which I did my student teaching uses homogeneous grouping so as to allow each class to proceed at its inherent rate of learning. The classes for students range from the strictly college preparatory groups to the industrial students, whose sole purpose in education is to learn a trade so that they might be able to function as fairly competent skilled workers when they take their place in society.

My teaching assignments included college preparatory and average groups, but my observation period consisted of observing a senior English class made up solely of boys who were in the industrial program. Strangely enough, I became more interested in the industrial group than the classes I was teaching. They had been branded as the "dummy group—the good-for-nothings in 12–6."

While observing the group, I got to know them by talking with them before and after class. I quickly received two impressions from them. First, they felt that nobody expected anything of them as far as schoolwork was concerned, and second, because they were branded as the "dummy group," many of them had fallen prey to a mild inferiority complex. The latter took concrete form in an incident which occurred about two weeks before Washington's birthday.

My cooperating teacher was looking for volunteers from that class for a short program which was to be put on before the student body on Washington's birthday. When nobody responded to his request, my cooperating teacher began to name "volunteers." The first designee refused flatly without an explanation for his action, as did several others who were named. It was Tom who responded for the whole group when his name was called: "You ain't gettin' me on that stage on no Washington's birthday. We get laughed at everyday for bein' the dummy group, and now you want the whole school to do it at once? Hell, no, you'll have to kick me outta this school first." The problem was now in the open, standing out as plain as the nose on Tom's face. Perhaps fortunately, before my cooperating teacher could reply, the bell rang, and the 12–6 "dummies" stampeded out of the room.

After they left, my cooperating teacher explained that getting this group to do anything was almost impossible. I asked if I could be of help. He said he would appreciate any help I could give him.

The following morning, I decided to go to the 12–6 gym class to participate with the boys in an effort to show them that I was still "one of the gang." During a break, I called Tom aside to talk to him. Since I knew he was the leader of 12–6, I felt if I won him over, the rest would follow. I told him the academic students just naturally poke fun at the lower group, this being part of human nature. But, I explained, by no means was his group inferior to any other in the school. I told him few, if any, academic students were capable of doing the things he and his group were doing in metal, woodworking, and automobile shops. I further explained everyone is blessed with different talents, and that each one is superior to someone else in something. Finally, I asked him if he would reconsider being in the Washington's birthday program, or at least apologize to my co-operating teacher for his crude remarks.

The following day, Tom raised his hand in class and was acknowledged by my cooperating teacher. "Y'know, Mr.——, I was thinkin' it over last night about the program, and it just hit me why the other kids make fun of us. We're the tough guys of the school, but we never had enough guts to be in a program because we were scared they would laugh at us. I changed my mind—put me down for that program. We'll show 'em." "Put me down too," bellowed another voice from the back of the room. Before long, there were enough volunteers for the program.

Days of rehearsal followed, and the skit took form. At last the big day arrived. When 12–6 made its appearance before the student body, a silence came over the auditorium, more out of astonishment than out of respect. The boys went through their paces perfectly, and when they finished, the auditorium was filled with whistles and applause.

It was an entirely new group that walked into class the following day. They were proud of themselves; my cooperating teacher was proud of them, and I felt a warm glow of satisfaction. This was the new 12–6, ready to take on the world, no longer feeling like "dummies."

## Points for Discussion

- *What would you do with a group of slow students to bolster their confidence?*

- *What present day procedures are in use which would eliminate "dummy" groups?*

## PROBLEM 67: A GIRL LACKS CONTROL OF HER VOICE

Although I enjoyed my entire student teaching experience, I obtained the greatest degree of satisfaction out of working with Florence. She was a fifteen-year-old girl in my tenth grade biology class. In a short time, I recognized her as a reticent girl who was ill-poised in any sort of recitation, refusing to answer any questions I asked her. Even though I used the Socratic approach, I could not draw an answer out of her.

Becoming increasingly concerned by her complete withdrawal from class participation, I checked her records. Personality and mental ability tests showed her to be normal. In talking with my master teacher about Florence, I found he knew a great deal about her family background because he was friendly with the parents. He assured me there were no domestic problems.

When I first began to teach, I told the class that an oral report would be required of each student. To test her reaction, and to see if I could find a clue to her problem, I called on Florence to give her report. Soon after she began to speak, the reason for her reticence became evident to me (since I was a science major). Due to hormonal changes during adolescence, vocal changes take place; these are more pronounced in boys than in girls. I deduced that Florence's vocal chords were thickening more than usual, causing her voice to deepen. After the chords tired, her voice began to crack repeatedly. Embarrassed by this lack of control over her voice, Florence presented a well-prepared report, hurried back to her seat to a chorus of giggles, and returned to her refuge of silence. I sympathized with her because I had had the same problem during adolescence.

I thought immediately of referring her to the speech instructor, but found that the school did not have one. Next, I found out that although the school had a visiting speech therapist, she was already over-loaded and could not take any new cases. I therefore decided to try to help her, after receiving permission from the principal. As I mentioned previously, I once had the same problem, and I remembered the exercises I went through to correct it.

Calling Florence aside, I asked her if she would be interested in learning how to control her voice. She reluctantly agreed. The therapeutic procedure was a rather simple one but it required great concentration. I assigned Florence nightly readings from either a magazine or the textbook. Every Friday during the activity period we read the assignments together.

Gradually, Florence began to soften the volume of her voice. By doing this, she could voluntarily increase the pitch. Also by speaking at a moderate pace rather than her usual rapid rate, she was able to prevent her voice from cracking. At times the exercises were grueling, but the end result made it all worthwhile. Both Florence and I were enthusiastic over her progress.

I think it is interesting to speculate what might have happened if Florence had been left on her own resources. Personally, I think her personality would have suffered greatly. Being afraid to speak for fear of being ridiculed, she might have developed neurotic symptoms, or, at the least, her social development would have been inhibited.

My work with Florence showed me how important it is for teachers to try to develop the *whole* student. The teacher must be more than "a textbook wired for sound," as some author put it. He must be, above all, a humane person, sympathetic to the needs of the pupils placed under his care. If he is, he will sample many of the intangible rewards of teaching.

## Points for Discussion

- *What avenues of help are open to pupils like Florence?*

- *What risks did the student teacher take in trying to treat Florence?*

## PROBLEM 68: A PUPIL'S SPECIAL ABILITY
## IN ART IS USED TO ADVANTAGE

As I look back over my student teaching, I recall a boy who presented a definite challenge to me as a teacher. Jim seemed a typical boy, average in intelligence and appearance, yet he was obviously gifted in the field of art, for he could create and reproduce images with the preciseness of a schooled artist. Nevertheless, Jim became a problem to me because he showed no interest in my English course; he simply drew pictures constantly, both in my class and in others.

During my first three days of student teaching, I observed Jim sketching instead of paying attention to English. Possible ways of handling the situation went through my mind all this time. The only certainty I arrived at was that I could not pass him on his artistic ability in an English class.

On the fourth day of class, I picked up the drawings on Jim's desk, tore them up, and threw them into the waste basket. Jim said not a word, but the rebellion surging up within him was evident. The ripping procedure was repeated several times in the next four weeks. Although his drawings in class decreased, he made no attempt to do his English assignments.

I then had a conference with him. He appeared indifferent to things around him, and showed that he was highly sensitive and individualistic. He wanted to do only the things that interested him, and I was unable to convince him that education is many-sided, and that art constitutes but one side of his development.

When the first six weeks ended, and there had been no satisfactory work forthcoming, in conscience I had to fail Jim. Shortly thereafter, I had the idea of trying to correlate his art work with classroom activities. I suggested to my cooperating teacher and principal that Jim be permitted to design the program cover for a coming school minstrel show. They agreed to give Jim and me a free hand in the matter.

I then held a second conference with Jim, and this one was successful. I explained to him that he could take over the design work for the whole project if he learned how to use words and punctuate properly. Having an inkling now of the part English could play in his art work, he started to bring in an assignment now and then. We began working together on various projects related to the minstrel show. All the while, his classwork slowly improved, and he passed the second six-week marking period.

It was a slow, laborious process to try to get Jim to accept the idea that an education would mean a great deal to him in the future. He by no means had accepted it fully by the time I completed my student teaching, but he had made a start. His other teachers told me that he was beginning to stir himself occasionally in their classes. I hope to return to visit the school next year. It will be interesting to see how Jim is doing at that time.

## Points for Discussion

- *What mistake did this student teacher make in his early relationship with Jim?*

- *What advice would you have given Jim concerning his special ability in the field of art?*

- *Distinguish between intelligence and talent.*

## PROBLEM 69: VERY LITTLE SUCCESS IS EXPERIENCED IN HANDLING A SLOW STUDENT

Bonnie was a trouble spot in my sophomore biology class. She had no interest in her work, and continuously annoyed the students who sat in her vicinity.

I decided to see if I could encourage her to do some work and participate in class activities. Since she seemed to resent all authority, I thought I would try winning her over by being kind. Ignoring her transgressions, I started to compliment her on any constructive thing she did, no matter how trivial. For the first few days, I found it difficult to control my anger because of the things she did, but after a time she became less obnoxious and even seemed to be trying to work with the rest of the class.

In checking her school records, I found that Bonnie had an I.Q. of 70. Although she had been promoted to the tenth grade, she had not passed any of her ninth grade courses. Now that she was placed in a class in which the pupils were far above her in mental ability, the chances were good that she would fail again.

After Bonnie started working in my class, I did not pay any particular attention to her until one day when I was giving a spelling test consisting of twenty-five biological terms. As I dictated the words to the class, Bonnie worked like a beaver and by her manner seemed to be doing well. That night, however, as I was correcting her paper, I found it full of writing which did not include a single word I had given on the test! I concluded that, not wishing to appear stupid to the rest of the class, she had merely pretended to take the test. The words she wrote on the paper were copies from material on the blackboard and posters on the wall. The paper made no sense at all.

The following day in class I contrived to have her read some written material to the class. She did poorly. After class I talked to her alone, and was shocked to discover that (in my opinion) her reading ability was no higher than that of a second-grader. Her reasoning ability also seemed very limited. She could not, for example, relate words to concrete objects after I showed her pictures of parts of the body, gave her the names, and asked her to name them. In short, written words seemed to have little or no meaning for her.

Apart from the fact that Bonnie was trying harder than she had previously, I was not successful in improving her as a student. I firmly believe that she is in her present dilemma because she was pushed along through the grades even though she did failing work. This state of affairs, in my opinion, is not the fault of the teachers, but of the system that permits such things to occur.

## Points for Discussion

- *Several errors of omission and commission were made in this case. Identify them. How would you correct them?*

- *Do you believe that pupils should be promoted even though they do substandard work? Why?*

- *Do you think the conclusion in this case is valid? Why?*

### PROBLEM 70: A BOY IS SELF-CONSCIOUS ABOUT AN EYE DEFECT

Sitting isolated in the back of the room, Samuel, an exceptionally good-looking boy of thirteen, let out a sarcastic laugh when my co-operating teacher first introduced me to the class. I noted that the class did not respond to Samuel's impudence. Rather, the students looked expectantly at the person who was to be their guide through the complex world of English grammar for the next few weeks.

After class, my cooperating teacher had this to say about Samuel: "He's a plague on all the teachers, and even the students don't like him. Don't pay any attention to him."

Idealistic and fresh from my college courses in methods and theories of teaching, I egotistically determined that, whereas others had failed in reforming Samuel, I, a missionary with a zeal for true education, would succeed. However, when I began teaching in earnest, Samuel's constant antagonism toward me and his class-mates caused my zeal to cool and my anger to burn. I had exhausted my supply of panaceas for disciplinary problems on Samuel to no avail. I began to agree with my cooperating teacher's remark: "He's a plague on his teachers."

One day, while I was reading Samuel's weekly theme, I noticed the following sentence: "When I was a kid, all the other kids used to call me "cross-eyes," and it really made me mad so I beat them up." I was quite surprised for I had not noticed any visual defect in Samuel.

As the class did more and more diagramming on the chalkboard, I would call on students to comment on the work of their fellow-students. Each time I called on Samuel, he would either refuse to answer or say, "I guess it's right," or, "I can't read his writing."

Remembering Samuel's theme, I wondered if the reason he refused to recite could have been, simply, that he had not been able to see the board clearly enough from his seat. But why, I asked my-self, did he not just admit that he was unable to read from that dis-tance instead of feigning ignorance? I determined to have a talk with him after class, and I did.

During our talk, I noticed for the first time that Samuel actually had a slight case of strabismus. The condition appeared to be very minor, and would not be noticed by a casual observer. As we talked, I noticed he was extremely conscious of it because he did not look at me directly in the eyes. From our conversation, I inferred that his detachment from people and his resentment of teachers was rooted in his belief that his visual defect marred his appearance, and vir-tually made him an outcast. However, his belief was inaccurate: the defect was hardly noticeable.

I told him his defect was barely and only occasionally percep-
tible, and that in fact, I had never noticed it myself until then. I tried
to assure him that it in no way detracted from his uncommon good
looks, and the reason, no doubt, why his classmates did not enjoy his
company was because of *his* antagonism toward them, and not
because of his minor visual defect. I suggested he have his eyes
checked by the school nurse, and I wrote a note to his mother, telling her of our conversation. Since Samuel's I.Q. scores were above
average, I suggested he strive to excel academically, thereby gaining respect and admiration from his fellow students. He nodded, and
said: "Thank you, I'll try to do better."

Both he and his mother must have taken my advice seriously,
for about a month later he got glasses. In the meantime, I had seated
Samuel nearer to the board. His recitations and interest in the class
improved, slowly at first, but more rapidly as my weeks of student
teaching drew to a close.

## Points for Discussion

- *What causes strabismus? Besides prescription of glasses,
  how else may it be treated?*

- *Comment on the way Samuel's defect affected his personality.*

## PROBLEM 71: A SUPERIOR SEVENTH-GRADE STUDENT
NEEDS AN ENRICHED COURSE

During most of my student teaching period, my greatest concern and
challenge was a seventh-grade boy with an exceptional mind. My
problem was to keep this boy working to his capacity at the same
time I was trying to give my other students their full opportunity to
learn.

Bill was a boy who was mentally developed far beyond his
chronological age. Whenever the class could not answer a question,
someone would chime in and say, "Ask Bill. He knows everything."
How true this statement proved to be!

Bill had keen judgment and could think rapidly. Most amazing
was his grasp of new material and his ability to put it to use. He
could detect mistakes at once, as I found out when he corrected me
several times in a most objective manner. He did not parade his
knowledge; he simply used it to enlighten the class and add understanding to the problem at hand. An example of the way he worked
was his weekly social studies report, which everyone in the class

had to make. Bill went to every source he could find, and presented not only the facts but also a comparison of the present with the past, and, at times, his opinions on what the future would bring.

Since the school had no planned program for superior pupils, I knew it was up to me to do whatever I could for him. My first step was to find out where his interests lay, and I discovered that he was very interested in my major field, which was history. At first I started to correlate his social studies readings with pamphlets for which I sent away. These I assigned to him and then asked him pertinent questions about them. He had no difficulty in correlating the readings with the matter at hand. I then went a step further. Several companies had sent me maps that I had requested, and we correlated these with the readings. Bill took it all in stride. Still later, I gave him assignments that were based exclusively on outside sources.

This was not very much to do for Bill, but I had no time for more because I had to think of the rest of the class. If nothing else, I hope I instilled the idea that knowledge does not end with reading the textbook. The textbook is a blueprint or a starting point; whereas the library, outside reports, and map studies are the extras that are the "delicious" parts of the learning process. I hope I have encouraged Bill to sample these delicacies.

## Points for Discussion

- *What would you do or say if a bright student kept asking you questions you were unable to answer?*

- *What else could have been done for Bill if he were in a special class for bright children?*

- *What other provisions do schools make for bright children?*

### PROBLEM 72:  A PUPIL WITH SEVERAL PHYSICAL HANDICAPS MAKES A GOOD ADJUSTMENT

As a student teacher I met several minor problems which I was able to handle without much difficulty. There was one student who made a deep impression on me, not because he was a problem, but because of the courageous way in which he adjusted to his physical handicaps.

Bob was a fourteen-year-old student in my World Cultures class. As soon as I noticed he was handicapped, I began to investigate his situation at the school. I talked with the principal, the school nurse, and a member of the faculty who worked with Bob on an individual basis. From these sources I learned the nature of his handicaps. I wanted this information so that I might understand him better, and so that I might take appropriate measures to facilitate learning for him.

From the sources I consulted I learned that Bob had a premature birth which resulted in some serious disabilities for him. He had coordination problems which may have resulted from damage to his motor control center, although there was no exact diagnosis for the cause of the problem. He also lost the sight of his left eye, a condition discovered soon after he was born. In addition, he developed spurs in his knees which caused him severe discomfort. To top it off, he also had a slight speech impediment. In the past, he received physical therapy treatments and, during the time I was student teaching, he was making visits to a local hospital for continued treatment.

Bob's mental ability tested as average, and he was doing satisfactory work in school. His reading ability test score was slightly below average, but this might have been due at least in part to blindness of the left eye.

Because of the nature of his disabilities, there was not much I could do to help him, but I did what I could. He had already been assigned a seat in the front of the room, so I did not have to be concerned about seating him where he could see and hear better. I did have a few problems with him in the beginning. His first test (a minor quiz) was a failure. The work he turned in was sloppy and poorly prepared. His participation in class was erratic. There were days when he was active and responsive while at other times he was neither prepared nor attentive. There were days when he was extremely restless (cold weather seemed to aggravate his condition) so I tried to give him opportunities to do work that would relieve his restlessness.

When he received the failing grade on the quiz, he was visibly upset. When I noticed this, I talked to him, telling him not to be concerned about the grade, and that with a little more work he would have no trouble making a passing grade. Since then, his work improved and he made very good marks on subsequent tests.

The most interesting thing about Bob was his social development. He appears to have made an excellent adjustment to his handicaps, although they are occasionally a reminder that he cannot react in a normal manner. One such instance occurred during a lunch hour when a classmate hid something of Bob's. I noticed that Bob was upset and frustrated because he could not retaliate. I walked over and attempted to handle their disagreement as a normal situation between two boys, without drawing attention to Bob's inability to stand up to his classmate.

On the whole, however, Bob is active in school and attends school functions regularly. For example, I saw him in attendance at most of the basketball games. After getting to know him better, I found him to be inquisitive, and to have a good sense of humor. His personality development, in spite of his handicaps, was proceeding normally. I never knew him to complain or whimper about his problems, and he never tried to draw sympathy to himself.

Bob's actions, problems, and progress provided me with an opportunity to gain helpful experience in dealing with students who have physical handicaps. Despite some early problems with him, I found working with Bob a pleasant and rewarding experience. He taught me a lesson, too. I don't think I'll ever feel sorry for myself again.

## Points for Discussion

- *Would you try to be objective or sympathetic with a student with physical handicaps? Why?*

- *Recall a physically handicapped person you know. What type of adjustment has that person made to life's problems?*

### PROBLEM 73: A STUDENT TEACHER SEES ADVANTAGES IN HOMOGENEOUS GROUPING OF SUPERIOR STUDENTS

During my term of student teaching I had the good fortune to be exposed to a homogeneous group of above average students, and a heterogeneous group, both of which were being taught by a teacher who used a modified version of the Dalton plan. During the first part of the school year, my master teacher had drilled the students on diagraming sentences, and on the rules of grammar. When I took over teaching, the classes were just beginning the section of the textbook containing the grammar handbook, in which seven chapters of exercises were to be worked by the students at their own rate of speed. The function of the teacher was to circulate among the pupils, giving them aid as needed.

The homogeneous group had very little trouble with this system. They moved along rapidly, rarely missed the unit deadline before they were tested on each chapter, and recited very well on the day for the customary oral check before the chapter test. This group also excelled in the written themes and oral reports which were required periodically.

The heterogeneous group, on the other hand, moved more slowly, frequently missed the chapter or unit deadline, and did not recite nearly as well on the oral check day. They depended heavily on my help during this oral work.

Needless to say, the test results of the homogeneous group were always much higher than those of the heterogeneous group. Some of the outstanding characteristics of the homogeneous group were: greater intelligence, maturity, dependability, aggressiveness, and perception. In a request for a written, anonymous criticism of my teaching, this group expressed keen insight into my problems as a student teacher. It was they who assured me that they "didn't bite teachers."

All in all, I found the homogeneous group superior in all classroom activities, as one would expect. In addition, I found it easier and more pleasant to work with them than with the heterogeneous group.

### Points for Discussion

- *What is the Dalton plan? Compare it with Individually Prescribed Instruction.*

- *How do those characteristics of superior children mentioned compare with generally known traits of such children?*

### PROBLEM 74: A POSSIBLE UNDETECTED BRAIN INJURY CHANGES A PUPIL'S LIFE

Student teaching was one of the most interesting and profitable periods of my life. I learned a great deal and I hope my pupils did likewise. Although I had my share of problems, they were of the usual type experienced by all teachers, and they were solved without too much difficulty. My cooperating teacher, however, had a problem which was so interesting and so unusual that it bears telling.

A few years ago, our school system received a sixteen-year-old boy who had transferred from a school in another state. The boy, Frank, had records with him which stated that he had been advanced to the tenth grade after having completed a "modified program." On the basis of the information Frank gave us, in addition to what appeared on the records, we concluded that he had attended industrial classes almost exclusively.

Frank was assigned to one of my less capable English classes. He seemed to be intelligent, but was very quiet and withdrawing, which I at first thought was due to the fact that he was in strange surroundings. I was to change my mind later.

He was in class only a few days when I discovered that he could not read a single word! In a private talk I had with him, he told me he had never learned to read, and the schools he attended were never able to teach him to do so. I showed him some printed material and pointed to two and three-letter words such as "to," "an," and "the." He was not able to identify a single one of them. Then I pointed to "a" in a sentence, and he identified it correctly. Further questioning revealed he could identify all the letters of the alphabet, but he could not associate them together to form a word. He could, for example, identify "t," "h," and "e" separately, but could not identify the word "the" when the letters were put together.

At some time in the past I remembered reading of cases such as Frank's. I thought it best to refer him to a psychiatrist at this point.

The psychiatrist confirmed the fact that Frank was unable to read. He gave him an I.Q. test of the nonverbal type, on which Frank scored an average I.Q. of 101. In reviewing Frank's past history, the psychiatrist unearthed a significant fact: Frank had been hit by a truck at the age of four, and he remembered that he had had a head injury. Putting together these and other facts, the psychiatrist made a tentative diagnosis of aphasia, which is a defect of association, affecting the visual center of the brain. Frank's head injury might have produced this defect. The psychiatrist further explained that in some cases of this type the individual is able to learn to read through the sense of touch instead of the sense of sight. In other words, he may be taught to read through the use of Braille.

Another interesting item brought out was the fact that Frank had held several part-time jobs, but gave each of them up after a month or two. Frank explained his frequent changes of employment by saying that he stayed on a job until his employer or fellow employees discovered he could not read. He had been so ashamed of his defect that he gave up each job when it was discovered. This feeling of inadequacy undoubtedly also explained why he was quiet and withdrawn.

The psychiatrist explained his findings to Frank, and suggested to him the possibility of learning to read Braille. Frank, however, was not interested in it. He said he had enough of school and was going to quit in less than a month, when he would be seventeen years of age. Frank's parents were consulted, but they also thought it best for him to leave school. This he did in a short time.

I think this case brings out an important point which a beginning teacher should always keep in mind. Frank's life could have been entirely different if some teacher during his early years had taken the trouble to refer him to a psychiatrist for a diagnosis of his reading deficiency. Either no one knew enough to do it, or no one cared. The result of this neglect was a life filled with obstacles and humiliation. How would you like to be held responsible for something like this?

## Points for Discussion

- *What other reason could be given for the fact that Frank had never been referred previously for a psychiatric examination?*

- *Is the fact that this is an unusual diagnosis a valid reason for failure to discover it? Explain.*

- *Was there a possibility that Frank's previous teachers simply categorized him as a mentally slow child? Why or why not?*

## PROBLEM 75: THE TEACHER TRIES TO EVALUATE INDIVIDUALLY PRESCRIBED INSTRUCTION

I had the good fortune of being exposed to one of the recent innovations in education—Individually Prescribed Instruction (IPI). One of the classes I was assigned to teach was a group of slow students in an IPI class. Since it required some specialized training to work with an IPI class, I worked closely with my cooperating teacher most of the time.

The class consisted of a group of sixteen slow students in seventh grade mathematics. The procedure in this class was altogether different from the way I conducted my other classes. The students were to go through levels of learning, in this case, Levels A through H. There were prescribed materials for each level; these were printed materials which had been developed at the Learning Research and Development Center at the University of Pittsburgh. The materials also included tests the pupils had to take at various points: pre-tests, curriculum-embedded tests, and post-tests. The tests were designed to uncover weaknesses students had in certain skills, to show progress in mastery of skills, and to determine whether there was sufficient mastery to move on to the next level.

My cooperating teacher had the assistance of two teacher's aides, one in each corner of the rear of the room. Along the rear wall of the room were specially designed racks to house the printed materials that were used to develop and measure each skill for each level of learning. I soon found that students were not only working at different levels, but also that students working at the same level were working toward mastery of different skills. Thus, it was possible for each pupil in the room to be working at a different task.

The system was a simple one and almost mechanical. A pupil worked out the exercises for a particular skill in math, then took it to one of the teacher's aides for correction. The aide marked the wrong answers, and designated the degree of mastery by circling a score at the top of the page. The pupil then returned to his seat, waiting for the teacher to examine his work. If the teacher found the score indicated mastery of the skill, she assigned work on the next skill to be mastered; if the score showed lack of mastery, the teacher prescribed additional work in that skill. This procedure was repeated for every pupil.

For the first few days that I observed the class, I marvelled at the endurance of my cooperating teacher. She quickly moved from one pupil to another, explaining things as pupils needed them, or giving them a prescription for the next skill to be mastered. I asked her why she didn't save her energy by having the pupils come to her desk instead of going to them. She replied, "I like to keep on top of them to keep them motivated and working. Also, it would create disorder to have them marching up to my desk."

I never took over that class as I did with my others. Instead I simply helped the cooperating teacher give the pupils individual attention. It took me some time to become familiar with the materials for making the individual prescriptions, but other than that I had no problems with IPI.

I can see advantages and disadvantages in using the IPI system. The obvious advantage is that each pupil works at his own ability level and rate of speed, and each pupil receives individual help. As a teacher, I worked harder with that class than the others while I was in school, but I did not have lessons to prepare because the materials were all prescribed and ready for use. Also, I did not have tests to correct because the teacher's aides did that, and they kept individual progress records on IPI flow charts. There were no problems of discipline because my cooperating teacher and I were moving around the room all the time, keeping the pupils busy. As for disadvantages, I think the lack of group activities and class discussion are shortcomings. I missed these activities, and I think they are necessary for the development of students. Another shortcoming is that we were locked into IPI materials, so that there was no room for the teacher's initiative, ingenuity, or judgment in teaching the course.

## Points for Discussion

- *What does research show about the effectiveness of IPI?*
- *As a teacher, would you like to make use of IPI? Why?*

## PROBLEM 76:  A CLASS OF MENTALLY SLOW PUPILS PRESENTS PROBLEMS

My first class was one in junior World History. It consisted wholly of slow students, and I might add, they were a rough-looking lot, because there were several football players in the group. I did not need to be clairvoyant to sense that the going would not be smooth.

From the first day of teaching this class, I was confronted with two problems. Some of the students were very poor in reading, and all of them were unable to express themselves clearly even when they knew the answers. I therefore adopted techniques of teaching which I thought would overcome these handicaps. Because their comprehension was slow, I decided to eliminate some of the material, retaining only the important information which they would definitely need in order to go on. Every day I drilled them on this material until they could comprehend it and answer my questions intelligently. To give them more opportunity to express themselves, I related the material to the problems which face us today, and then had a class discussion on it.

With this program well on its way, I was still confronted with the problem of getting the students to read their assignments from day to day. It seemed that most of them were lazy, refusing to read —probably the reason many of them were poor readers. To remedy this defect, I gave daily quizzes on the assignment of the previous day, a procedure which worked fairly well. Most of them began to read, with the result that we were able to have more class discussion, as well as better responses to my questions.

The biggest challenge in this class was the disciplinary problem. Most of the boys were football players with little interest in school work. About fifteen minutes after the class began, they would get restless and start to "cut up." I knew I could never coerce those boys to study because they were much bigger than I. I tried keeping them busy, I asked questions of the offenders, and I threatened to lower their marks, but none of these measures had a lasting effect.

## Discussion

- *What would you do with this slow group?*

## PROBLEM 77: A SUPERIOR STUDENT IS DISLIKED BY HIS PEERS

Let us call him Joe. He is a senior in high school who is academically exceptional. In looking over his personal file, I found that since seventh grade he has received almost all A's, with an occasional B in a minor subject, such as gym. Throughout the file it was reported that his work habits, integrity, self-control, and self-confidence were superior. His Stanford-Binet I.Q. was listed as 133.

Referred to by many of his teachers as "intellectually oriented," the problem with Joe appears when we look over the part of his file devoted to social adaptability. He was given poor ratings there, and it was this that first brought my attention to Joe. Why, I asked myself, when everything was so promising for him—good physical appearance and health, excellent grades, and the choicest colleges pursuing him—did he appear to be a social outcast among his peers? Others were cool in manner towards him, and he had noticeably few friends.

Before trying to do something for him in my small way, I tried to discover his interests. This proved interesting for I found that Joe seemed to participate only in those things that he could perform by himself, never in anything that was a team effort. The only activities listed for him were debating and camera club. There were several unflattering remarks, describing him as "self-centered," "selfish," and "one who gets along with those who display the same position and high standards as he does. Does not get along with less gifted children."

I talked with the guidance counselor as well as two teachers who knew him well. My purpose was to get their personal view of Joe's problem. They related that Joe's problem of creating friendships seemed to have become serious in about the ninth grade, and they wondered if the death of his father when he was in the seventh grade might have had much to do with it.

At this point, I asked Joe if he would come to see me after school to talk about his future. He said he would like this. We met, and during our discussion I was able to find out that he had had a very close relationship with his father, as they had spent unusually great amounts of time together. They had camped, fished, and travelled together. Joe's father had even taken him along on business trips whenever he could. Thus evolved an extremely close relationship.

In thinking about it later, I felt that Joe's close ties with his father contributed to two problems: (1) he did not develop the childhood friendships necessary to all children because he spent so much time with his father; and (2) the constant companionship of an older person, plus his high intelligence, developed in him a mature and serious outlook that was beyond his years, thus making it more difficult to socialize with children his own age.

## Discussion

- *What would you do to help Joe with his social relationships?*

### PROBLEM 78: A STUDENT TEACHER FINDS IT DIFFICULT TO ADAPT HIS METHODS TO A HETEROGENEOUS GROUP

The greatest difficulty I had during student teaching was the matter of trying to teach the bright, the average, and the dull in the same classroom. I had to go fast enough so the bright pupils would not be bored, yet slowly enough so the dull students could understand. The problem was to explain things so that each pupil could understand, whether putting figures on the chalkboard, or using illustrations or maps, or referring to the textbook. On any specific question, what some understood, others could not; hence, it was necessary to find different ways of explaining the same point. I discovered while the majority of students found my illustrations and examples sufficient for understanding, there were a few superior students who were more than saturated and a few slow pupils who needed ten times as much explanation in order to understand the work involved.

I tried to adapt myself to the situation as well as I could. In an attempt to satisfy the superior students, I inserted, whenever possible, more difficult and complicated problems for them to work out. Moreover, I relied on the superior students for answers and explanations to problems which baffled the rest of the class.

For the below average students I gave additional explanations in class whenever the others were engaged in written work. I also gave them additional attention during the short study periods at the end of the class.

Although this system worked out fairly well, I never felt that I had spent enough time with the superior and the below average pupils.

## Discussion

- *Describe the procedures you would use in a heterogeneous class.*

## PROBLEM 79: A STUDENT TEACHER DISLIKES HOMOGENEOUS GROUPING OF DULL STUDENTS

During the course of my student teaching I had an opportunity to note the way in which classes were arranged according to individual differences. The aim of this arrangement, of course, was to try to fill the various needs of all the pupils.

I taught four different classes: two sophomore groups, one junior group, and one class made up of juniors and seniors. The first three groups consisted of students who, on the whole, were above average. The fourth class—the one combining juniors and seniors—I would class as poor, although the word "dull" would probably describe them more accurately.

After teaching these various groups, I came to the conclusion that grouping pupils together has more bad points than good. I think too much emphasis has been placed on individual differences, and that grouping them together creates many problems. On the basis of my short teaching experience, I came to the following conclusions:

1.  A class consisting soley of dull students is more difficult to motivate.
2.  It is more difficult to maintain discipline in a classroom with dull students.
3.  Some teachers pass most of the pupils in a dull class because to fail them reflects on their teaching ability.
4.  In a dull class, all the students are aware of their mental level, and therefore feel it is not necessary to show any initiative.

### Discussion

- *Describe the procedures you would use in a homogeneous class.*

## PROBLEM 80: A MENTALLY SLOW CLASS LACKS KNOWLEDGE OF SIMPLE FACTS

I had no really serious problems during my period of student teaching, but I did find it a considerable challenge to teach a mentally slow class that was assigned to me. The class to which I refer was a ninth-grade class in history. My cooperating teacher had told me not to expect as much of them as of the civics class which was also assigned to me. His was the understatement of the year.

After the first week, I gave them a short quiz on the physical make-up of Pennsylvania. One of the questions involved the identification of Pennsylvania cities. Among the answers it was common to find listed such cities as Chicago, San Francisco, and Detroit. With the exception of two students, all thought the Mississippi River was located in Pennsylvania. As far as English usage was concerned, I cannot see how they were allowed to pass beyond the fifth grade. In a later test I was to find that only three students out of twenty-three knew who was President during the Civil War, and there were some who did not know who won the war.

## Discussion

- *What would you do if you were assigned to teach this class?*

## SELECTED READINGS

Barbe, Walter B. *The Exceptional Child.* Washington, D.C.: The Center for Applied Research in Education, Inc., 1963.

Brickman, William W., and Lehrer, Stanley, eds. *Education and the Many Faces of the Disadvantaged.* New York: John Wiley and Sons, Inc., 1972.

Cruickshank, William M., and Johnson, G. Orville, eds. *Education of Exceptional Children and Youth.* Englewood Cliffs, New Jersey: Prentice-Hall, Inc., 1967, parts II and III.

Garrison, Karl C., and Force, Dewey G., Jr. *The Psychology of Exceptional Children.* New York: The Ronald Press Company, 1965.

Kirk, Samuel A. *Educating Exceptional Children.* Boston: Houghton Mifflin Company, 1972, chapters 3, 4, 6, and 9–11.

L'Abate, Luciano, and Curtis, Leonard T. *Teaching the Exceptional Child.* Philadelphia: W. B. Saunders Company, 1975, sections IV and V.

Love, Harold D. *Educating Exceptional Children in Regular Classrooms.* Springfield, Illinois: Charles C. Thomas, 1972.

Smith, Robert M., and Neisworth, John T. *The Exceptional Child.* New York: McGraw-Hill Book Company, 1975, part V.

Stoumbis, George C., and Howard, Alvin W. *Schools for the Middle Years: Readings.* Scranton, Pennsylvania: International Textbook Company, 1969, part IV.

# 6

# Problems of Evaluation

The problem of evaluating a student's progress in learning is one that causes sleepless nights even for seasoned teachers. The difficulty stems from the controversial nature of evaluation techniques, and from the fact that the same techniques may be used by different teachers with varying degrees of accuracy and conscientiousness. Every teacher has his own philosophy of grading, strongly believes in it, and may bristle when it is challenged.

For the student teacher, evaluation presents even greater problems. Because of his lack of experience, he is not sure whether his test items are too difficult or too easy. At the start, he has no way of knowing whether the test as a whole is too long or too short. He wonders how much credit to give for a partially correct answer, or whether to give credit at all. Should he use questions of the essay type or the objective type? How will he make up a final grade? Even if he has formulated his answers to some of these questions, he will wrestle with the problem of applying his policies to particular cases. Moreover, his philosophy of grading may differ from that of the teacher or teachers under whom he is doing student teaching, which in itself is a very frustrating experience.

These problems, nevertheless, are not insurmountable. If the beginning teacher works closely with his supervisors at the start, he can avoid mistakes and serious problems during his first weeks of teaching. The beginning teacher can be sure that he *will* make some mistakes, and that he *will* be uncertain of his evaluation procedures, but he should console himself with the thought that the whole problem of evaluation very often poses serious questions even to the cooperating teachers under whom he is training.

**EVALUATING BY TESTS**

In the evaluation of his students' progress, the beginning teacher is faced with two major questions. First, should he use essay type tests or objective type tests? Second, what factors should he consider in grading a pupil's progress? A brief discussion of each of these problems follows.

*Advantages and Disadvantages of Essay Type Tests.* Although the essay type test has been attacked in many ways, the two chief criticisms are that its evaluation is a subjective process, and that it provides too limited a sampling of the pupil's knowledge. Those who object to this type of test point out that since several correct responses may be possible to a single question, it is therefore very difficult for the teacher to judge each answer on a comparable basis. Or, they say the teacher may mark an answer incorrect simply because it does not agree with his "preconceived notions." Moreover it has been pointed out that the same paper, graded by different teachers, may receive a wide range of different ratings. It is also held that because they take a longer time to answer, only a few essay questions can be asked during a class period; therefore, such a test samples too limited a portion of the pupil's knowledge. Other criticisms of the essay type test take the following forms: in grading a paper, the teacher may be influenced by his personal opinion of the pupil, by the appearance of the paper, by the quality of handwriting, by his mood at the time, or by the degree of his fatigue.

Proponents of the essay type test have strong arguments for its use. They hold that this type of test better measures certain mental processes, such as ability to organize, synthesize, compare, contrast, interpret, and evaluate. Furthermore, an essay type test calls for greater effort and mastery on the pupil's part because he must produce the entire answer himself, instead of simply making a choice from the alternatives provided for him in an objective type test. In addition, it is argued that the essay type test enables the teacher to judge a pupil's ability to express himself, and that it gives the pupil needed practice in written expression. (See problem 92.)

*Advantages and Disadvantages of Objective Type Tests.* The objective type test consists of items that can be answered by a word, letter, number, or some other symbol. The objective type test is so widely used that it needs little explanation.

It is claimed that the objective test eliminates the shortcomings of an essay type test. In the first place, it eliminates subjectivity because there is only one correct answer possible to each question; anyone provided with a scoring key would arrive at the same grade. In the second place, because the questions can be answered with a word or a symbol, they do not take much time to answer; consequently, a large number of questions can be asked during a class period, thus permitting wider sampling of the pupil's knowledge. Objectivity of scoring, and a larger sampling of material constitute two of the chief advantages of the objective test—and these are said to be lacking in the essay type test. Opponents of this type of test counter by saying that in order to achieve these advantages, it is necessary for the objective test to sacrifice other things: the pupil is deprived of the opportunity to express himself, and to show how well he can organize, synthesize, evaluate, and so on. Opponents further state that although objective items can be constructed so that they call for evaluation, comparison, etc., they cannot do it as well as the essay question. (See problem 92.)

*Combination of Essay and Objective Type Items.*   The question of what type of test item to use is not an "either-or" proposition. Both types can and should be used. By a combination of essay and objective items the advantages of both can be incorporated into a test. The use of a large number of objective items provides a wide sampling of the material, while the inclusion of one or more essay type items provides evidence of the pupil's ability to express himself in terms of the knowledge he has gained. Actually, the nature of the material, or the teacher's purpose, will dictate the type of test he will give. If the teacher has been drilling his students on factual material, an objective test will suffice to provide evidence of mastery. However, if the teacher's purpose is to determine how well the pupils can interpret and apply that material, the essay type item will be more appropriate.

*Components of a Grade.*   All beginning teachers struggle with the question: "What factors shall I consider in grading a pupil's progress?" Although a considerable portion of a student's grade will be determined by the scores he has made on the various types of tests given him, other factors must also be considered in the evaluation of his progress, such as the quality of his homework, other written assignments, projects, and oral work in class. What percentage of the grade should be allotted to each of these elements cannot be stated categorically because the amount of homework, written work, oral work, etc., varies with subjects and teachers. For example, since there would be a great deal more emphasis on oral work in language classes than in other classes, a greater portion of the final grade would be assigned to oral work than, for example, in a chemistry class. Similarly, some teachers assign major projects, while others do not; in some cases, more homework is given than in others; some courses include laboratory work, but many do not. In the last analysis, then, the weight of each type of activity would have to be determined by the teacher himself because of the fact that his classroom and learning activities differ from those of other teachers.

In making up an interval or a final grade, then, the teacher must first decide on the components of the grade, and then assign each component a certain weight. The following is illustrative of this procedure, with the apportionment of the weight distribution for each component merely suggestive.

### Components of a Final Grade

| | |
|---|---|
| Final examinations | 30% |
| Major tests | 30% |
| Homework | 10% |
| Oral work | 10% |
| Special project | 10% |
| Short quizzes | 10% |
| | 100% |

A system of grading such as this has several advantages because it takes into consideration many phases of the individual's work. It gives recognition to his class work and independent work. It rewards him for daily preparation, and for his ability to assimilate, correlate, and interpret large units of work. Moreover, since it embraces several elements, the student must do well in all phases in order to merit an evaluation of "superior." This fact encourages the student to be active continuously, rather than to coast along until it is time for an infrequent test. (See problem 86.)

There are many other problems inherent in the evaluation of pupil progress. Following are some suggestions on evaluation which, if implemented by the beginning teacher, should save him many headaches and heartaches in the process of trying to assess his pupil's progress.

### GENERAL SUGGESTIONS ON EVALUATION AND TESTING

*Explain Your Grading Policies to Your Students.* When he first meets a class, and at regular intervals thereafter, the teacher should explain the factors that he will consider important in evaluating a student's progress. He should also explain the relative weight each type of activity will carry in determining the final grade. This procedure will go a long way toward eliminating misunderstandings and discontent among the students when they receive their grades. It will also reduce to a minimum such comments as, "I should have had a B, but he gave me a C."

*Set Reasonable Standards.*   Although there is a reasonable amount of consistency on the standards set by teachers, there are exceptions. It is a known fact that pupils have to work very hard to attain the standards set by some teachers, whereas they can reach the goals set by others with a minimum of effort. Similarly, some teachers give tests which are regarded as "impossible" by the students, yet the tests of others are classified as a "push-over." Teachers who fall into those extremes would do well to re-examine their standards, procedures, and evaluation techniques. In all cases, goals should challenge the pupils, but should be attainable. In the case of teachers who consistently give low grades, the answer might lie in tests of unreasonable difficulty, standards that are too high, or even poor teaching techniques. On the other hand, a teacher who consistently gives high grades might do well to raise his standards and to refine his tests. The beginning teacher should strive to reach the mean between the extremes. With some experience, he should be able to do so.

*Base Your Grades on as Much Objective Evidence as Possible.*   There are several persons to whom the teacher may have to justify a grade. First, he will have to justify it to himself. His conscience will be clear if he has objective evidence to support his judgment; evidence such as the results of major and minor tests, written assignments, homework, and special projects. Next, a pupil may ask the teacher to justify the grade he gave him, and the teacher can easily do so if he has the supporting objective evidence to show the pupil. Sometimes, too, an irate parent (who may not have received all the facts from the student) may enter into debate with the teacher over the grade given to his offspring. In this case, a teacher need only say, "Let's look at the record," to convince the parent that a just grade was awarded.

*Be Sure Pupils Understand Test Directions.*   Some pupils do poor work at one time or another simply because they misunderstand what is to be done—especially in taking tests. Before permitting his pupils to begin a test, the teacher should explain any special directions or procedures appropriate to it. He should have his tests mimeographed or otherwise reproduced, and should include written directions. This has the advantage of permitting pupils to refer to the directions as often as they deem necessary.

*State Your Questions Clearly.*   The teacher should take great care in constructing test questions, being sure the terminology is appropriate to the pupils' level of understanding. Questions should relate to a single idea, problem, or project. The shot-gun approach, wherein the teacher calls for several answers within one question should be avoided because it confuses the pupils. (See problem 88.)

*Base Your Tests on Important Material That Has Been Taught Thoroughly.*   The teacher's purpose in giving a test is not to trip, trap, or befuddle the student, but rather to evaluate how well he has assimilated, and how well he is able to apply, the things the teacher regards as important for the pupil to know. It is unfair as well as purposeless to question the student on items that received passing mention in class, or which appeared in obscure footnotes. The fact that the teacher spent little or no class time on such items indicates that he himself regarded them as relatively unimportant, and he therefore should not include them on a test. As an exception to this, the teacher *would* be justified in including material not taught in class if he were testing on outside readings or anything assigned as extra-class work.

*Always be Alert While Pupils are Taking a Test.*   While administering a test the teacher should not occupy himself with other tasks at his desk, such as correcting papers or reading a book. He should be standing so that he can see all members of the class clearly, and he should walk quietly up and down the aisles occasionally to be sure that pupils are not using aids of various types to help them answer test questions. When the teacher stands in front of the room, it is amazingly simple for him to discern the slightest irregular movement on the part of a pupil, such as a slight turn of the head in the direction of a neighbor's paper. A common maneuver by some pupils who wish to cheat is to rest the forehead on the cupped hand, thus shielding the eyes from the teacher. If the teacher moves to the side of the room, he can usually determine whether the pupil's eyes are directed toward a neighbor's paper, or whether he has merely adopted a position of rest. Another type of pupil who bears observation is the one who looks up at the teacher frequently. Some pupils do this to see whether or not the teacher is attentive, or whether it is safe for them to try to copy from their neighbors. Other pupils, trying to supply information to their friends, hold their papers up in front of them, as if they were reading them. There are, of course, other familiar devices for cheating, such as writing information on the hand or arm, or on pieces of paper which are hidden on the student's person.

It is likely that most pupils do not attempt to cheat on tests, and they resent that some pupils are permitted to do so through the carelessness of the teacher. Their resentment is due to the fact that their grades were earned, whereas some few, dishonest pupils received comparable grades even though they did not study. Their resentment is understandable. (See problems 84, and 99.)

*Make and Use a Scoring Key.*   Before correcting a test, the teacher should set down the correct answers on a copy of the test. There are several advantages in doing this. The scoring key will save him a great deal of time in correcting the papers, especially if the test contains a large number of objective type items. In the case of an essay type test, the key will eliminate the danger of the teacher forgetting certain points, and it will make the correction more objective.

*Review Test Questions With Pupils.*   The teacher should correct and return the test papers as soon as possible. When he does return them to the class, he should explain the correct answer to each question. Such a procedure shows the pupils their errors, and contributes to their understanding of the material. It also reduces the number of questions from individual students who seek explanations as to why their answer was incorrect. An effective technique the teacher may use in going over a test is to call on students who gave good answers, asking them to read their answer to the rest of the class. This not only shows the rest of the pupils that a complete, correct answer was possible to a question, but also may serve as an incentive to some of the other members of the class to strive for such answers on future tests.

*As a Rule, Do Not Change a Grade.*   It is assumed that a teacher has arrived at a grade conscientiously, whether it is a grade on a test or a final grade. Some students, however, will approach the teacher in an effort to obtain more credit than the teacher gave them. In such cases, unless the pupil can point out a definite error on the part of the teacher, an explanation should be given the student as to why he did not receive more credit. Unless the teacher remains firm on the grade he gave, he leaves himself open to the reputation of being lenient in such matters, and he will be approached by an increasing number of pupils who will seek grade changes even though they do not deserve them. (See problem 83.)

*Do Not Allow Personal Feelings to Enter into a Grade.* There is the danger of a "halo effect" in grading. Whether the teacher likes or dislikes a student should not influence the grade he gives him; a grade should represent a level of achievement. The teacher who dislikes a pupil might be tempted to grade that pupil's paper more severely than he would the paper of a student he likes. This is inexcusable because the same standard should be applied to all. (See problems 82, 87, 90, and 100.)

*Keep Pupils Informed of Standing and Progress.* When a teacher returns a major test to the class, he should provide data which enable the individual to see how he stands in relation to the other members of the class. It takes the teacher only a few minutes to make up a general frequency distribution of the number of students who scored in particular categories. If, after returning the tests, the teacher writes the distribution of scores on the chalkboard, it helps each pupil to interpret his score. The following is an illustration of this simple procedure.

**Distribution of Grades Made on a Test**

| | |
|---|---|
| 90–100 | 3 |
| 80–89 | 7 |
| 70–79 | 15 |
| 60–69 | 2 |
| 50–59 | 1 |
| Total | 28 |

A distribution of this type immediately shows a pupil his relative position in scores made on the test. The distribution can be made even more discriptive and more helpful to the student by using intervals of five instead of ten.

A similar procedure might be used in keeping the pupils informed of their progress in class work, or on more frequent short tests. At the end of each week or two, the teacher can give each pupil a grade representing his average, and then place on the chalkboard a distribution of the pupils' averages, thus showing the individual his position in relation to the work being done by the others.

Knowledge of progress has been found to be an incentive to learning. If the pupils know where they stand as they go along, they are spurred to a greater effort than when they do not have this information. It is poor practice to keep the pupils uninformed or guessing about their progress.

*Give Pupils Benefit of the Doubt.*   In making up a final grade, if the teacher finds that a pupil is in a borderline category (say between a D and F, or between a C and C+ ), the pupil should be given the benefit of the doubt and should be awarded the higher grade. Evaluation techniques and tests are not so refined as to be infallible in measuring a pupil's progress. There is always a margin of error in measurement of achievement, especially when progress is measured by the tests constructed by a beginning teacher. Moreover, in the case of some pupils, indiscernible, subtle, intangible forces may have prevented a pupil from doing his best on a test, or may have slowed down his progress during a portion of the course. Consequently, if the beginning teacher is agonizing in doubt over a borderline case, he should resolve the doubt in favor of the pupil.

● ● ●

The illustrative problems of evaluation which follow are not, on the whole, serious problems. They are, however, representative of typical questions and problems experienced by the beginning teacher.

### PROBLEM 81: A STUDENT TAKES ADVANTAGE OF A "NO FAILURES" POLICY

I wish I could report success with Jimmy, but I can't. He is a sophomore in my biology class who is a lackluster student of average intelligence, and who is indifferent to school work. His main extra-curricular activity is attending dances, and his main interest is girls. He prides himself on his ability to enchant females who, incidentally, do not find him at all repulsive. Hence, every night is "date night" for Jimmy.

In the classroom, Jimmy has a reputation of being obnoxious and complacent. Since he desires attention constantly, he is continually annoying both the teachers and the conscientious students. Consequently, his mother has been notified several times of his unruly behavior.

As his biology teacher, my first impression of him was optimistic—he seemed cooperative and sincere. After about a week, however, he became haughty and obstreperous. I immediately had a talk with him about his conduct, and he promised to behave. In order to increase his interest in class, I gave him minor duties to perform, such as distributing paper, setting up equipment, operating the camera, etc. Unfortunately, none of this helped him do better work. He failed his first test miserably.

I had another talk with Jimmy to discuss his scholastic problems. He stated tersely that he hated biology and all other sciences. My attempts to explain to him the importance of sciences today made no impression at all. He bluntly stated that he would not study.

Consultation with Jimmy's other teachers did much to further enlighten the situation. Jimmy's father had guaranteed the boy a "good-paying job" as soon as he graduated. Naturally, therefore, Jimmy enrolled in the easiest curriculum, and he did the minimum amount of work. In addition, his father allowed Jimmy to use the car (a flamboyant convertible) any night he pleased. Jimmy's mother was similarly lenient and unconcerned about her son's social life. Jimmy eventually became a V.I.P. among many of his classmates.

In class, Jimmy's deportment continued to deteriorate. I again tried several ways to get him to be interested and active. I gave him simple questions to answer, then complimented him. When he passed a quiz, I was generous with praise. I gave him items to deliver to the office, and even let him help me with the class demonstration. All to no avail. He progressively became more and more fractious, so I isolated him. Even this did not help.

Again I had a talk with Jimmy about his conduct. This time I uncovered the key to the whole problem of his lack of application in class. We had talked for several minutes, when Jimmy finally culminated the discussion with this statement: "I flunked almost all of the tests Mr. _____ (my cooperating teacher) gave me the last few intervals, and he gave me C's. He doesn't flunk anybody, and you won't flunk me because he has it over you!" Jimmy was right—he didn't fail because Mr. _____ had it "over me."

Finally, after repeated warnings, I had to send Jimmy to the principal's office, an action that was inevitable because of his misconduct. Following a reprimand by the principal, Jimmy presented me with no disciplinary problems. Intellectually, however, he remained at a standstill. Yet, to his delight and my dismay, he continued to pass.

## Points for Discussion

- *How much authority should a student teacher have in determining a student's grade?*

- *What are the advantages and disadvantages of a "no failures" grading policy?*

## PROBLEM 82: PUPILS ACCUSE A STUDENT TEACHER OF PREJUDICE IN GRADING

I had been sailing along smoothly in my student teaching until I handed out the grades for the first marking period. The day after the students received their grades, there was an unusual atmosphere in the class—nothing that could be pinpointed, but an air of resentment throughout. Nobody seemed to care to do any work, or even to make an attempt to cooperate in the class work. I was just about to shrug it off as "just one of those days," when I found a clue to the reason for the trouble.

Just after the bell ended the class, I overheard one girl tell another that I was prejudiced. That comment hurt me, because above all things, I wanted to be fair with the students. I called the girl to my desk and asked her to explain her comment, but she kept evading the issue. I kept pressing, until she finally admitted what was bothering her. She and her girlfriend had identical averages, but she had received a B on her report card, while her friend got an A. The fact that she and her friend were intense rivals added to her resentment. They were attractive, popular, and both had very good grades. She felt that since they both had the same average in my class, I liked one better than the other.

The first thing I did was to check their averages and grades. My record book showed that I had given *both* girls a B. It occurred to me that one of the girls might have been lying to make the other jealous. I then checked the record cards. The cards showed that the girls had spoken the truth. One of them *did* recieve a grade of A.

I made one final check with my cooperating teacher, explaining the whole situation to him. He said he had forgotten to mention to me that he had changed one grade to an A because of the fine work the girl had done for him before I took over the class. He told me that I was free to announce in class that it was he who had changed the grade. When I took his advice and made the announcement, the problem seemed solved because since then there has been no evidence of resentment.

## Points for Discussion

- *Should the cooperating teacher have the right to change a grade given by the student teacher? Why?*

- *How can teachers guard against being prejudiced in awarding grades?*

### PROBLEM 83:  A STUDENT THINKS HER GRADE ON A TEST IS TOO LOW

During student teaching, I found that making up a good test was more difficult than I thought it would be. First I had to decide what kind of test items to use. To provide variety, I decided on true-false, completion, matching, and essay items. I eliminated multiple choice items because they take too long to make up. Then I had to go through the material several times, picking out material that would be appropriate for each type of item. Next, I found that I had to re-write many of the items to make them clearer. The final step was typing the test in proper format and reproducing it. The whole process took at least 2–3 hours.

Despite the fact that I was scrupulous in making up a test, I found that students make errors of interpretation, or do not read the questions carefully, with the result that they score lower than they should have. Sometimes when this happens, it may provoke a disagreement between the pupil and the teacher. I had a case of this kind on the very first major test I gave.

The test consisted of fifty objective items, and three essay type questions in which I asked that *explanations* be given. I expected that the test would keep the class occupied for the whole period, but I announced: "If you finish your test early, turn it in to me and start your next assignment."

To my surprise, one of the students in the class, Susan, brought her test paper up to my desk after thirty-five minutes. I thought she wanted to ask a question about the test, but, instead, she told me she had finished.

"Are you sure you answered the questions completely?" I whispered.

"Yes," she replied, and returned to her seat.

Only one other student finished the test early, just a few minutes before the fifty-minute period expired.

Curious to see how Susan did on the test, hers was one of the first I corrected. She did well on the objective items, but poorly on the essay question. Instead of giving explanations in the essay questions, she simply enumerated facts without elaborating on them. I therefore deducted five points from each of the three answers.

I returned the tests during the next class period. After class, Susan came to me and asked why I deducted points from her essay answers. I told her that she should have read the questions more carefully because they called for explanations. I asked her if she knew the difference between "explain" and "list."

"Yes," she replied. "When you explain you give reasons, when you list you don't."

"Do you understand now why I deducted points from your answers?"

She said she did, but her next comment showed that she had something else on her mind when she came to me about the test.

"I don't think that was the real reason you deducted points. You deducted them because you were mad at me for finishing my test so early!"

I assured her that I would never do such a thing, and that the thought never entered my mind.

"I don't believe you," she replied, and walked away.

Susan never acted quite the same toward me after that. I noticed that she finished early on the next test I gave, but she did not turn it in to me. She did not want to take the chance that I would "get mad" at her again; which, of course, I never did or would—not for that reason anyway.

## Points for Discussion

- *What should the student teacher have done prior to the test to minimize misinterpretation of questions?*

- *What kinds of test items will you use in your tests? Why?*

- *What are the advantages and disadvantages of essay type test questions?*

### PROBLEM 84: A STUDENT CLAIMS HE IS CHECKING HIS ANSWERS, NOT CHEATING

I had a rather peculiar situation in one of the classes I was teaching. When I gave my first major test, I noticed that Donald was staring intently at his neighbor's paper. My first thought, of course, was that he was cheating in order to make a satisfactory grade. Not wanting to draw attention to Donald, I simply issued a general warning: "Keep your eyes on your own paper." Donald heeded the warning.

Curious about Donald's ability level, I checked his records. I found that he had an I.Q. of 115, and that he was at least a B student in all of his courses. In view of this, I saw no reason why he should have to copy to pass a test. A thought that crossed my mind was that his good marks were the result of expert cheating. Another possibility was that he was just lazy, and depended on his neighbors to pass tests. I was determined to find the answer.

The next time I gave a test I separated the students, and at the same time maneuvered Donald into a seat close to my desk. The separation prevented Donald from cheating. To my surprise, he scored the fourth highest grade in the room. His high score shattered my theories about him being lazy, or that his high grades were due to copying.

At this point, I decided to have a talk with Donald. I told him that I had seen him looking at his neighbor's paper repeatedly during the first test. He responded by admitting that he had looked at the other student's paper, but he also stated that he wasn't cheating. He contended that he had all his answers already written, and that he was only checking his answers because he wanted a perfect paper. I told Donald that although he didn't have the intention of copying every answer from his fellow student, his method of checking his paper was considered cheating. I further told him that he was capable of attaining an above-average grade without checking his answers with those of this neighbor. I cited the last test, on which he received the fourth highest grade even though he was separated from the other students. Finally, I told him that checking his answers that way had become a habit with him, and unless he broke the habit he might get into serious trouble in the future. He said he would try to break the habit.

To help him break the habit, I separated him from the rest of the class during the next two tests. His scores on both tests were in the upper fifth of the class. Then, on the next test, I used a normal seating arrangement. Donald glanced at his neighbor's paper only once. After class, he told me that he was trying to break the habit, but he felt a little insecure about not being able to check his answers. I told him that this feeling of insecurity would decrease each time he passed a test without looking at a neighbor's paper.

### Points for Discussion

- *How would you handle a student who told you he was simply checking his answers with those of a neighbor?*

- *Discuss the types of penalties that may be imposed on a student who has been caught cheating.*

### PROBLEM 85: DAILY QUIZZES ARE FOUND TO IMPROVE WORK

Before I started to teach my class in algebra, I talked to my cooperating teacher about introducing my own method of teaching. His method consisted of giving very long homework assignments, with oral questioning on the assignments of the previous day, and an hour-long test at the end of each chapter. I told him I would like, instead, to try the following procedures: short homework assignments to be done in class during the last portion of the period, the preceding day's homework to be checked in class, and any problems causing difficulty to be explained on the chalkboard; and, after all the problems had been checked and explained, a short quiz involving two or three problems, to be given daily. My cooperating teacher gave me permission to put this plan into effect.

I explained the new procedures to the class. They were very much in favor of the shorter homework assignments, but raised many questions on the daily quizzes. I told them the purpose of these quizzes would be to show me how well they were grasping the material as we went along, so that I would know whether or not it was necessary for me to spend more time on the material we were studying.

Because we were in the middle of a chapter when I started to teach, I did not put the new plan into effect for over a week, and when I tested the pupils on that chapter, the results were very poor. Not a pupil received 100 percent, and the average grade was 62 percent.

When we began the next chapter, I put the new plan of study into effect. The daily quizzes I gave usually consisted of two or three problems, one easy and the others more difficult, to provide for individual differences. The results I obtained were as follows:

1. The pupils began to do their own homework, since they realized that copying homework did not prepare them for the daily quizzes.

2. The first daily quiz showed three students who did not get a single problem correct, and only four who got both problems correct.

3. The results on the tests improved steadily, so that on the fourth daily quiz only five pupils out of twenty-seven failed to get all the problems correct, and those five had two of the three problems right.

4. When I gave them the full-hour test on the chapter, two students received 100 percent, one pupil was below 60 percent, and the class average was 84 percent.

I cannot make any general conclusions on the daily quiz method because I used it for only a relatively short period of time. Before I left, however, I asked the students for an anonymous, written criticism of the method, and they unanimously stated that they liked the idea of small assignments. Seventeen of them liked the daily quiz because it gave them an indication of how well they were absorbing the material. As I said, these results are inconclusive, but I do know that I shall continue the method when I obtain my first assignment as a teacher.

## Points for Discussion

- *What is the purpose of homework?*
- *Should pupils be permitted to do their homework in class?*
- *State the advantages and disadvantages of giving daily quizzes.*

## PROBLEM 86: THE STUDENT TEACHER EVOLVES A GRADING SYSTEM

One of my greatest problems during student teaching centered around the testing and grading of my students. I had heard and read arguments about the relative merits of essay and objective tests, but I had not arrived at any definite conclusions of my own.

Since I liked the idea of essay questions which gave the pupils a chance to express themselves, the first test I gave was of that type. The results were a sharp reminder to me that I was teaching high school, not college, students. I made the mistake of asking questions that were highly abstract. I further discovered that high school pupils do very little reading, and as a whole, they seemed to study for mastery of facts, giving little attention to evaluation and interpretation. I therefore changed my tests to include a large number of objective items, making use of the following types: true-false, multiple choice, matching, completion, and identification. The results of tests of that type were much better than they had been on the essay questions, thus, my testing problem was solved.

The next question that bothered me was: "What shall I consider when making up their grades?" I felt that a grade should not be based on test results alone, but I wasn't sure what else should be included. After much mental wrestling with the problem, I devised the following chart, which I used as my chief guide in making up grades:

| | |
|---|---|
| Major tests | 30% |
| Minor tests | 20% |
| Oral report | 10% |
| Homework | 10% |
| Recitation | 20% |
| Attitude | 10% |

With this chart to guide me, I felt that I would be able to give a just grade to every student because it took into consideration all aspects of his work. Also this chart permitted me to justify any grade I gave. Several students questioned me about the grade I gave them, but every one of them was satisfied after I had explained the system to him and showed him what he had earned in each category. The system worked well, and I intend to use it in the future.

### Points for Discussion

• *This student teacher adjusted his tests to the idea that his students were studying for facts instead of ideas. What should he have done?*

• *Evaluate the grading chart described in this problem.*

• *What elements should go into making up a final grade? Why?*

### PROBLEM 87: A STUDENT IS RESENTFUL BECAUSE HIS GRADE WAS LOWERED

Frank was a student in my literature class who seemed to hate authority. My cooperating teacher told me that she was actually a little afraid of him because of his violent outbursts of temper in the class, and because he towered over her in size.

The day I took over teaching the class, one of Frank's best friends was sporting a black eye as a result of a friendly argument they had had. I picked up this bit of information from some of the students in the hall. I also learned that all of Frank's classmates respected him because of his ability to handle himself physically.

I soon discovered that Frank was also a mentally superior boy, intelligent in reading, reasoning, and in expression. I was therefore amazed to see that his mark in the course was a D. When I asked my cooperating teacher the reason, she replied that Frank's attitude in class lowered his grade.

One day I stopped Frank in the hall and started a discussion on football. I knew he was keenly interested in sports because all of his oral reports were on that subject. During the course of our conversation, I asked him why he lacked interest in school work. He unhesitatingly said that he disliked my cooperating teacher and her policies. His chief objection was that he had a B average for the month, but because he had some sort of argument with her, she had lowered his mark to a D. Also he pointed out that there were many members of the class who deserved better grades but did not receive them because of the school's policy of issuing only a limited number of A's. He said all the students resented this policy.

I promised Frank that if he would work, he would get whatever grade he earned, in spite of school policy. I gave him enough work in and outside of class to keep him busy and out of trouble. He took it all in stride, doing everything I asked of him. When the next grading period came along, I talked to my cooperating teacher about his grade. She said she was impressed with his change of attitude, and agreed to raise his grade to a B.

Ever since Frank received his just grade, his conduct has been ideal in class. At the present time, my cooperating teacher considers him to be a shining light in her coming production of *Macbeth*. Even his classmates seem pleased with his change because peace now reigns in the classroom.

## Points for Discussion

- *Do you think the teacher was justified in lowering Frank's grade? Why?*

- *What do you think of the student teacher's promise to do something "in spite of school policy"?*

- *State advantages and disadvantages for a grading system that is based on the "normal curve."*

### PROBLEM 88: A BRIGHT PUPIL TEACHES THE STUDENT TEACHER TO BE CAREFUL IN MAKING UP TEST ITEMS

Mark was a gifted student in my freshman Spanish class. It was a pleasure to have him as a student, and he taught me a lesson I will never forget.

Mark was the kind of student every teacher dreams about. He was intelligent, enthusiastic, and industrious. Whenever I asked a question, Mark was always the first person to raise his hand. After I discovered his capability, I challenged him with the more difficult questions and assignments. For example, if I sent students to the chalkboard for drill exercises, I would save the most difficult exercise for Mark. Nine times out of ten he would write the correct answer.

I discovered how really clever and intelligent Mark was after I gave my first test. The test was on grammar. However, we had also taken up the story of Ponce de Leon in class. Midway through the test, I suddenly decided to give the students a bonus question on the story, so I wrote the following question in Spanish on the chalkboard: "Who discovered the fountain of youth?" As I wrote the question I wasn't thinking of how I worded it. All I wanted was the answer, "Ponce de Leon."

When I got to correcting the papers, I noticed that Mark's answer to the bonus question was, "No one." And he was right! No one discovered the fountain of youth, because there is none. This would have been a good trick question if I had thought of it and wanted to trick the students, but it took a clever student like Mark to show me the error that I and the rest of the students did not see. All of the other students responded with my expected answer of "Ponce de Leon."

I could go on endlessly extolling Mark's virtues. He caused no disciplinary problems—I never heard a peep out of him except when he volunteered or was called upon to recite. When he did recite, there was no hesitation, and there was always the correct answer. Mark was mainly interested in the sciences, and there is no doubt in my mind that he has what it takes "upstairs." I think a bright future is in store for this young man.

Although I shall remember Mark mainly as an exemplary student, I shall also remember the lesson he taught me on that bonus test question I gave. From that point on, I wrote and rewrote my test questions until there was no possibility of misunderstanding or misinterpreting the items.

## Points for Discussion

- *What are the characteristics of a good test question?*

- *Many students feel that teachers ask "tricky"questions. What is a "tricky" question?*

## PROBLEM 89:  THE STUDENT TEACHER BETS
##                  A FAILING PUPIL THAT HE CAN PASS

Ted was a student in my ninth-grade Civics class. A borderline student, he was troublesome in the classroom. He seized every opportunity to make a wise or humorous remark. He was constantly turning around to talk to his neighbor, thus disturbing our class work. When I called on him, he would move from side to side in his seat, and make no attempt to answer. I had to keep reminding him to stand up when I called on him. As far as study was concerned, he showed no signs of exerting himself in that direction, but he always managed to make a bare seventy on the hour-long tests I gave. Whenever I gave a test on the day's assignment, however, he always failed. I tried to make things easier for him by asking him to repeat a correct answer given by another pupil. This device did not help, and my patience was becoming threadbare.

One day while I was teaching class, Ted constantly disturbed the procedure by turning around and talking. I stopped class several times and stared at him. He only looked at me and smiled. I changed his seat to a front one, thinking it might help to quiet him, but he still insisted on turning around and entertaining a few of the students. I had only one resort left; I told Ted to see me after class.

When class was dismissed, Ted presented himself at my desk. I told him that I had had enough of his foolishness in class. He immediately went on the defensive and told me he "wasn't doin' nuthin'." "That's just the trouble," I said, "you aren't doin' anything." I told him that if he didn't change his tactics in class, I would have no alternative other than to fail him. "Why should I study?" Ted replied. "I failed almost all my subjects last interval. Besides, you just told me I'm going to fail, so why should I study?"

When Ted walked out of the room, I realized I had handled him in the wrong manner. When I went home that night, I averaged his marks. He had an average of seventy-two for the second interval.

The next day, Ted was very quiet in class. After I got the class studying an assignment, I went to Ted's seat and asked him to step out into the hall. I told him I had averaged his marks, and that his average was seventy-two. "I'm going to make a bet with you," I said. "You told me you couldn't pass this course. I'm going to prove to you that you *can* pass. You prepare your lesson everyday, and I will ask you one question each day. This will build up your average. I'm going to show you, Ted, that you can pass yourself. It's entirely up to you." He agreed, we sealed the bet with a handshake, and we went back into the classroom.

From the results to date, it is evident that Ted kept his end of the agreement. He had his work prepared everyday, and his attitude in class changed completely. In fact, he helped me keep the other students in check by telling them to keep quiet. I am happy to report that Ted passed the second interval with an average of eighty-five, and that in his last hour-long exam he had one of the highest grades in class. He appears to be very proud, because he proved to himself that he was able to do better than just passing work.

Points for Discussion
_____

- _Discuss the statement: "You can pass yourself."_

- _What should the student teacher have done sooner than he did? Why?_

**PROBLEM 90: A STUDENT THINKS HIS**
**TEACHERS ARE UNFAIR IN GRADING HIM**
_____

While I was observing my cooperating teacher, I noticed that a few students showed little interest in their work, especially Tim. He acted as if he didn't have a care in the world, and spent most of his time in class playing with his pencil. Just by observing him, one could tell that he was floating away on his imagination.

Before I started to teach the class, I had a talk with my cooperating teacher about Tim. She told me he was a junior, repeating the biology course I was to teach. She also told me Tim had the ability to do above average work if he applied himself. I then went to see the school counselor who told me that the results of standardized tests verified that Tim had above average ability. The counselor told me that Tim came from a well-to-do family, and that his father was a college graduate. His family background, then, was not responsible for his poor attitude in school.

When I started teaching, there were two weeks left in the marking period. Up to that point, his grades constituted a failure for the period. For the first few days, Tim did absolutely no work for me. I had a few private talks with him which didn't accomplish anything. Tim just didn't want to be bothered. This went on for the remaining two weeks of the marking period, and I was just about ready to give up on him.

When the marking period came to an end, I had another talk with Tim. I told him he had failing marks for the period. I pointed out that because of his low marks, his poor attitude, and his lack of participation, there was no possibility that he could get a passing mark for the period. It was during this discussion that I hit paydirt in discovering the reason why Tim did not work. He said: "Even if I did work, I would fail anyway. The teachers don't grade me on what I do—they grade me on what they think of me." He went on to say that the teachers were against him and wanted to fail him. I told him this was untrue; teachers are there to help students, but they needed the cooperation of students to do so. I told him I also wanted to help him, and if he did his work, I would give him the mark he earned. Tim looked at me as if he was trying to analyze my sincerity. Then, apparently satisfied, he said he would "give it a try."

Now that Tim knew I was interested in him, his attitude in class improved greatly. As the days passed, we built up a friendly relationship. He began to apply himself and participate in discussions. His assignments were turned in regularly, and his biology drawings were perfect. Of three short quizzes I gave, he received a perfect mark in two. Also, on two full-period tests, he averaged 88. At the end of the marking period I averaged his marks. I found he had an average of 91, which was a good strong B.

When I told Tim his average, he asked me if he would receive the B, or if I would drop his grade "like the other teachers did." I reminded him of our agreement that he would get the grade he earned, and that he had earned the B. He seemed very pleased with his accomplishment, and thanked me for helping him.

Without a doubt, this was my greatest achievement in student teaching—getting a student to work hard enough to change from an F to a B in one marking period. My greatest disappointment was to learn that some teachers let their personal feelings influence their evaluation of a student's achievement. I think that practice is unfair, and it certainly doesn't stimulate a student to do better work.

### Points for Discussion

- *Evaluate the student teacher's last statment.*

- *Evaluate the statement: "A pupil's conduct automatically affects his achievement."*

### PROBLEM 91: THE STUDENT TEACHER GIVES HELP TO A PUPIL DURING A TEST

A problem I experienced concerned a boy in my class who was a chronic trouble-maker and who consistently failed in his school work. I received information to this effect from my cooperating teacher before I started to teach the class.

Only a few class periods went by before I realized my problem child was above average in intelligence. During those first classes I also learned that he seemed to have a deep sense of inferiority because he had known only failure in his school work. His misbehavior was very likely a reaction to the tensions that had built up within him because of his failures.

Since he had above average intelligence, and therefore, should have been doing good work, I tried to think of some way of getting him to experience success. I felt that once he had started to taste success, he would work for additional helpings of it.

The problem was solved after I decided to help him on the first few tests I gave the class. As I walked around the room during the test, I stopped at his seat and gave him a few helpful hints, believing that since he had tasted nothing but defeat, passing a few tests would encourage him and instill the confidence which he so greatly lacked. This experiment seemed to solve the problem. After I stopped giving him help, he continued to pass the tests, and received an average grade for the subject.

## Points for Discussion

- *What do you think of giving a student help during a test?*

- *What might be the reaction of the other students who were taking the test?*

- *What other measures might have been taken to provide the pupil with success experiences?*

## PROBLEM 92: THE STUDENT TEACHER PREFERS ESSAY QUESTIONS

The greatest problem I met, and one still unsolved, concerns giving tests which are fair to all, but which, at the same time, indicate the true ability of the students. In my opinion, tests should not be the only criterion for marks.

The first test I gave was of the true-false type, and I permitted the students to correct their own papers. After rechecking the papers myself, I came to the conclusion that some students are not above correcting papers to their own advantage.

For my next test, I used a variety of items, including true-false, matching, and fill-in questions. Even though I corrected the papers, the results were not satisfying to me. Students who showed very little interest, and even less ability, came up with high grades. In spite of close vigilance on my part, the grapevine system was apparently operating efficiently.

On another occasion, I isolated several of the suspected pupils, but their marks still remained high. I therefore concluded that objective type tests were conducive to guessing, and that my pupils were good guessers.

The last test I gave was of the essay type, with questions which required evaluation on the part of the pupils. The results were most gratifying, because those pupils who were inattentive in class showed the poorest results. I therefore feel that the essay type test is best for evaluating a student's knowledge, and that this type of test, together with oral questioning in class, should give the most satisfactory results.

### Points for Discussion

- *What are the advantages and disadvantages of permitting pupils to correct their own papers?*

- *State the advantages and disadvantages of objective type tests.*

### PROBLEM 93: A PUPIL GRADED LOW IN EFFORT REFUSES TO DO ANY WORK

I first noticed Carl at the time I was making an assignment in my History class. As I explained the assignment, his face went through some of the most amazing contortions ever witnessed by man. His facial expressions alternately portrayed agony, disgust, and despair. Each day as the assignment was made, he would act as if it were a personal punishment for him. I ignored these antics because no matter how much he complained or made faces, he was always prepared.

At the end of the first marking period, I gave Carl a C, but wrote on his report card that his effort was only fair. The day after the cards were distributed, he came up to my desk and bluntly told me, "If you say I don't try, then I won't." He turned and walked back to his seat before I could say anything.

I had a quiz scheduled for that day, and gave it as usual. When I collected the papers, I noticed that Carl's paper had only one printed statement on it: "I don't try, so I won't try."

When I asked Carl about his statement, he shouted: "Why should I do any work when I don't get credit for it?"

I directed him to leave the room. "Go to the principal, and tell him that you do not want to do any work."

After class I went to see the principal. He told me that Carl was one of the problems that the school had learned to live with. Carl and his whole family, it seems, were rebellious against authority and the suggestions of others. Homework was considered by Carl as a means of harassment.

The next day, I asked Carl to remain after class. Our conversation went something like this:

"All right, Carl, why did you act as you did yesterday?"

"Because you said I wasn't trying, and I was."

"What grade did you get?" I asked.

"I got a C," he replied disdainfully.

"Is that the best you can do?"

"No, I can do at least B work."

"Why don't you then?"

"I will."

"How?" I asked.

"I'll work harder."

"And how will you do that?" I persisted.

"By trying harder, I suppose," he replied uncomfortably.

After his own admission that he was not trying hard enough, I tried to help Carl get over his belligerent attitude by giving him special attention in class. I went over his papers with him carefully. I gave him special little jobs around the classroom. I tried to give him recognition when I was explaining material, by asking him, "Is that right, Carl?" He would usually smile, and nod his head in approval.

I would like to be able to report that he became a good student, and that he got over his resentful attitude, but such was not the case. He still makes faces when assignments are given out, and he is still not trying as hard as he should. Worst of all, since I started treating him as someone special, he expects attention all the time and becomes extremely upset if he does not get it. When his attention wanders, I make a comment such as, "You're not here, are you, Carl?" The class laughs, and Carl smiles. So I have the feeling that Carl is at least learning to live with the world, and that soon his attitude and work will improve.

## Points for Discussion

- *How would you explain to a pupil the factors that entered into a grade you gave him for "effort"?*

- *In giving special attention to a student, what should the teacher keep in mind regarding the needs of the class?*

## PROBLEM 94: A PUPIL TRIES TO TAKE ADVANTAGE OF A POLICY OF AUTOMATIC PROMOTION

John was transferred to my English class from another. The reason, as I found out, was that since he could not get along with the other teacher, he had been sent to the principal's office so frequently that he seemed like one of the staff.

For the first few days I had no trouble with him, but then I noticed that he was reading magazines instead of studying. When I told him to put the magazines away, he replied that he found them more interesting than English. I pointed out to him that he was free to read as many magazines as he liked outside of school, but that while he was in my class I expected him to study English. He reluctantly put his magazines away.

The next week he became noisy. When he would not do his work and continually bothered his neighbors, I told him to see me after class. When we were alone, I told him that although I was disappointed in his conduct, I would always be willing to meet him halfway if he did his work. I asked him to give it a try.

"Why should I work?" he replied. "I always get a 70 on my report card anyway."

I told him that in my class he would get only what he earned. The following week he made a 60 on a test I gave. Since it was just about time for an interval grade, I gave John a 68 on his report card. Indignant, he came to see me about his grade. I explained the reasons for it, and once again told him that he would not get a passing mark unless he earned it.

John changed quite a bit after that. He worked and he behaved himself. Occasionally I would call him aside after class and compliment him on a good piece of work he had done. His next mark was 88. When he received his report card, he came up to thank me. I told him there was no reason to thank me, inasmuch as he had earned the grade. From that point on, he was no longer a problem.

### Points for Discussion

- *Evaluate tests and grades as incentives to learning.*

### PROBLEM 95: THE STUDENT TEACHER DECIDES THAT SPELLING AND GRAMMAR SHOULD NOT ENTER INTO A PUPIL'S MARK

Giving a pupil an interval grade has occasionally proved to be a complex task for me. There is no problem in grading the student who continuously does excellent daily work, whose homework is always turned in, and who has done good work on test papers. A serious question arises, however, when a student is excellent in class, but has difficulty with written expression and grammar on tests. For example, one of my students of above average intelligence who does superior class work made ten errors in spelling and grammar on a test I gave, but all his answers were correct. I gave him a B instead of an A.

Whether or not I was justified in lowering his grade bothered me, and I asked several teachers in the school their opinion on the matter. Their answers developed along two lines. One group of teachers said that an A student is one who is excellent in every respect, including spelling and English grammar, and who has an above average grasp of the subject matter. This group agreed that I was justified in lowering the mark to a B. The other group contended that if a student does A work in subject matter, his grade should not be dropped to a B because of his weakness in spelling and grammar. This group held that spelling and grammar should be graded only in spelling and grammar classes, and that, therefore, I was not justified in lowering the grade of the student in question.

I thought and thought about the problem, and finally decided that lowering of a student's grade does nothing to improve his facility of expression if he does not have it in the first place. On the other hand, giving him the higher grade may serve as an incentive for him to continue to do good work. Although this is what I concluded, I am by no means sure that I am right.

## Points for Discussion

- *What other reasons might be given for making spelling and grammar errors on a test?*

- *How do educators feel about deducting credit for spelling and grammar errors?*

## PROBLEM 96:  TEXTBOOK QUESTIONS CONFUSE A SLOW PUPIL

Dora was a sixteen-year-old, ninth grade student, who was doing poor work in a class of slow students. Going to and from school alone, she did not even enjoy the companionship of other girls. Her appearance and dress were average, although she made no attempt to conform to the styles adopted by the other girls.

Dora attracted my attention the first time I called on her, for she would not reply to the questions I asked her. Later questioning produced at least the verbal response of "I don't know," but nothing more. Each time I called on her she would turn her head aside, with a half-smiling, half-puzzled look. The few times that I pulled out an answer from her she would look around to see if anyone was laughing at her.

Clearly, she had personality problems, and I spoke to my cooperating teacher about her. He told me that she had regular appointments with the guidance department in an effort to improve her social and emotional adjustment. Feeling that I could add nothing to what was being done in that direction, I turned to another phase of Dora's problems.

I noticed that she had been doing very poor work on the major tests that had been given in class. The tests used were ones that appeared in the textbook, each test consisting of fifty objective type questions. Her marks on the past four tests had been 22, 30, 34, and 50. One day I kept Dora after class to go over some of the test items in the textbook with her. I discovered that although she had a passable knowledge of the subject matter, she was confused by the terminology of the test questions. When I explained the questions, she generally could give acceptable answers. This insight led me to the conclusion that the low marks of Dora and some of the other pupils were not entirely due to the fact that they were slow pupils, but at least partly due to the type of test they were given.

### Points for Discussion

- *Describe the measures you would take next in this case.*

### PROBLEM 97: GRADING IS BASED ON A PUPIL'S I.Q. RATHER THAN ON ACHIEVEMENT

The thing that bothered me most during my student teaching was how to grade a slow pupil who is in a heterogeneous class. In one of my classes I had a girl with an I.Q. of 74, who worked harder than anybody else in the class, but always received a failing mark.

I talked the problem over with my cooperating teacher. She told me that she too felt sorry for the girl, but that it would be unjust to the pupil, to the other pupils, and to the school to give the girl a passing mark if she did not meet the standards for one. It would be unfair to the pupil to have her think she was meeting standards when she was not; it would be unfair to the other pupils if the teacher raised the mark of one, and not the others; and, finally the reputation of the school would suffer if students were given passing marks for poor work.

I still was not satisfied. After giving several tests, I found that my slow pupil never made higher than a 60. However, I reasoned that 60 represented the highest mark she could possibly make with her limited capacity for learning; in other words, she was working to full capacity. Since she was doing as well as she could, I felt she deserved the passing mark of 70 more than a pupil with an I.Q. of 120 deserved a mark of 80, because the latter was *not* working to his capacity. I am not sure that I did the right thing, but I gave her a 70 for every marking period while I was at the school.

### Discussion

- *Evaluate the arguments used by the student teacher and the cooperating teacher.*

### PROBLEM 98:  THE STUDENT TEACHER EXPERIMENTS WITH TESTS AND GRADING

Among the problems facing the new teacher is that of testing procedures. There are many kinds of standardized tests that can be used, but they are not appropriate for use by a beginning teacher who faces a heterogeneous group.

During the course of my student teaching I used several types of tests. At first I used the unit type of objective test that accompanied the textbook, but this I found unsatisfactory for two reasons. The tests were too difficult for my particular age group, with the result that half the class received failing grades. Also, I was informed that an answer sheet had circulated among the members of a small clique—a contention which was supported by the fact that about a quarter of the students scored above 90 percent even though they were doing only average class work.

I next tried using oral quizzes and a weekly test of my own. I discarded these because the oral quizzes were too time-consuming, and the weekly tests did not cover enough material.

From there I went to the essay type test, but found the results unsatisfactory. The students were not familiar with this type of test, and did not know what was expected of them. Although the results included a few good papers, the majority of them were almost worthless.

Since I found so many weaknesses in testing, I decided to include as many other things as possible in making up a grade for a student. I gave weight to things such as attendance, class participation, written work, conduct, outside projects, reading proficiency, and oral questioning. These, along with test results, gave a rounded picture of the student's progress in learning.

### Discussion

• *Evaluate the student teacher's grading system.*

### PROBLEM 99: A STUDENT IS CAUGHT CHEATING ON A TEST

Cheating, as any teacher knows, is likely to take place from time to time. The question I wish to raise is whether it should be dealt with harshly or sympathetically.

My first case of cheating occurred during the first test I gave my class. I had enough space to seat the students in every other seat, which I did in order to minimize the opportunity for cheating. While I was standing at the back of the room, I noticed that Peter, a pupil seated in the row next to the windows, was continually looking at his hand. I walked over to him and told him to show me what he was hiding. When he showed me his hand, I found that he had written all over it some possible answers to test questions. Becoming angry, I told him to throw his paper into the wastebasket and wash his hands. With the eyes of his classmates upon him, he was deeply ashamed and humiliated.

The following day, Peter came up to me after the class period was over to say he was sorry he had cheated. He begged to be permitted to take the test over, promising that he would never cheat again. He said: "My father will murder me if he finds out. Please! If you do this for me, I'll be the best pupil you ever had."

### Discussion

• *Describe what you would do next in this case.*

### PROBLEM 100: THE COOPERATING TEACHER INSISTS ON A LOWER GRADE FOR A BELOW AVERAGE PUPIL

I was told that Mike, a pupil in my seventh grade grammar class, was well below average in intelligence. After observing him a few days I could see that he was lagging behind the class, and that he could scarcely read. What was I to do with him—ignore him, as I was told to do? I decided I would at least try to help him.

Mike was fifteen years old, and went with the "cool" crowd. He had frequently-combed long hair and dressed in unorthodox fashion. Though his manners were crude, he certainly was not the trouble-maker I was told he would be.

When I first noticed Mike, his whole appearance repulsed me. His actions were crude, and he just sat sprawled in his seat, not even listening to what I was saying. When I tried reprimanding him, he ignored me.

My relationships with the other pupils improved as I went along. As I helped other pupils, Mike slowly started to accept me, and even began to volunteer comments and answers. I then started asking him questions I knew he could answer. This device seemed to have the effect of showing his classmates that he was not as stupid as they had thought. His manners also began to show improvement.

Time came for the first marking period. Since Mike had been trying, and since he was passing his tests, I gave him a C. The coop-erating teacher, however, thinking that this was too great a jump in his grade, changed it to a D. Mike had been expecting the C I prom-ised him, but I told him that in order to get it, he would have to do as well for the cooperating teacher as he had been doing for me. He agreed to try.

Mike continued to do passable work, and his conduct improved all the time. Even the principal, who had observed several of my classes, commented on his improvement. At the next grading inter-val, I again gave him a C, but once again my cooperating teacher dropped it to a D, saying that although he was doing passing work, it still could not be considered of C caliber.

## Discussion

- *How would you handle this impasse on Mike's grade?*

**SELECTED READINGS**

Adams, Georgia Sachs. *Measurement and Evaluation.* New York: Holt, Rine-hart, and Winston, 1964, chapter 10.

Bloom, Benjamin S., Hastings, J. Thomas, and Madaus, George F. *Handbook on Formative and Summative Evaluation of Student Learning.* New York: McGraw-Hill Book Company, 1971, part 2.

Ebel, Robert L. *Measuring Educational Achievement.* Englewood Cliffs, New Jersey: Prentice-Hall, Inc., 1965.

Gronlund, Norman E. *Measurement and Evaluation in Teaching.* New York: The Macmillan Company, 1971, parts II, and V.

Howard, Alvin W., and Stoumbis, George C. *The Junior High and Middle School: Issues and Practices.* Scranton, Pennsylvania: Intext Educational Publishers, 1970, chapter 15.

Lien, Arnold J. *Measurement and Evaluation in Learning.* Dubuque, Iowa: Wm. C. Brown Company, 1971, chapters 5, 9, and 10.

Nunnally, Jum C. *Educational Measurement and Evaluation.* New York: McGraw-Hill Book Company, 1972, part II.

Stanley, Julian C., and Hopkins, Kenneth D. *Educational and Psychological Measurement and Evaluation.* Englewood Cliffs, New Jersey: Prentice-Hall, Inc., 1972, chapters 9, 10, and 13.

TenBrink, Terry D. *Evaluation, A Practical Guide for Teachers.* New York: McGraw-Hill Book Company, 1974, chapters 2 and 13.

# 7

# Problems of Adjustment to School Personnel

In his relationships with personnel of the cooperating school, the student teacher is in a hybrid category. The relationship is neither that of teacher-teacher nor teacher-pupil, but rather somewhere between the two, and something of both. The student teacher is on a higher plane than that of a pupil, but on a lower plane than that of the personnel with whom he will be associating because he has not yet achieved their professional status. It is important that he remember this fact in his dealings with the personnel of the cooperating school to which he has been assigned. Although he will usually be treated as a professional associate, at the same time he will be expected to remember that he is subject to the authority and decisions of the school administrators and cooperating teachers.

In making the transition from college student to student teacher, there are courtesies, policies, and procedures to be observed by the student teacher. If these are observed carefully, his stay in the cooperating school will be a pleasurable and profitable experience. If they are not observed, college and cooperating school supervisors may decide that he lacks desirable professional qualifications, and withdraw him from the student teaching program.

After meeting the cooperating school administrator who is in charge of student teachers, the student teacher is assigned to his cooperating teacher. The cooperating teacher is a person of demonstrated superior teaching ability who, through precept and example, can make significant contributions to the professional development of the beginning teacher. The student teacher should remember that even though he is permitted to act in place of the cooperating teacher, and to exercise more and more authority in the classroom as he progresses in student teaching, the cooperating teacher still bears the responsibility for the proper instruction of his class. Since this is so, he can insist that the student teacher stay within the guidelines and procedures set by him for the instruction of the class. The cooperating teacher will insist on thorough preparation for each class, will require the student teacher to submit written lesson plans which will be evaluated before the lesson is taught, and will make suggestions for changes in these plans whenever they are appropriate.

In all his actions and comments, the cooperating teacher is motivated by his desire to help, not criticize. He is interested in helping the student grow into a teacher who will be a credit to the profession. Invariably, if the student teacher cooperates, the cooperating teacher will be patient and understanding because he recalls that *he* needed and received help when he was a student teacher. He also recognizes it will take the student teacher some time to adjust his thinking to the other side of the desk.

The student teacher is expected to reciprocate by being conscientious and thoroughly prepared everyday. Since he is engaged in fashioning the most precious thing on earth—human beings—nothing but his best is good enough. He must remember he is taking the place of a thoroughly experienced teacher; therefore, he must wor'. very hard if he is to approximate the results achieved by him. The student teacher should keep in mind that his pupils are depending on him, and should he neglect his duty, the training they should have received from him might be lost to them forever.

In addition to maintaining good relationships with the cooperating teacher, it is obvious that the student teacher should be able to get along with his pupils. If he does not, there will be a block in the learning process. It is well known that pupils work harder and more willingly for a teacher they like than for one they dislike. If implemented, many of the suggestions made in previous chapters on maintaining discipline, motivating pupils, dealing with emotional problems and individual differences, and evaluating student progress should result in good relationships between the student teacher and cooperating school personnel. Though they need not be repeated here, it is possible to focus on a few basic suggestions within the present context.

## SUGGESTIONS FOR DEVELOPING GOOD RELATIONSHIPS

*Be Neat.*   A teacher who is habitually neat makes a favorable impression on the supervisors and teachers in the school, as well as on his pupils. Neatness begins with the person of the teacher. Clothing should be clean, pressed, and if possible, should reflect current styles. Female student teachers have the special problem of toning down their attire to the point where it will not attract more attention than the learning task at hand. Teachers who are tastefully dressed not only serve as an example to other teachers who might have become careless in the matter, but they may influence many of the pupils to dress more appropriately. It is an intangible influence which the teacher has no way of measuring, except as he notices obvious changes in the appearance of some of his pupils. The teacher can be sure, however, that if his appearance is untidy, he will be censured, even by the untidiest of his pupils.

Neatness also extends to the appearance of the classroom. The teacher should make an effort to keep his classroom tidy at all times. Scraps of paper should be picked up by him and the pupils. Their desks and the teacher's desk should be kept neat. Displays should be arranged attractively. The bulletin board should be current and uncluttered. The chalkboard should be erased when not in use. In other words, a general picture of cleanliness and order should meet the eye when one enters the classroom. The teacher should insist that the pupils leave the classroom or laboratory in the same condition as they found it. Actually, the pupils themselves might be less likely to create disorderly conditions in such an environment.

A neat teacher, then, promotes this trait by precept and example. In general, this quality results in better relationships between the beginning teacher and the personnel of the school because it is a habit which is admired, even if not cultivated, by all.

*Be Courteous.* Courtesy implies conformity to accepted rules of behavior, and consideration for the rights of others. By the time the college student has arrived at the student-teaching stage, he is expected to have absorbed enough manners, morals, and culture to act habitually in a courteous manner. Courtesy is an indispensable ingredient for harmonious relationships with others.

Courtesy begets courtesy. The beginning teacher who is habitually courteous will find the personnel of the school responding in like manner. Therefore, it is to his personal advantage to cultivate this type of behavior. Furthermore, it is his duty to do so, because he could not expect to develop in his students a quality which he does not practice or possess. (See problems 103, 105, and 106.)

*Be Punctual.* Punctuality signifies reliability. If the beginning teacher reports to school on time, begins and ends his classes punctually, and is prompt at school affairs, he will earn the title of dependability. Great emphasis is placed on this quality by school administrators. They want to be able to feel they can rely on a teacher to be at his post at the appointed time. One of the surest ways for a student teacher to arouse ill feelings is to be lax on this point. One administrator became irritated with a student teacher because the latter walked into the building each day just a minute or two before the final bell rang. The student teacher reached his class on time—just on time. The administrator was vexed because, as he put it, "I expect my regular teachers to report into the building twenty minutes before classes start, and I see no reason why a student teacher should not be able to do the same."

Punctuality may also affect relationships with other teachers. This is particularly true in the matter of dismissing classes on time. The over-zealous or the inconsiderate may hold their classes beyond the bell to finish up material under discussion at the time. Since pupils have very little time between classes, they usually straggle in late for the next class, thus making it difficult for the teacher to begin class smoothly. Naturally, this is very irritating to the teacher whose class is thus disrupted. The beginning teacher, therefore, would be wise to be scrupulous about dismissing his class at the sound of the bell. Keeping a class overtime cannot be justified because, as one veteran teacher stated, "No teacher is discussing a matter of such urgency or world-shaking importance that it could not wait until the next class period to be finished."

Punctuality has its effects on pupils too. If the teacher begins work promptly at the bell, pupils will extend themselves to get to class on time, and will immediately settle down to work. Lack of punctuality on the part of the teacher fosters a similar trait in the pupils, represented by remarks such as, "She doesn't care if I'm late," or, "He never starts class on time." Such an attitude on the part of the students brings disorder to the classroom. It also deprives the students of learning the habit of promptness, which is so important throughout life, and which is closely linked with considerateness for the feelings and time of others.

*Do a Little More than is Expected of You.*   School officials plan a definite program of observation, teaching, and other activities for the student teacher. It is, of course, important that he adhere to this schedule and discharge his duties conscientiously. Even if he does, it is possible to distinguish between a beginning teacher who performs only the duties expected of him and one who gives something extra without being asked to do so. Teaching is a life of service. It is that little extra contribution by the student teacher that marks him as one who is properly motivated toward teaching, and as one who is likely to be happy in his work with young people. He need not be told to do these things; he seeks them out voluntarily. He will offer his help in taking charge of a study period, giving pupils extra help, assisting with a school play, or in any one of a host of activities. He will ask permission to attend P.T.A. meetings and faculty meetings, and will offer his services at school functions. This spirit of service will be noticed by administrators, teachers, and pupils. The beginning teacher will be admired for it, and it will favorably influence his relationships with all concerned.

*Discourage Pupils From Becoming Emotionally Involved With You.*   In the chapter on discipline, it was noted that the teacher should be friendly but not familiar with his pupils, in order to avoid loss of dignity on the part of the teacher, and in turn, loss of respect from the pupils. An extension of this idea not previously discussed concerns emotional involvement between a pupil and the teacher. It sometimes happens that a pupil becomes emotionally attached to a teacher to an undesirable degree. One of the problems outlined later in this chapter describes a girl who spent all her time gazing at the male student teacher with "starry eyes." This experience was very disconcerting and distracting to him, and he wisely took immediate measures to bring the young lady back to reality. Female student teachers sometimes find themselves the object of a "crush" by an adolescent boy. In cases of this type, it is necessary for the student teacher to be very tactful, so as not to embarrass the pupil who is emotionally involved. In a private talk with the student, the teacher may point up facts such as the necessity for professional relationships, their difference in age, and the transitory nature of emotions. The pupil should be made to feel that the teacher is highly complimented by the student's regard for him, and that he will look forward to working with the pupil on a *friendly* basis. Conversely, it is self-evident that the teacher should never permit himself to become romantically associated with any of his pupils, nor should he seek to date them after school hours. (See problems 101, 111, and 120.)

*Take Pupils' Remarks in Stride.*   Just as any public figure is discussed by the general population, so will a student teacher be discussed by his pupils. Usually, students' comments are far removed from the teacher's ears. Sometimes, however, he may overhear a comment as he is walking through the hall, or as the students are leaving the room. At times, too, comments made by students may reach him through indirect sources such as friends, relatives, or acquaintances who relay the stories to him.

Although some of the things the beginning teacher hears about himself may be pleasant enough to buoy his spirits, an occasional unpleasant remark of criticism may reach his ears. Whether he is praised or criticized by a pupil, the beginning teacher should try to view such comments objectively, and if possible, forget them. He should remember he cannot be all things to all pupils, nor should he try to be. His personality, regulations, and procedures will not be equally appealing and effective with all his students, and he must expect that in the process of upholding his standards and procedures he will leave an occasional student dissatisfied or disgruntled. Although he should try to develop more favorable attitudes in those students, it is essential to his mental happiness as a teacher to realize that all teachers are criticized by pupils at one time or another. To rephrase an old adage: a teacher can expect to interest all the pupils a great deal of the time, and some of the pupils all of the time, but he would indeed be a unique teacher if he kept all the pupils interested all the time. (See problem 102.)

*Do Not Criticize Cooperating School Personnel.* It is quite likely that a student teacher may occasionally observe an act or procedure in the school that could be justifiably criticized. Although criticism may be justified, it should *never* be given by the student teacher. He should not make negative comments about the school, the supervisors, or the teachers to anyone, with the possible exception of his college supervisor, who can advise the student concerning his difficulties and who will maintain a discreet silence about what he is told. If the teacher criticizes one teacher in the presence of another, or if he makes negative comments about the administration, he will arouse antagonisms which will shatter the cooperative relationship which existed between the student teacher and the personnel of the cooperating school. The student teacher will find himself facing an attitude of hostility, manifested by comments such as, "That young upstart! Who does he think he is, criticizing us?"

The beginning teacher must bear in mind there is no such thing as a perfect school, administration, teacher, or person. If one searches for weaknesses, he will find them. The student teacher can be sure that teachers and administrators are aware of their shortcomings and are continuously trying to overcome them. To be criticized by a neophyte can have no other effect than to arouse resentment. (See problem 109.)

*Accept the Suggestions of the Cooperating Teacher.* During the course of his teaching, the student teacher should keep an open mind to evaluative comments made by the cooperating teacher. These comments will be both positive and negative. The cooperating teacher tries to view him objectively as a total teaching personality, directing his comments toward him as a future teacher. The student teacher should accept the fact that the cooperating teacher is trying to help him through constructive criticism. In fact, it is quite likely that the student teacher would be one of the first to admit that a cooperating teacher who failed to criticize when necessary would not be performing his duty either toward the student teacher or toward the teaching profession in general.

As a rule, the student teacher need not be apprehensive about problems with personnel of the cooperating school. If he is courteous, open-minded to suggestions, cooperative, and conscientious, his relationships with them will be on a high plane. He will find that administrators and cooperating teachers will do everything within their power to make his student teaching experience a pleasant and profitable one. (See problems 104, 108, 112, 116, 118, and 119.)

• • •

The problems which follow are illustrative of some of the difficulties which might be encountered by the student teacher in his relationships with administrators, cooperating teachers, parents, and pupils. These cases show that in some instances problems arose because of the thoughtlessness of the student teacher, while in others they were brought about by factors over which he had no control. Whatever the cause, it is evident that once a problem arises, the solution depends on the common sense, courtesy, sympathy, and understanding of the parties involved.

### PROBLEM 101: A YOUNG STUDENT DEVELOPS A "CRUSH" ON THE STUDENT TEACHER

In my tenth grade history class, I ran into a problem which was very embarrassing to me. The source of the problem was a girl named Mary.

Mary was a very attractive, petite girl with a winsome smile. Not long after I began student teaching, I noticed she spent most of her time looking at me. Every time my eyes met hers, she smiled. I do not want to appear to be egotistical, but I think she smiled at me with something more than friendliness. Since she sat in the front of the room, I could not miss her starry-eyed glances, which became very disconcerting and distracting to me while I was trying to conduct class. Whenever we met before or after class, she greeted me with a meaningful "Hello-o-o."

I did not know quite how to go about discouraging her attentions without hurting her feelings. I tried calling on her more than I did the other pupils, hoping she would miss the answers and pay more attention to her work. However, she knew all the answers! Finally, I decided there was no other way out of the problem than to talk with her.

One day I kept her after class. Since I could not tell her directly that I thought she had a "crush" on me, I approached the whole thing indirectly. I asked her reaction to the course and to student teachers. She said she liked the course very much. As far as student teachers were concerned, she said she liked them on the whole, but that some were better than others. I then tried to give her an insight into the problems student teachers have in adjusting to all levels of personnel in the high school, dwelling at length on the teacher-pupil relationship. I told her we form many friendships while we are student teaching in the high schools, but that we must always keep our relationships on a professional basis, for our own good and for the good of the students. I asked her if she thought this was a good policy. She agreed that it was. I thanked her very much for her opinions, telling her that they helped me understand the students' problems better, and that I hoped what I told her helped her see our problems a little better. "I understand," she said.

Apparently she did understand the purpose and the tone of the conversation because, from that time forward, our relationship was that of teacher-pupil. She was friendly, and she still smiled, but "that look" had disappeared from her pretty face.

### Points for Discussion

* *The relationship between a student teacher and his pupils should be on a professional basis. Describe this type of relationship.*

### PROBLEM 102: A STUDENT TEACHER RECEIVES THREATENING TELEPHONE CALLS

My first four days of student teaching had gone along very nicely. During the evening of the fourth day, while I was preparing my lesson plans, I received a telephone call. When I picked up the receiver, a heavily muffled boy's voice greeted me.

"This is one of your students," the voice said. "We're going to throw you out the window tomorrow."

For a moment I was speechless. Then I said, "Is this your idea of a joke?"

"This is no joke," replied the voice. 'We're going to throw you out the window tomorrow." There was a click as the boy ended the conversation.

I slumped into a chair, not knowing what to make of the call. I was sure that someone was merely trying to frighten me, but then how could I be certain? What was I to do?

During the next half-hour I received three more calls. As soon as I heard the muffled voice, I hung up without saying a word. After the fourth call came through, I decided to call my cooperating teacher. I needed some definite course of action for the next day's class, but I could think of nothing constructive. I disliked calling the teacher at home, but to me, this was an emergency. After all, my classroom was located on the third floor, and I did not relish the idea of sailing out a window from that altitude.

When I phoned my cooperating teacher and explained my plight, she did not seem properly disturbed. She asked me if I had had any special difficulties with my students. I told her that we were getting along very well.

"What should I do?" I asked.

"Nothing," she replied. "If you get any more phone calls tonight, leave your phone off the hook. When you go to class tomorrow, act as if nothing happened, and nothing will."

She told me to try to forget about the calls and to get a good night's rest. Frankly, I was almost as surprised at her lack of concern as I was at the phone calls.

Shortly after we had finished the conversation, another call came through. After hanging up, I disengaged the phone, and then I busied myself with preparations for the next day.

When I went into my classroom the next day, I tried to appear calm, although I must admit my heart was thumping. As I conducted classes, I looked at the pupils carefully, trying to find the guilty-looking faces, but I found none. My cooperating teacher was right. Nothing unusual happened.

When I talked the matter over further with her that day, she mentioned that there was nothing really unusual about receiving occasional anonymous phone calls from students. She said that it was simply an expression of a distorted sense of humor on the part of some pupils.

"I have received my share of anonymous calls," she continued. "Some of them have been social, some romantic, and one was like yours—threatening. The best thing to do is to ignore them. If the students involved see that they do not disturb you, they will not continue to make the calls."

Again she was right. I received no more calls during the remainder of my student teaching. Teaching became a wonderful experience. I shall never forget, though, how near I was to panic the night I received those phone calls.

### Points for Discussion

- *How would you have handled the telephone calls this student teacher received?*

- *Formulate a policy for dealing with phone calls from pupils who identify themselves.*

### PROBLEM 103: PUPILS APPRECIATE BEING TREATED AS YOUNG ADULTS

When I began student teaching, I was assigned two groups of commercial students, one seniors and the other sophomores. I was a little wary about taking over the senior group, because for the most part they were only three or four years younger than I. I didn't believe there would be any problem with the sophomores.

Much to my surprise, no problems developed in the senior class. When I walked into the class for the first time, I treated them respectfully as mature, young ladies and gentlemen, and they reciprocated by treating me with respect. Throughout my student teaching, I never had to raise my voice in that class. In fact, I achieved something I believed almost impossible in a commercial class. I got them to read a novel and write a book report on it. They even enjoyed it. So that was my senior class, whom I enjoyed teaching from beginning to end.

The problem children were the sophomores. I had heard about this group before I took over the class, so I thought I was prepared for them. I walked into class with my best austere manner and began laying down the laws. I later realized that this was a mistake, and the only thing it accomplished was to create resentment on the part of the students. I believed them to be children who had to be scolded and deprived of privileges, just as any child who misbehaves. When a student became a little too loud, I would single him out and reprimand him in a harsh tone of voice. This produced no results for two reasons: it brought sympathy for him from the rest of the class, and secondly, the reprimanded student wanted to show the class he was not afraid, so he repeated his misbehavior. In fact, the rest of the class joined him in misbehaving.

Roy was a case in point. One day while I was teaching the class, I kept hearing a rubber ball hitting the floor. From my position in the front of the room, I could not see who was causing the disturbance, but students were looking at Roy. Roy's friends thought his act was hilarious, so he kept it up. I tried to pay no attention to him, hoping that he would see that his prank was not bothering me. It didn't work. He kept it up until I had to ask him and his friends to stay after class.

After class, I talked to the boys and found them to be very "human." I asked each one why he was trying to annoy me. No one answered. I asked each one if he was interested in school. All replied in the negative. Finally, I asked them what they planned to do after finishing high school. Each replied: "I'm going into the service." I followed up by asking them if they were going to make the service a career, and when they replied in the negative, I asked what they planned to do after the service. One said he would try to get into the State Police, another said he would work for his father, and the third wanted to be a mechanic.

I saw an opening to try to reach at least one of them. I told the one who wanted to join the State Police that they investigate high school records, and talk to many people who knew the person applying for the position. This he did not believe, but when I told him I had a brother already in the State Police, he took my word that what I had said was true. We then became involved in an informal discussion that lasted about fifteen minutes. When it ended, we parted with a good feeling toward each other.

I had no more trouble with them in class. The laughing and showing off was gone, and they behaved in class. For my part, I began treating them and the other students more like young adults than like children. This had reciprocal effects. They seemed proud to be shown respect, and returned the same.

### Points for Discussion

- *Do you think students regard teachers as a friend or as a foe? Give reasons for your answer.*

### PROBLEM 104: THE STUDENT TEACHER IS SELF-CONSCIOUS IN THE PRESENCE OF THE COOPERATING TEACHER

My biggest problem confronted me *before* I actually began to teach. After I had observed my cooperating teacher for a few days, my confidence in my teaching ability began to shrink. It shrank more with each passing day. The reason for this diminishing confidence was that I began to compare myself with my cooperating teacher, and I did not like what I saw. She was a lady who had been teaching for eighteen years. Her class moved along like clockwork, with never a lag. She made the subject so interesting that the pupils seemed to hang on her every word. Obscure points she made clear by drawing on a wealth of examples. The whole class was *alive*.

I knew that when I took over the class I could never hope to conduct it half as effectively as she did. My anxiety was centered around questions such as, "How will the pupils react to me after having a superior teacher?" and "What will the cooperating teacher think of me when she is observing me?" I could think of no favorable answer.

Ordinarily, I was to have started teaching after a one-week observation period, but at the end of the week I told the cooperating teacher I was not quite ready to begin, and asked for an extension of another day or two of observation. This was granted. Then I asked for another day, and another, until the second week was consumed. Yet instead of gaining confidence I became more fretful.

On the last day of the second week, my cooperating teacher had a talk with me and asked why I kept postponing my first day of teaching. Feeling that it would be best to be frank with her, I poured out my anxieties. She listened and, after I had finished, smiled sympathetically.

"I suspected that was the reason," she said. "You know," she continued, "I felt exactly the same way when I started to teach eighteen years ago. That feeling almost cost me the happiest eighteen years of my life, because I thought I could never become as good a teacher as my master teacher, and if I could not become that good, I did not want to become a teacher at all. My master teacher assured me I had no cause to worry because this was a common, and normal, feeling among student teachers. His reassurance was all I needed."

I began to feel better. Here was a teacher of high ability who had felt inferior when she started, and probably her master teacher had felt the same way.

She told me something else that added to my confidence. "You forget," she said, "that there is a difference of eighteen years of experience between us. It is quite likely that after you have taught for eighteen years, you will be a better teacher than I am right now."

I could see that I had made two mistakes. The first was in not realizing the cooperating teacher would be understanding when she observed my teaching, and the second was in making a comparison for which there was no common basis.

The following week I began teaching. Although I know I didn't do as good a job as my cooperating teacher, I was consoled with the thought that I was doing the best I could, and that some day I might have a student teacher under me who felt as I did.

## Points for Discussion

* *What qualifications should a cooperating teacher have? Why would the answer to this question have dispelled the doubts of this student teacher?*

## PROBLEM 105: A SARCASTIC COMMENT AROUSES THE WRATH OF A PARENT

I had been exasperated with Frank for a long time because of the careless errors he had been making on written assignments and tests. Although he knew how to do things correctly on the assignments, and he knew the material on the tests, he simply rushed through things in a slipshod manner.

I had talked to Frank several times about being more careful with his work, but apparently I had made no impression on him. One day when my patience was low, I put a note on a test paper of his that I had just corrected. It read: "A fine paper! Are you this sloppy in everything?"

The day after I returned the papers, the principal called me into his office. He told me that Frank's father was furious about the comment I had put on his son's test paper, especially since Frank was always neat in appearance. The father considered the remark a slur on his family environment. "Anyone who would make a remark like that is not fit to be a teacher," he told the principal. "I'm going to the school board about it."

The principal had not been able to soothe his wounded feelings. He suggested that I see Frank's father to try to persuade him not to take the matter to the school board. That night I went to the father's home. We talked the matter out, and I apologized for any insult that might have been implied in my remark. He was still coolly resentful, but he said he would permit the matter to drop. I was pretty well shaken up by the visit, but relieved to know that he would not make a further issue of it.

I guess I shouldn't have written what I did, but I still don't see that it was such a serious matter. I simply wanted to jolt Frank into some orderly work. I did learn a lesson though. Hereafter, I shall be very careful about what I put down in writing because it always remains there for someone to interpret—or misinterpret.

### Points for Discussion

- *Do you agree with the student teacher that what he had written was not a serious matter? Why?*

- *What do you think of the father's attitude?*

- *What effect does sarcasm have on an individual?*

### PROBLEM 106: A GIRL RESENTS A TEACHER'S JOKE

My problem deals with a very intelligent girl and also a very sensitive girl. Her name is Ellen. She is a student in my eighth grade history class, although the problem actually began in a health class. Ellen is a very bright student who can easily comprehend and retain material. She always answered my questions, often giving detail not called for. She herself often asked very good questions. Up to this time, she had maintained the second highest average in my history class.

Ellen's homeroom teacher was absent for two weeks because of illness, and during that time I was asked to take over the girls' health class. Instead of having a study period I decided to go on with the material. It was a very informal class, the students relating many of their personal experiences to the material. For example, when we were discussing skin burns, a girl told us about her neighbor who had been burned in his own back yard. I allowed free discussions and we got along very well.

The next week I was asked to take over the class again. At this particular time they were on fats, oils, and minerals in general. I asked Ellen to read the section on fats, telling her in a joking way that this was a subject very appropriate to her (since she was rather plump). Although I meant it as a joke, Ellen took it seriously. Immediately she walked out of the room with an air of wounded pride. I didn't think much of it because I imagined most young people are wounded one minute and recover in the next. This, however, was not the case with Ellen.

After fifteen minutes, I sent another girl after Ellen, but Ellen would not come back with her. I dispatched another girl after her with strict orders to bring her back. When Ellen came, she walked right past me as if I had never existed. Throughout the remainder of the class she ignored me, turning her back on me no matter what direction I faced.

I went home that day thinking Ellen would forget about my remark. I was wrong again. Things became even worse. She was just like a statue in class. When I asked her a question she would always answer, "I don't know."

Another example of her resentment toward me concerned a picture of the student teachers which was posted by the principal on the hall bulletin board. The day after the incident I noticed my picture had been rubbed out. I didn't have to ask who had done it. However, this incident didn't bother me so much as the fact that Ellen's work in history was slowly but surely deteriorating. I tried calling on her more often in class, hoping to stimulate her into giving some answers instead of saying "I don't know." When I called on her, she read as if it meant nothing to her.

Finally, I had a private talk with Ellen. I apologized for saying she was "fat," telling her that I was merely trying to make a poor joke. She told me I was just apologizing because the rest of the class had noticed her resentment. I assured her this was not so, that I was sincere in my apology. We talked for quite a while. I must have been successful in convincing her because the next day I noticed a slight change in her attitude. Within three days after our talk, things were back to normal. She continued the high-quality work of which she was capable, and came out with the highest grade in the class.

## Points for Discussion

- *Should a teacher ever joke in class? If so, under what conditions?*

- *Discuss the emotional sensitivity of girls as compared with that of boys.*

## PROBLEM 107: TEACHERS DO NOT RELATE TO A "WISE GUY"

I had heard a great deal about teachers who "label" students on the basis of their reputation. When they get such a student in class, they throw up a barrier between themselves and the student, making it impossible for communication to take place. I saw this happen while I was student teaching, and it saddened me a great deal. Specifically, I saw it happen with Tony.

Before I started to teach the class in which Tony was a student, I was filled in on his reputation. Tony was having a great deal of trouble in school. He constantly cut classes and played hooky. During the current year, he had already missed forty days of school. When he was in school, it was not long before he was dismissed from class or sent to the principal. Many letters were sent to Tony's mother who often had to appear in school on his behalf. Tony had been sent to detention countless times, but it did not improve his conduct. He used four-lettered words in class, and referred to one of his teachers as either "Blondy" or "Baby." Almost all his teachers noted that he is constantly loud and disruptive in class.

By the time I took over the class, I found myself resenting Tony, and mentally labeling him a "wise guy." This is exactly what I said I would never do, but Tony's past performance made it very easy to fall prey to labeling him. I realized I had to do something to overcome my attitude and give Tony some kind of chance to prove himself.

I had some talks with Tony. These talks, plus conferences I had with the guidance counselor, revealed that Tony had attended a private school for eight years. He had done well through the sixth grade, making grades of B and C which correlated well with his I.Q. of 101. Then in junior high school, his grades fell to C and D, and he was expelled from the private school. His grades declined to D and E in public school, and it seemed certain that he would fail his present junior year.

In his talks with me, Tony told me that his teachers never really cared for him, but were more concerned with giving orders. So he decided to get even with his teachers by giving them a "hard time." In our discussions, he came through to me as a person with a basically good nature, but he held the pessimistic view that he had no control over what will happen to him. I told him he had as much control over his own life as anybody else, and urged him to give his teachers a chance to show their concern for him. He replied that he would be willing to give them the chance, but he knew they were not interested.

I did show interest and concern for him in my class, and I know that he knew it. Not once did he cause me a problem. In fact, he participated greatly and made worthwhile contributions. Unfortunately, the concern I showed for him may not have come soon enough.

It is too late for some teachers to change their opinion that Tony is a hopeless case. I had talks with them about Tony, but had no success in altering their views about him. To them he is a "wise guy" who has to be treated accordingly. It is really a shame because all

Tony needs is some concern from others and another chance—a chance which none of the other teachers are willing to give him. Unfortunately, unless he gets some time and understanding from his teachers, I don't think Tony will finish high school.

### Points for Discussion

- *Can you recall a "wise guy" that you went to school with? How was he treated by your teachers?*

- *The student teacher blamed the teachers in this case. Do you think they should shoulder the blame? Why?*

### PROBLEM 108: TWO COOPERATING TEACHERS ARE CONTRASTED BY THE STUDENT TEACHER

The majority of cooperating teachers with whom I came into contact during my period of student teaching were honest, capable, patient people who enjoyed their work. There were of course exceptions, but these were few. I suppose there are one or two teachers in every school system who do not belong there. They are impatient, lose their tempers, spend a great deal of time shouting at the pupils, and are disciplinarians of such nature that they would have made better law enforcement officers than teachers. This type of teacher seems to forget that he is dealing with restless, energetic, curious, and sometimes humorous students who do not always live up to the rules and regulations of an adult world.

I know two teachers who exemplify extremes of motivation for the teaching profession. One of them regarded his ninth graders as pests and told me one day, "They are brats who have to be ruled with an iron hand. I actually feel sorry for you, just starting out in your teaching career. I would never go through it again."

The other teacher, who maintains discipline just as well or better, held that the prime requisite for anyone entering the teaching profession is a love of young people and a desire to help them in every way possible. An example of the way she handles pupils is shown in her conduct the day a boy smuggled a turtle into class and let it wander around the floor. She calmly told the boy to remove the reptile from the classroom. Later she gave him a private sermon that made him sorry and embarrassed for what he had done. After classes that day she remarked to me, "He's all boy, isn't he? God love him."

What would the other teacher have done with this "brat"? Would the results have been any better? Would they have been as good? Which of the two would children confide in? There isn't much choice, is there?

I am convinced that teachers are wonderful people. They have as high a degree of purity as that well-known soap. The future of our children and our nation is in good hands.

## Points for Discussion

- *Think back on the teachers you had when you were in high school. What qualities did your good teachers have? For what reasons did you dislike certain others?*

- *What qualities do you think a teacher should have to be happy in the teaching profession?*

## PROBLEM 109: THE STUDENT TEACHER THOUGHTLESSLY CRITICIZES ANOTHER TEACHER

I had been told never to criticize anything or anybody in the school system in which I was doing my student teaching. Much to my sorrow, I made one slip, and it was just that—a slip of the tongue. I had not intended to be critical. What I said was just a matter of conversation.

My student teaching was going along fine, and everyone seemed satisfied with the work I was doing. I had a schedule which called for teaching some classes and observing others. About two weeks before my training period was to terminate, I was assigned to observe a teacher with whom I had no dealings before.

Mr. X was a man who was nearing retirement age, and I must honestly say that I did not learn anything from observing him, unless it was what *not* to do. His history class was the most boring I had ever seen. He had the pupils read from the textbook, one after the other, and occasionally he added a comment of his own. Not only did he show no enthusiasm, he appeared bored all the time. Often his mind seemed to wander. Strangely enough, the pupils paid attention and caused him no trouble. This man, I thought, does not belong in the classroom.

After observing him about two days, I happened to be talking with another teacher in the school. When asked how things were coming along, I replied that I was learning a great deal from everyone. Then I stupidly added, "That is, everyone except Mr. X. I think even I could do a better job."

Why I added that comment I'll never know. The teacher to whom I was talking bristled, and shot back, "If you ever become half the teacher Mr. X was, you would still be one of the best." With that he turned on his heel and walked away.

Apparently what I said was circulated among the faculty, because there developed a cool, almost frigid, relationship between me and them. Also, they seemed to go out of their way to show me that I was not doing as good a job of teaching as I thought I was. Whatever I did, there was a better way to do it, and I was always told about it.

I could not understand why the faculty felt so strongly about an innocent remark, but I was determined to find out. Not wanting to approach the teachers, I sounded out the students on Mr. X. I soon got my answer. Mr. X was regarded as one of the most efficient and best-liked teachers by the pupils and faculty alike. Three months before, however, his wife died, and he had been in a state of semi-shock ever since.

Needless to say, I gave myself a well-deserved tongue-lashing. I could scarcely look anyone in the eye during the remaining few days of my student teaching. I shall never criticize anybody again, and shall always keep in mind that appearances often belie the facts. I was happy that this episode happened so near the end of my student teaching. On the last day, I folded my tent and silently stole away.

### Points for Discussion

- *Besides criticizing a teacher, this student teacher made another mistake. What was it?*

- *What do you think of the attitude and action of the faculty? Were they justified? Why?*

- *What should a student teacher do about deficiencies he uncovers in the cooperating school?*

### PROBLEM 110:  A STUDENT TEACHER
### SEEKS PREFERENTIAL TREATMENT

Although I had been told by college officials that my student teaching assignment would be arranged for me in a particular school, and that I was not to make any contacts with high school personnel until I was told to do so, I thought I would help matters along. I had personal reasons for wanting to be assigned to this particular high school.

Since there were two school board members whom I knew very well, I contacted them and asked them to approve the request of the college for me to do my student teaching in their district. They told me that the request was already in, and that the school board had already approved it. At my request, they said they would get in touch with the superintendent and ask him to place me in the building I desired.

With my mind relieved, I settled back to wait for student teaching to begin. My peace of mind was short-lived. I was called in by the college supervisor who told me that he had received a phone call from the superintendent of the school district. The college supervisor let me know in forceful terms that I had disobeyed instructions, that I was guilty of unethical practices, and that he therefore doubted that I was a suitable person for the teaching profession. I was stunned. I had no idea that the college would be informed of my actions, and I certainly did not want to do anything that was unethical. I explained my actions to the college supervisor, and my reasons seemed to make an impression on him. He informed me, however, that no matter how strong my reasons were, they did not excuse my actions. He would think the matter over, he said, and let me know the next day whether or not I would be granted permission to do student teaching. After a day that was filled with all sorts of flights of imagination, I went to see him. Permission was granted. I was to teach on a probationary basis.

My troubles did not end there. The superintendent of the district and the high school principal both resented the fact that they had been asked by members of the school board to give me a preferential assignment. Word of what I had done even filtered down to the teachers. Everybody seemed to have the idea that I wanted to "coast along" in my student teaching. Determining to show them otherwise, I worked very hard, and volunteered for many extra assignments. This, in addition to their learning the real reason why I wanted to teach in their school, gradually relaxed their stern looks. Even so, I could feel there was some underlying resentment remaining.

I finished my student teaching without encountering any other major problem, but I certainly learned my lesson about the advisability of going through proper channels, even though I had what I thought was a legitimate reason for not doing so. You see, my wife was expecting our first addition to the family. I wanted to be near her, just in case . . .

## Points for Discussion

- *Do you think this student teacher had a valid reason for acting as he did? Why?*

- *How could he have accomplished the same result through the use of different means?*

## PROBLEM 111: THE STUDENT TEACHER UNWITTINGLY DATES A STUDENT

Things went along very smoothly during my period of student teaching until the night I was to act as a chaperon at a school dance. Just as I was getting ready to leave home to pick up another male student teacher, I received a phone call from Judy, one of my pupils. She told me that the girl who was to give her a ride had become ill, and asked if I would mind giving her a ride to the dance. I told her I would.

I picked up my co-worker, and then we stopped by to pick up Judy, and proceeded to the dance. Judy thanked me very much for taking her to the dance, and at the same time asked if I would also take her home after it was over. Since she did not have a ride, I told her I would.

The dance went along well, and all the pupils seemed to be enjoying themselves. Although I did not dance, I was having a good time watching the others. About an hour after we arrived, however, one of the pupils came up to me to say that Judy was crying. I asked what was wrong.

"You took her to the dance," the pupil answered, "and you haven't even asked her for a dance."

I was amazed and shocked. Apparently Judy had told the other girls that I had asked her to the dance, and then ignored her. What was I to do?

Mrs. G., one of the regular teachers at the school, was also chaperoning the dance. I immediately went to her and explained all the circumstances of the problem. Mrs. G. said she would talk to Judy, and that she herself would give her a ride home.

They next day I went directly to the principal's office and laid the incident before him. He called Judy in while I was there, talked to her kindly, and explained all the implications of her actions. Judy said she knew she was wrong, and apologized. That ended the incident.

I am thankful that the matter ended well. There is one other thing I am very thankful for, and that is that I had the other student teacher with me when I picked up Judy. Otherwise, she might have made up some very embarrassing stories about the ride from her home to the school.

## Points for Discussion

- *How would you have handled the telephone call from Judy? What would you have told her?*

- *What would you have done at the dance? Suppose Mrs. G. had not been present to handle the situation?*

- *Explain the type of social relationship that should exist between a teacher and his pupils.*

### PROBLEM 112: THE QUESTION OF HOW LONG A COOPERATING TEACHER SHOULD OBSERVE THE STUDENT TEACHER

The question of how long a cooperating teacher should remain in the room is an important one. Since I taught under two cooperating teachers who represented extremes on this point, I am in a position to draw some conclusions on the relative merits of long and short stays by them.

Teacher A very seldom remained in the room. In a sense, this was good because it gave me the feeling of handling a class on my own. It also caused me to feel more relaxed, knowing that I was not being observed. Since he was not in the room to observe me, however, he could not give me help where I needed it, and I believe a student teacher can learn a great deal from the criticisms offered by an experienced teacher. Yet, he obviously cannot teach you the tricks of the trade unless he is in the room with you.

Teacher B, on the other hand, was seldom out of the room. Although his continuous presence made me nervous in the beginning, I soon got to the point where I even forgot his presence, for this teacher was a great help to me. He gave me important tips on such little things as ventilation, lighting, and seating arrangement. He discussed mistakes I made in teaching right after class, while they were fresh in his mind. He told me, for example, how to send students to the chalkboard when there is limited board space. Most important, he showed me techniques of teaching his subject that he had picked up throughout the years.

My conclusions? Though I learned more from Teacher B, as one would expect, I thought he stayed in the room too much. There is a happy medium between the two extremes. Although Teacher A taught me a lot in our conferences, he could have helped me more with the mistakes I made in the classroom. Teacher B helped me a great deal more in all ways except one: if he had been the only cooperating teacher I had, I would not have had enough experience in handling a class by myself.

## Points for Discussion

- *What are the functions of the cooperating teacher?*

- *Using your answer to the previous question as a basis, evaluate the arguments presented in this case.*

## PROBLEM 113:  THE STUDENT TEACHER
## TRIES TO MEND BROKEN FENCES

You never know what kinds of problems you will face in student teaching. I ran into a problem that made me feel like I was a cross between a public relations man and a shuttle-diplomat.

Two weeks after I began teaching, I noticed that a boy in one of my classes was absent each Friday. Upon checking with my cooperating teacher, I discovered that for the past several weeks this same boy, Fred, had not attended school on Friday. My cooperating teacher said that he had noticed Fred to be a shy boy who lacked confidence. Fred's cumulative record confirmed this information and also recorded that he was dependable, worked hard at everything he tried, and was very nervous. In all his years at school he was in generally good physical health. His grades were average, and he had an I.Q. of 95.

I decided to have a talk with Fred. When I asked him about his being absent every Friday, he at first said nothing, but after I pressed the issue he said he always felt sick on Friday. Since he was shy and hesitant, and since I wanted to remain on friendly terms with him, I did not pursue the matter any further for the moment.

The next day, I asked three of Fred's classmates to remain after class, and asked them if they knew why Fred was absent every Friday. I could tell from their expressions that they knew the reason, but they were reluctant to speak. I told them the only reason why I wanted to know was that I wanted to help him if he had a problem. Finally, one of them blurted out that Fred was afraid to go to school on Friday. He had had a run-in with the shop teacher, and the teacher destroyed Fred's project. Since by nature Fred was a fearful and nervous boy, this incident fanned his anxiety to the point that he was afraid to meet the shop teacher again.

I wondered if I should talk to the shop teacher about it. He might tell me, as a student teacher, to mind my own business! I decided to chance it. The teacher did not seem to mind my asking about Fred. He confirmed that he had destroyed the project, adding that the same treatment had been administered to others deserving it. It was intended as a punishment, he said, and he certainly didn't mean to scare him away from class.

I then had another talk with Fred in which I told him I understood his situation, and I asked him to give me his version of what had taken place. His account was similar, but he added that the shop teacher didn't want him in class again. I told him that most likely this was untrue, and urged him to have a talk with the shop teacher. I tried to explain to him that he had an unfounded fear that was building up in him.

Following that, I had another talk with the shop teacher, asking him if he would talk with Fred to help him rebuild his confidence in himself and in his teachers. He promised to do so the next day. This he did, but the result was unsatisfactory—it only widened the gap between them.

At this point, Fred's parents decided to look into the situation. They had a vigorous talk with the principal with the result that Fred received dispensation from attending shop for the rest of the term.

This really did not solve the problem. Fred ran away from the situation and nothing was done to help him overcome his basic shyness and anxiety. However, it did eliminate further confrontation with a situation that might have aggravated Fred's emotional problems. Anyway, I took the first step. Maybe someone else can take the next one.

### Points for Discussion

- *Was the shop teacher justified in destroying a project as a means of punishment? Why?*

- *How far should a student teacher go in trying to reconcile problems caused by other teachers?*

### PROBLEM 114: A TEACHER DISLIKES TEAM TEACHING

There are all sorts of variations of team teaching. When I began to teach, I was exposed to one of them in an American Heritage course. The team consisted only of my cooperating teacher and me. After having been part of a teaching team, I am not sure that I like it.

My cooperating teacher took responsibility for teaching our heritage through history, and I cross-fertilized it with American literature. It took us many hours of planning to integrate the two. We sifted through a great deal of material, trying to correlate the literature of a period with its history. We had to plan when and what each of us would teach, what type of assignments we would give the pupils, and we had to collaborate on the types of tests we would give them. During marking periods we had to reach a decision on the grade to be awarded to each pupil.

I realize that I had to do all these things in the other courses I was teaching, but there was one important difference. In the other courses, I was captain of my own ship, setting its course and guiding its progress. In the team-taught course, I was a co-captain, but I didn't feel like one because I was a student teacher.

The problem in team teaching, as I see it, is one of adjustment between members of the team. Countless judgments have to be made on course content and procedures to use, and there is not always agreement on what should be done. My cooperating teacher and I had many disagreements, which were almost always resolved in his favor. Since I was only a student teacher, I finally agreed to everything he wanted to do, even though I know that many of my suggestions had merit. It was a discouraging experience.

As I mentioned before, team teaching can take many forms. Teams can be composed of from two to twenty members; they can use an interdisciplinary approach, or they can use specialists within a single discipline; and, they may or may not use aides. I know, too, that studies have shown some of them to be successful. Claims have been made that pupils get a higher quality of instruction, that teachers extend themselves more when working with colleagues, that pupils are exposed to the influence of more teachers, and that there is more accurate assessment of pupil progress.

From my brief experience with team teaching, I would say the advantages claimed for team teaching are an ideal that can be achieved in few cases. I think it takes a great deal more of a teacher's time, can cause friction and resentment among colleagues, and I am not sure that it produces a better learning situation for the students.

## Points for Discussion

- *Discuss the advantages and disadvantages of team teaching.*
- *Would you like to be a member of a teaching team? Give reasons for your position.*

## PROBLEM 115:  THE SON OF A SCHOOL BOARD MEMBER ASSUMES HE DOES NOT HAVE TO WORK

My first impression of John was that he was the slowest, laziest pupil in my physics class. As my period of observation progressed, I found him to be even more than that: he was the trouble-maker of the class as well. After making a few inquiries about him, I found out he was the son of a member of the school board. I was also told that he depended on his father to make sure that the teachers passed him. It would not have seemed so bad, but he was depending on being passed without doing *any* work.

When I started to teach the class, John tested my patience. He never prepared his homework, and was noisy most of the time. Although he could not answer questions I gave him, he interrupted the class by blurting out incorrect answers to questions I asked of other pupils. He seemed to have no respect for his classmates, himself, or teachers.

His lack of work showed up on the tests I gave the class. He was lowest in the first three tests, scoring a zero on one of them. Feeling that something had to be done, I had a private talk with him one day. I asked him if he had any special problems that I could help him with. He replied that he had no problems, and that he liked school very much. I encouraged him to try to do better work. He said he would.

Even though John sounded sincere and convincing about trying harder, he soon was back to his old role. On the next test I gave, his score was again the lowest in the class. I reprimanded him in the presence of the class, telling him I was very much disappointed in his work. Not long after, I was in charge of a study hall which was largely attended by senior girls. John's presence was soon manifested by his trying to make an impression on these girls. Once again I reprimanded him publicly. I deliberately mentioned his low marks and told him that he could not afford to waste time. This brought laughter from the girls, which seemed to settle him for the remainder of the period.

From that time forward, John changed. He no longer caused trouble in class; instead, he became attentive. He even began to ask sensible questions, and made an honest effort with his assignments. His test scores improved to the point where he was making passing marks instead of being the lowest in the class. At the next marking period, as a reward, I gave him a passing grade. This seemed to be just what he needed. It showed him he had the ability to pass on merit, instead of depending on the influence his father might try to exert in his behalf.

## Points for Discussion

- *Assume this boy's father approached you to change his son's grade. What would you tell him?*

- *Explain the kinds of problems that are created for a teacher by having a pupil in class who is related to school personnel.*

## PROBLEM 116:  THE STUDENT TEACHER BECOMES UNNERVED BY THE CONTINUAL INTERRUPTIONS OF THE COOPERATING TEACHER

During the first few weeks of my student teaching I was faced with what I considered a grave problem. I felt that my cooperating teacher was trying to show how much she knew, and how little I knew, about teaching English.

My first few days of teaching went along fairly smoothly. I was well prepared and began to feel at ease before the class. Before each day's teaching began, I conferred with my cooperating teacher, showing her my lesson plans and explaining to her the procedures I intended to use. She approved them, making no suggestions for changes.

During my second week of teaching, Mrs. B. interrupted me in the middle of an introductory lecture I was giving the class on the works and style of Chaucer. She suggested I skip the introduction and go on with the story. I was disturbed by her interruption, but I thanked her and carried out her suggestion.

I would not have minded if her unsolicited comment had ended with that one instance. She continued her unexpected remarks and interruptions, however, for the remainder of the week. Besides creating boiling resentment within me, she was making it difficult to maintain order in the classroom.

During our daily conferences, I especially emphasized what I was going to do and say in class. She offered no objections during our talks; she saved them, and voiced them verbally before the entire class, I could scarcely withhold my desire to give her a verbal blast in return.

I did not know how to solve the problem. Mrs. B. was a good teacher. She had just been called out of retirement because the school needed her services. I could not hope to compete with her thirty-two years experience.

## Disscussion

- *What would you do about Mrs. B's interruptions?*

### PROBLEM 117: A PUPIL THREATENS TO HIT
### THE STUDENT TEACHER WITH A CHAIR

I had only one serious problem while I was student teaching, but it was a "hairy" one. It concerned a senior boy who not only was doing poor work in his studies but also was a disciplinary problem of long standing. Most of his teachers had some sort of trouble with him. He had been in serious trouble three times, and expelled once. On one occasion after the principal used corporal punishment on him, the boy circulated a petition to have the principal discharged. The teachers all agreed that he was a serious problem. In fact, I can quote one teacher as saying that the boy was a "psycho."

My problem occurred while I was supervising a study hall period. In the study hall were a large number of sophomore girls, and only one boy, our problem senior. I had been there only about five minutes when a commotion arose from the side of the room where the boy was located.

Immediately I directed the boy to change his seat to the other side of the room. He asked me why I was picking on him, and refused to move. I did not pursue the matter, and returned to my desk to continue correcting papers. No sooner had I sat down, however, than he made some abusive remarks about me which were loud enough for me to hear, and which caused the girls to titter nervously. When I rushed over to him, demanding that he repeat his remarks, he grabbed a chair and told me that if I touched him he would break the chair over my back. He also said that he hated student teachers and that he would "get" me after school.

### Discussion

- *What would you do next?*

### PROBLEM 118: THE COOPERATING TEACHER'S
### SON BECOMES A PROBLEM

I had a problem which might have been amusing had I not been in the center of it. It involved my cooperating teacher and his son who was in one of my classes.

During the days I was observing my cooperating teacher, we had many conferences during which he expounded at length his theories in education. He apparently had come up the hard way in life, which probably accounted for the fact that he was a stern disciplinarian. According to him, the only way to handle a disciplinary problem effectively was to use corporal punishment and, at the same time, lower the grade of the offender. He unhesitatingly blamed parents for the misdeeds of their children, holding that lack of discipline in the home was responsible for their misdeeds.

The humor, or perhaps irony, of the situation was that his son was in one of my classes, and Junior was no angel. He turned out to be a disciplinary problem not only to me but also to his other teachers. Though he had above average ability and was earning high grades, he constantly interfered with classroom procedures by talking, throwing things, and distracting the others. I tried in several ways to get him to behave, but had no success. Finally I threatened to lower his grade if he did not pay attention, and when he continued his disruptions, I lowered his grade for the six-week marking period.

To my amazement, my cooperating teacher swooped down on me with a barrage of reprimands for lowering his son's grade, maintaining that it was unjust and discouraging to a student to lower his grade for disciplinary reasons. The family circle was complete when the mother also visited the school to see me. She pointed out that her son was above reproach, both as a student and as a gentleman.

In view of what my cooperating teacher had told me about his policies, I thought he would be the last person to complain about my action. The matter did not end there. He stayed in my classroom every minute from that time on, constantly correcting me and interfering with my teaching procedures.

## Discussion

- *How would you handle this situation?*

## PROBLEM 119: THE COOPERATING TEACHER GIVES THE STUDENT TEACHER NO AUTHORITY IN GRADING PUPILS

A cooperating teacher should work closely with and support his student teacher. Otherwise, someone is sure to suffer.

I had a class in which there were many repeaters. Most of the boys in it had taken the course the year before and had failed it. When I first started to teach the class, I had no discipline problem, largely because the students thought I would be the one to give them their grade. I don't know how it came about or what prompted my cooperating teacher to do so, but she told them in my absence that she would be the only one to have a say on their grade. Once the class was told this, my discipline problems began.

I tried everything I could think of to quiet the students, but they paid little attention to me. I tried asking questions of those students who were talking or causing trouble, but they either remained silent or said "I don't know." I gave some students extra work to do, but they would not do it. When they failed to do the extra work, I told them I would deduct points from the grade they made on their next exam. They paid no attention to that because they knew that it was the policy of the regular teacher not to fail anyone unless he was absent from school most of the time.

Finally, I decided to change their seats. I arranged them in such a way that each trouble-maker was surrounded by girls, and that no two buddies sat near each other. For the first few days, some of the students resented having had their seats changed, but they eventually accepted it, and my troubles decreased.

Being a student teacher, I didn't want to challenge my cooperating teacher's policy on grading. However, I did ask her why she didn't give me any authority in the matter, pointing out that all of my fellow student teachers were not only allowed, but expected, to grade their pupils.

"Cooperating teachers have different policies," she told me. "Even though you took over my class, the school authorities hold me responsible for the pupils' progress, so I want to grade them myself."

## Discussion

- *How would you respond to the cooperating teacher's last remark?*

## PROBLEM 120: THE STUDENT TEACHER IS ENCHANTED BY A STUDENT

Only by chance was Bill chosen from a group of students to guide me to my newly assigned classroom. From that moment on, he was to be an important factor in the education of a new student teacher.

Bill found his chore an ideal vehicle to display his talent. He soon made it known to me that he was clever, witty, and as charming as only a red-haired, freckled-face boy in the seventh grade can be.

As the prospect of handling a class made me nervous, I was grateful for any display of assistance or friendship. Bill grabbed my hand with innocent abandon and speedily guided me to my destination. The long walk down the hall was made short by Bill's rapport.

His natural talent for conversation, aided by his youthful exuberance, unconsciously put me at ease. He not only aided me in gaining my composure but also lessened my nervousness. This in return made me grateful to Bill, and created a false sense of security and a false sense of obligation. It was more than comforting to discover that Bill was going to be a member of the class to which he was leading me.

From then on, Bill and I displayed our friendship to each other. As each day progressed, Bill's remarks became more clever. I even committed some of his profound remarks to memory so that I could repeat them to my cooperating teacher and my contemporary student teachers. I even introduced Bill to some of the teachers who were unfamiliar with this prodigious "find" of mine.

Bill's popularity soon harmed him more than it benefited him. Each day he became more and more uninhibited. He soon proved to be a "ham" among a room full of "hams." I soon realized all the students were becoming seasoned veterans in the battle of getting attention.

Bill would always be the first one to greet me when I entered the classroom, and he would proceed to ask me for special favors. He wanted the privilege of emptying the wastebaskets, getting more writing paper, going on special errands, etc. Besides consuming valuable time, these devices also prompted other students to follow suit and to compete with Bill in the game of special favors, becoming the center of attention, and wasting time.

## Discussion

- *How would you handle Bill if he were your student?*

## CONCLUSION

The problems presented in this text offer ample evidence that teaching is at once a challenging and rewarding profession. It is challenging in that each day unfolds new situations in which the teacher can apply his knowledge, skill, and ingenuity in helping human beings become all that is possible for them to become. Its rewards are indescribable. Who can put into words the feelings of a teacher when the dawn of understanding breaks over the faces of his pupils, or when a pupil's energies are diverted from open rebellion to close cooperation, or when the eyes of pupils glow with respect and admiration, or when the teacher sees his pupils grow in many subtle ways?

Such are the rewards and the challenges of teaching. They are experienced by every conscientious and selfless teacher, and are waiting to be sampled by the beginning teacher. If the student teacher reaches for them with an open heart and open hand, he will soon find his heart welling with emotional satisfaction, and his hand closing over many rich rewards.

## SELECTED READINGS

Brembeck, Cole S. *Social Foundations of Education.* New York: John Wiley and Sons, Inc., 1971, chapter 15.

Burrup, Percy E. *The Teacher and the Public School System.* New York: Harper and Row, 1972, chapter 9.

Crow, Lester D., and Crow, Alice. *The Student Teacher in the Secondary School.* New York: David McKay Company, Inc., 1964, chapters 3 and 5.

Evans, Ellis D. *Transition to Teaching.* New York: Holt, Rinehart and Winston, 1976.

Hamachek, Don E. *Behavior Dynamics in Teaching, Learning, and Growth.* Boston: Allyn and Bacon, Inc., 1975, parts III and V.

Noar, Gertrude. *The Junior High School—Today and Tomorrow.* Englewood Cliffs, New Jersey: Prentice-Hall, Inc., 1961, chapter 3.

Richey, Robert W. *Planning for Teaching.* New York: McGraw-Hill Book Company, 1973, chapters 5 and 7.

Ryan, Kevin, and Cooper, James M. *Those Who Can, Teach.* Boston: Houghton Mifflin Company, 1972, chapter 7.

Van Til, William. *Education: A Beginning.* Boston: Houghton Mifflin Company, 1971, chapters 19 and 20.

# Index

Acceleration, 146–147
Adjustment
  illustrative problems of,
    217–241
  teacher to school personnel,
    211–241
Aims
  and motivation, 68
  statement of, 12–13
Apology as punishment, 36–37
  illustrative problem, 46–47
Assignments in lesson plan, 14
Astigmatism, 140–141
Attention as a prerequisite for
    discipline, 30
Attention-getting
  constructive use of, 108
    illustrative problems, 89–90,
    115–116
Auditory defects, 141
Automatic promotion
  illustrative problem, 203–204

Behavior, extremes of, 110
  illustrative problems, 120–121,
    131–132
Belligerent attitude of teacher,
    10–11
  illustrative problem, 47–49
Benefit of doubt to students, 187
Brain injury
  illustrative problem, 169–171

Cheating on a test
  illustrative problems, 53–54, 208
Chronic infections, 142
Class discussion and discipline
  illustrative problem, 37–39
Comments by pupils about teachers,
    215–216
  illustrative problem, 218–220
Compensation, 106–107
Competition as motivation, 73
  illustrative problem, 87–89
Computer-assisted instruction,
    146, 147
Consideration
  as motivation
    illustrative problem, 97–98
  in scoring a test
    illustrative problem, 99
Cooperating teacher
  and grading
    illustrative problem, 239–240
  interruptions by
    illustrative problem, 237
  traits of
    illustrative problem, 227–228
Corporal punishment, 37
  illustrative problem, 42–43
Courtesy as a teacher, 213
  illustrative problems, 220–221,
    223–224, 224–225
Criticism of others by teachers, 216
  illustrative problem, 228–229

Daydreaming, 106
Deducting academic credit as
    punishment, 36
Defense mechanisms, 105–109
Delay in handling problems, 21
Delinquent student, problem of
    handling
    illustrative problems, 61–62,
    135–136
Detention as punishment, 35
Discipline, 27–66
    definition of, 28
    illustrative problems of, 37–66
    questionable procedures, 45–46
    standards of, 29
    suggestions for maintaining,
    29–32
Discretion, lack of, 4–5
Dismissal from class as
    punishment, 36
    illustrative problem, 49–50
Disorderly pupils, handling of,
    32–37
Disruptive pupil
    illustrative problem, 64–65
Drill, neglect of, 17
Drop-out, motivation of
    illustrative problem, 77–79


Economically deprived, motivation
    of
    illustrative problem, 79–80
Emotional adjustment, 103–137
Emotional control, teacher's lack
    of, 7–8
Emotional involvement
    by students
        illustrative problem, 217–218
    by teachers
        illustrative problems,
        231–232, 240–241
Emotional maladjustment
    contributing causes of, 103–105
    elimination of cause of, 111
        illustrative problems, 117–118,
        118–119, 120–121
    illustrative problems of, 112–137

Emotional problems
    suggestions for handling,
    109–111
    symptoms of, 105–109
Encouragement as motivation
    illustrative problem, 82
Enthusiasm and motivation, 68
Epilepsy, 142
Essay type tests, 180
    illustrative problem, 201–202
Evaluation, 179–209
    illustrative problems of, 187–209
    testing suggestions, 182–187
Examples in motivation, use of, 70
Excel, desire to, 72
Experience in motivation,
    capitalizing on
    illustrative problem, 95
Expression, errors in, 3–4
Extra work as punishment, 36
Eye defect, self-consciousness
    about
    illustrative problem, 164–165
Eyeglasses, self-consciousness
    about
    illustrative problem, 154–155


Failure
    desire to avoid, and motivation,
    72–73
    to solve a student's problem
        illustrative problem, 59–60
Fear of teachers by student
    illustrative problem, 233–234
Fighting in classroom
    illustrative problem, 46–47


Grade
    changing, 20, 185
        illustrative problem, 190–191
    changing by cooperating teacher,
    20–21
        illustrative problem, 208–209
    components of a, 160–161
        illustrative problem, 194–195
    resentment over a
        illustrative problem, 195–196

Grades and personal feelings, 186
  illustrative problems, 189,
    195–196, 199–200, 208–209
Grading
  on basis of I.Q.
    illustrative problem, 206–207
  effort of student
    illustrative problem, 202–203
  errors in grammar
    illustrative problem, 204–205
  policies, 182–183
  standards of, 183
  student challenge of
    illustrative problem, 190–191
  student resentment over
    illustrative problem, 199–200
  subjectivity in, 20
  system, evolution of
    illustrative problem, 194–195
  and use of objective evidence,
    183
Group influence on pupil
  illustrative problem, 49–51
Group leader, winning over of
  illustrative problem, 41–42

Help, teacher's failure to seek, 22
Heterogeneous grouping, 145–146
  illustrative problem, 175
Home, broken
  illustrative problem, 134–135
Home conditions as a cause of
    emotional problems
  illustrative problems, 112–113,
    121–122, 126–127, 128–129
Homogeneous grouping, 145–146
  of slow students
    illustrative problem, 176
  of superior students
    illustrative problem, 168–169
Homogeneous versus
    heterogeneous grouping,
    145–146
Humor, sense of, and discipline,
    32
  illustrative problem, 39–40
Hygiene of teacher, 4
Hyperopia, 140

Identification, 107
Illness, feigned
  illustrative problem, 132–133
Illness, unexplained
  illustrative problem, 118–119
Illustration, use of, 17–18
Imprudent firmness by teacher
  illustrative problem, 51–52
Individual differences, 139–177
  illustrative problems, 151–177
  learning disabilities, 150
  mental differences, 144–150
  physical differences, 139–143
Individual help, disproportionate, 6
Individually prescribed instruc-
    tion, 146, 147
  illustrative problem, 171–172
Information from other sources on
    emotional problems,
    110–111
  illustrative problems, 112–113,
    115–116, 118–119
Interests and motivation, 72
  illustrative problems, 85–87,
    92–93
Introvert
  illustrative problem, 130–131
Isolation as punishment, 35

Joke, misuse of
  illustrative problem, 224–225
Jumping to conclusions in
    emotional problems, 109–110
Justice in dealing with pupils,
    31–32
  illustrative problem, 82

Laboratory problems
  in biology
    illustrative problem, 43–45
  in languages
    illustrative problem, 62–63
Learning disabilities, 150
Lecture, overuse of, 14–16
Leniency in handling problems, 10
Lesson plan, sample of, 15
Lesson planning, improper, 12–14
Lighting, improper, 9

Malnutrition, 141–142
Manner, unprofessional, 6–7
Mannerisms in teaching, 4
Meaningfulness and motivation, 69
Mental ability, differences in,
    144–150
Mentally slow
  illustrative problems, 152–154,
      158–159, 162–163, 173, 176,
      176–177
  suggestions for dealing with,
      149–150
  traits of, 149–150
Mentally superior
  illustrative problems,
      151–152, 155–156, 156–157,
      165–166, 168–169, 174–175
  suggestions for dealing with,
      147–148
  traits of, 147–148
Mistakes of beginning teachers,
    1–25
  in attitude toward theory
      courses, 23–24
  in classroom environment,
      8–9
  in classroom procedures, 11–19
  in discipline, 9–11
  in evaluation, 19–21
  in handling problems, 21–23
  in personal traits, 2–8
Morale, teacher's, 24
Mother
  death of, as a cause of
      problems
    illustrative problem, 134–135
  source of emotional problems
    illustrative problem, 127–128
Motivation, 67–102
  illustrative problems, 75–102
  suggestions on, 68–75
Myopia, 140

Neatness as a teacher, 212–213
Negative approach of teachers, 7
Neurosis, 109
Note-taking by pupils, 18–19

Objective type tests, 180–181
Objectives, behavioral, 12–13
Objectivity in handling emotional
    problems, 111
Observation by cooperating
    teacher
  illustrative problem, 232–233
Only child, as a problem
  illustrative problem, 120–121
Open classroom, 146
Over-age pupil, problem with
  illustrative problem, 63–64
Overprotection by mother
  illustrative problem, 55–56

Pace in teaching and motivation,
    69
Parental influence as motivation,
    74
Parents as an aid in discipline, 34
Participation
  in experiments as motivation
    illustrative problem, 81
  motivation in
    illustrative problem, 84–85
Personalized system of instruction,
    146, 147
Physical defects, 139–143
  suggestions for dealing with,
      143–144
Physical deformities, 142–143
Physical handicaps and adjust-
    ment
  illustrative problem, 166–168
Praise as motivation, 73
Preferential treatment of students
  illustrative problems, 229–230,
      236–237, 238–239
Prejudging students
  illustrative problem, 54–55
Prejudice in grading
  illustrative problem, 189
Preparation
  as a contribution to discipline,
      29–30
  teacher's lack of, 11–12

Private talk
  in handling problems, 32–33, 110
    illustrative problems, 83, 117–118, 118–119, 124, 126–127
  in motivation
    illustrative problem, 83
  with the student, 21
Procedures in lesson plan, 13
Procedures, variety of
  and discipline, 30–31
  and motivation, 70–71
    illustrative problems, 81, 84–85, 87–89, 95, 99–100
Programmed instruction, 146–147
Progress of students, knowledge of, 73, 186
Projection, 106
Projects as motivation
  illustrative problem, 99–100
Promotion, automatic
  illustrative problem, 187–188
Psychosis, 109
Punctuality as a teacher, 213–214
Punishment
  forms of, 32–37
  as motivation, 74
Pupil activity and discipline, 30
Pupils
  knowledge of, 5–6, 31
  treatment as adults
    illustrative problem, 220–221

Questioning
  and discipline, 33
  technique of, 16–17

Rationalization, 105–106
Recognition, desire for, and motivation, 72
Referral of emotional problems, 111
  illustrative problem, 131–132

Regulations, lack of, 10
Relationships
  with school personnel, 211–241
  suggestions for improving, 212–217
Repression, 108–109
Reproof
  in handling disorderly pupils, 33
  as motivation, 74
Reputation of students
  illustrative problem, 225–227
Responsibility, teacher's neglect of, 22
Review, functions of, 17
Reward as motivation, 74
Ringleader, winning over of
  illustrative problem, 41–42

Sarcasm by teacher, 33
  illustrative problem, 223–224
Self-consciousness of teacher
  illustrative problem, 221–223
Sense of humor and discipline
  illustrative problem, 39–40
Service, spirit of, in teachers, 214
Shyness
  illustrative problem, 124
Slow students
  involvement in dramatics
    illustrative problem, 158–159
  lack of success with
    illustrative problem, 162–163
  special attention for
    illustrative problem, 152–154
  traits of, 149–150
Special ability in art, use of
  illustrative problem, 161–162
Special attention as motivation
  illustrative problem, 95–97
Special talent, use of, in motivation
  illustrative problem, 85–87
Strabismus, 141
Student teachers, student dislike of,
  illustrative problem, 57–58

Stuttering
   illustrative problems, 113–115,
      124–125
Suggestions, acceptance of,
      216–217
   illustrative problems, 221–223,
      227–228, 232–233, 237,
      238–239, 239–240
Superior student
   as a challenge to the teacher
      illustrative problem, 156–157
   with "cross-eyes"
      illustrative problem, 164–165
   disliked by peers
      illustrative problem, 174–175
   and enrichment
      illustrative problem, 165–166
   example of well-rounded
      illustrative problem, 155–156
   lack of challenge of
      illustrative problem, 151–152
   traits of, 147–148
Supplies, distribution of, 9

Team teaching, evaluation of
   illustrative problem, 234–235
Telephone calls, threatening
   illustrative problem, 218–220
Television programs as motivation
   illustrative problem, 92–93
Temperature, classroom, 9
Test questions, dictation of, 19
Testing
   aiding a student during
      illustrative problem, 200–201
   during class recitation
      illustrative problem, 58–59
   and grades, experimentation
      with
      illustrative problem, 207–208
   use of textbook questions for
      illustrative problem, 205–206
Tests
   construction of
      illustrative problem, 196–197

cheating, 184–185
   illustrative problems, 191–192
      197–198
clarity of directions, 183–184
   illustrative problem, 196–197
daily, as an incentive
   illustrative problem, 192–194
as a deterrent to disorder, 33
as an incentive to a failing
      student
   illustrative problem, 197–198
as motivation, 75
review of questions, 185
unreasonable, 19–20
use of scoring key, 185
Theory courses, students' attitude
      toward, 23–24

Untidiness in classroom, 8

Value of subject as motivation, 72
   illustrative problems, 93–94,
      100–101
Ventilation, classroom, 9
Violence, threats by student
   illustrative problem, 238
Visual defects, 140–141
Vocabulary in teaching, 2–3
Vocational students, motivation of
   illustrative problem, 75–77
Voice
   lack of control by student
      illustrative problem, 159–161
   in teaching, 2

Withdrawal, 107–108
   illustrative problems, 122–123,
      127–128, 130–131
Worksheets for use with illustra-
      tive problems, samples
      of, 25–26
Worry as a cause of emotional
      problems
   illustrative problems, 117–118,
      136–137